SERVICE

KIERON GILLEN | WRITER

ANTONIO FUSO | ARTIST

CHRIS O'HALLORAN | COLORIST

SIMON BOWLAND | LETTERER

JOSEPH RYBANDT | EXECUTIVE EDITOR

MATT HUMPHREYS | ASSISTANT EDITOR

MONEYPENNY

JODY HOUSER | WRITER

JACOB EDGAR | ARTIST

DEARBHLA KELLY | COLORIST

SIMON BOWLAND | LETTERER

JOSEPH RYBANDT | EXECUTIVE EDITOR

ANTHONY MARQUES | ASSISTANT EDITOR

NATE COSBY | PACKAGER & EDITOR

SOLSTICE

IBRAHIM MOUSTAFA | WRITER & ARTIST

JORDAN BOYD | COLORIST

SIMON BOWLAND | LETTERER

JOSEPH RYBANDT | EXECUTIVE EDITOR

ANTHONY MARQUES | ASSISTANT EDITOR

NATE COSBY | PACKAGER & EDITOR

IAN FLEMING'S

JAMES BOND 007

CASE FILES

M

DECLAN SHALVEY | WRITER

PJ HOLDEN | ARTIST

DEARBHLA KELLY | COLORIST

SIMON BOWLAND | LETTERER

NATE COSBY | PACKAGER & EDITOR

TULA LOTAY | COLLECTION COVER ARTIST

GEOFF HARKINS | COLLECTION DESIGNER

RIAN HUGHES | 007 LOGO DESIGNER

MICHAEL LAKE | EDITORIAL CONSULTANT

SPECIAL THANKS TO

JOSEPHINE LANE, CORINNE TURNER, JONNY DAVIDSON & DIGGORY
LAYCOCK AT IAN FLEMING PUBLICATIONS LTD.
& JONNY GELLER AT CURTIS BROWN

DYNAMITE®

NICK BARRUCCI | CEO / Publisher
JUAN COLLADO | President / COO

JOE RYBANDT | Executive Editor
MATT IDELSON | Senior Editor
ANTHONY MARQUES | Associate Editor
KEVIN KETNER | Assistant Editor

JASON ULLMEYER | Art Director
GEOFF HARKINS | Senior Graphic Designer
CATHLEEN HEARD | Graphic Designer
ALEXIS PERSSON | Production Artist
CHRIS CANIANO | Digital Associate
RACHEL KILBURY | Digital Mutimedia Associate

BRANDON DANTE PRIMAVERA | V.P. of IT and Operations
RICH YOUNG | Director of Business Development
ALAN PAYNE | V.P. of Sales and Marketing
PAT O'CONNELL | Sales Manager

www.DYNAMITE.com | Online
/Dynamitecomics | Facebook
/Dynamitecomics | Instagram
dynamitecomics.tumblr.com
@dynamitecomics | Twitter

IAN FLEMING PUBLICATIONS LIMITED

ISBN13: 978-1-5241-0678-2
First Printing 10 9 8 7 6 5 4 3 2 1
www.IANFLEMING.com

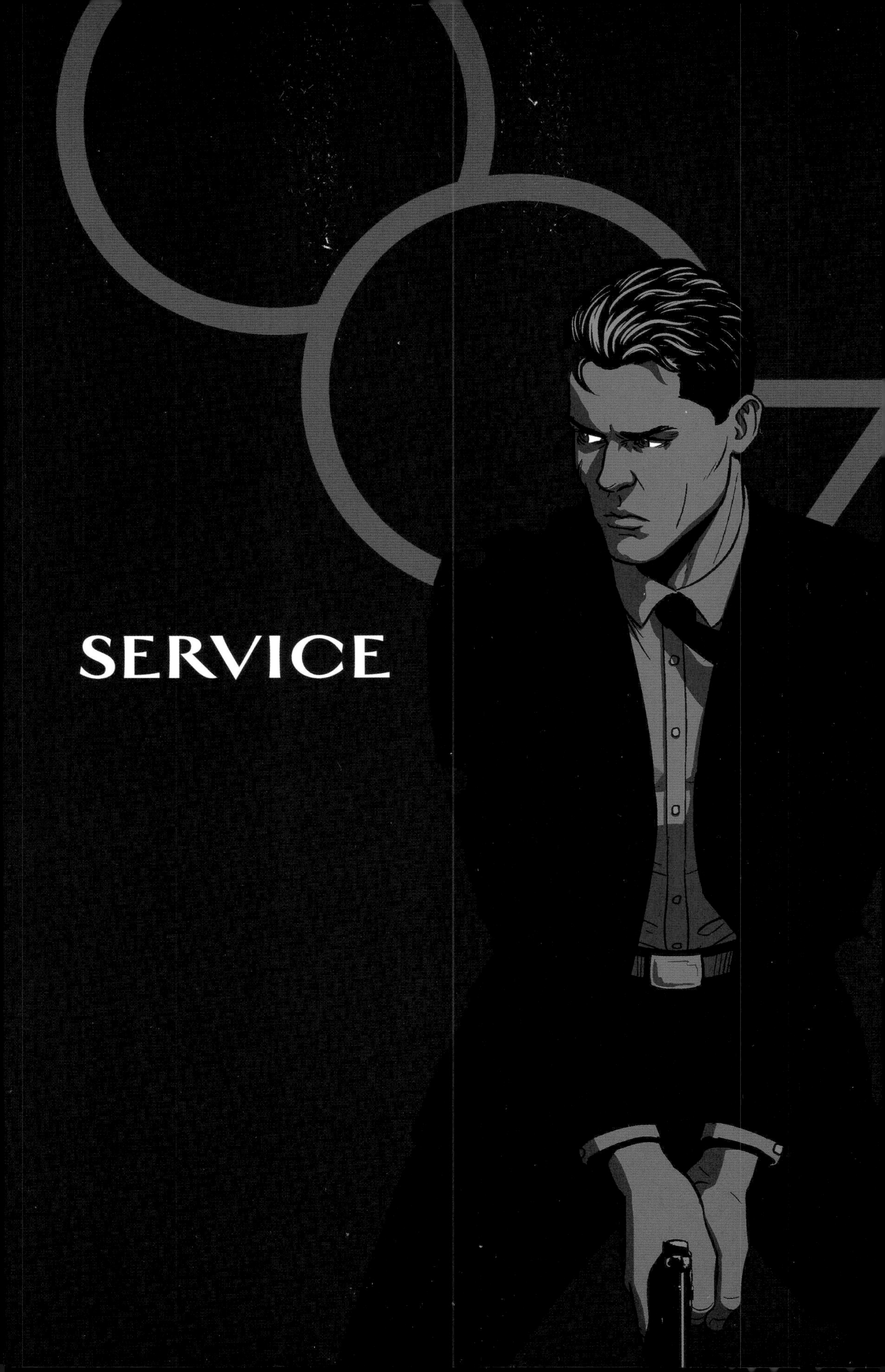
SERVICE

JAMES BOND: SERVICE
COVER BY JAMIE McKELVIE

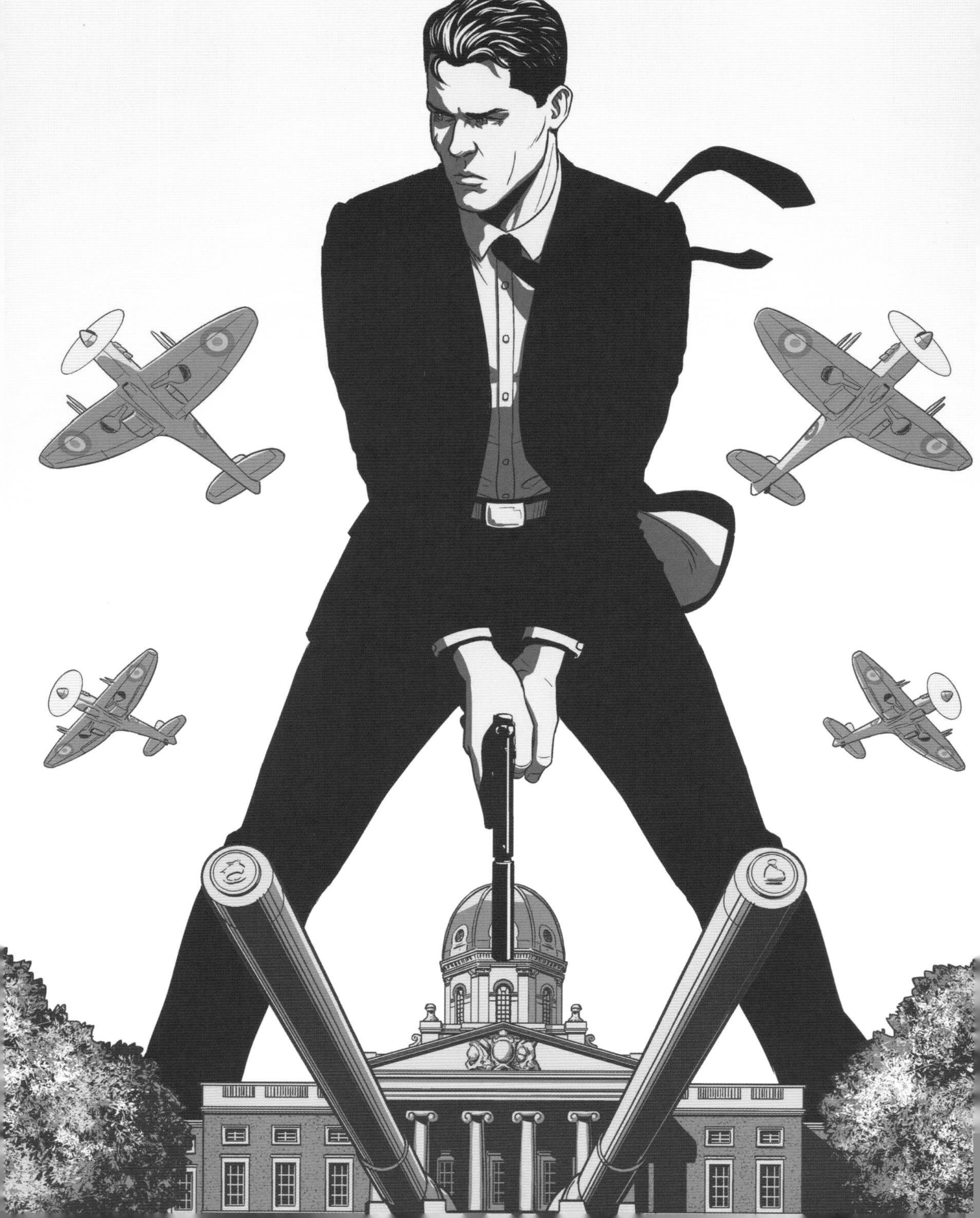

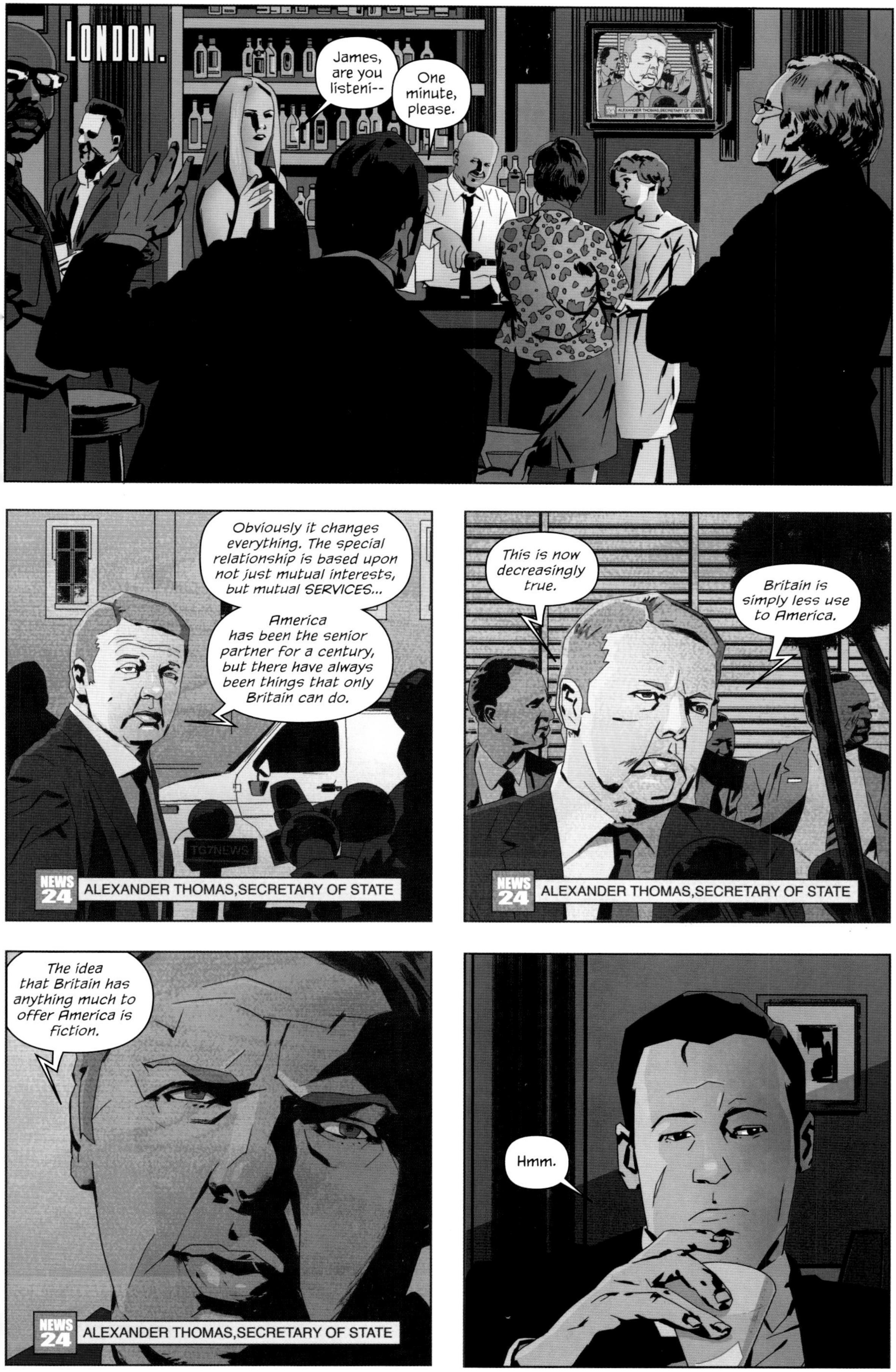

LONDON.
James, are you listeni--
One minute, please.
ALEXANDER THOMAS, SECRETARY OF STATE
Obviously it changes everything. The special relationship is based upon not just mutual interests, but mutual SERVICES...
America has been the senior partner for a century, but there have always been things that only Britain can do.
TG7NEWS
NEWS 24
ALEXANDER THOMAS, SECRETARY OF STATE
This is now decreasingly true.
Britain is simply less use to America.
NEWS 24
ALEXANDER THOMAS, SECRETARY OF STATE
The idea that Britain has anything much to offer America is fiction.
NEWS 24
ALEXANDER THOMAS, SECRETARY OF STATE
Hmm.

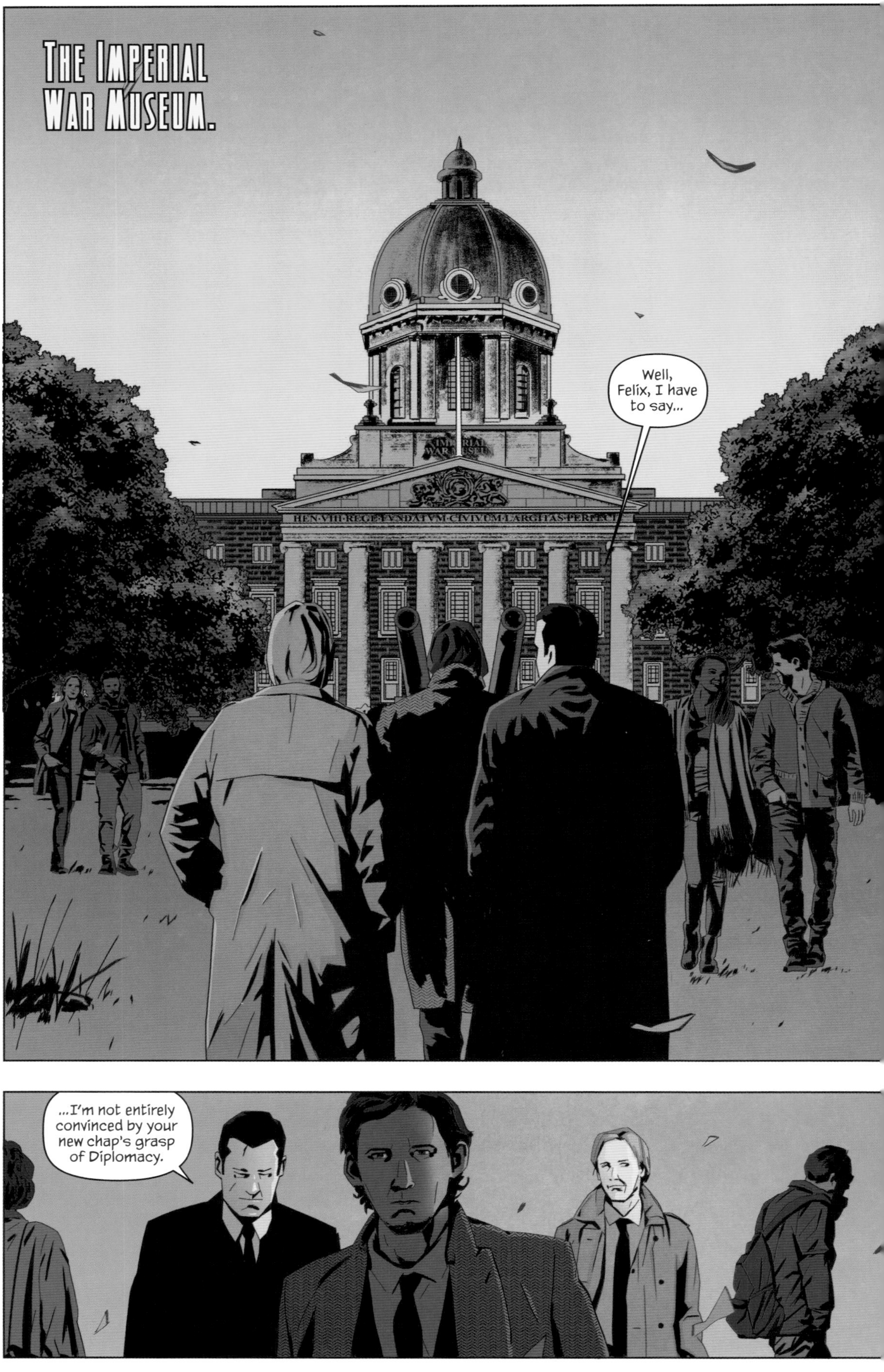
THE IMPERIAL WAR MUSEUM.
Well, Felix, I have to say...
...I'm not entirely convinced by your new chap's grasp of Diplomacy.

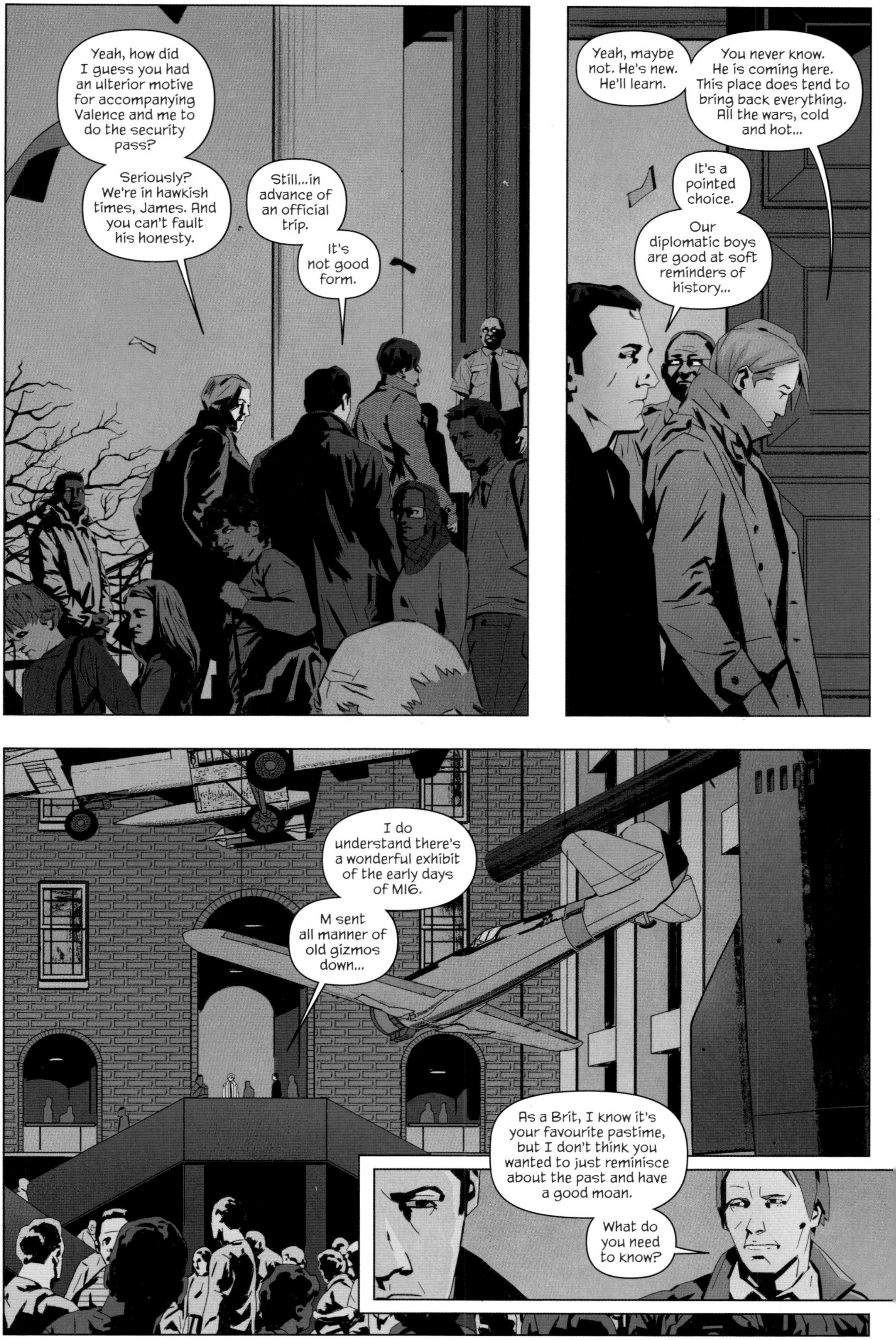

Yeah, how did I guess you had an ulterior motive for accompanying Valence and me to do the security pass?
Seriously? We're in hawkish times, James. And you can't fault his honesty.
Still...in advance of an official trip.
It's not good form.
Yeah, maybe not. He's new. He'll learn.
You never know. He is coming here. This place does tend to bring back everything. All the wars, cold and hot...
It's a pointed choice.
Our diplomatic boys are good at soft reminders of history...
I do understand there's a wonderful exhibit of the early days of MI6.
M sent all manner of old gizmos down...
As a Brit, I know it's your favourite pastime, but I don't think you wanted to just reminisce about the past and have a good moan.
What do you need to know?

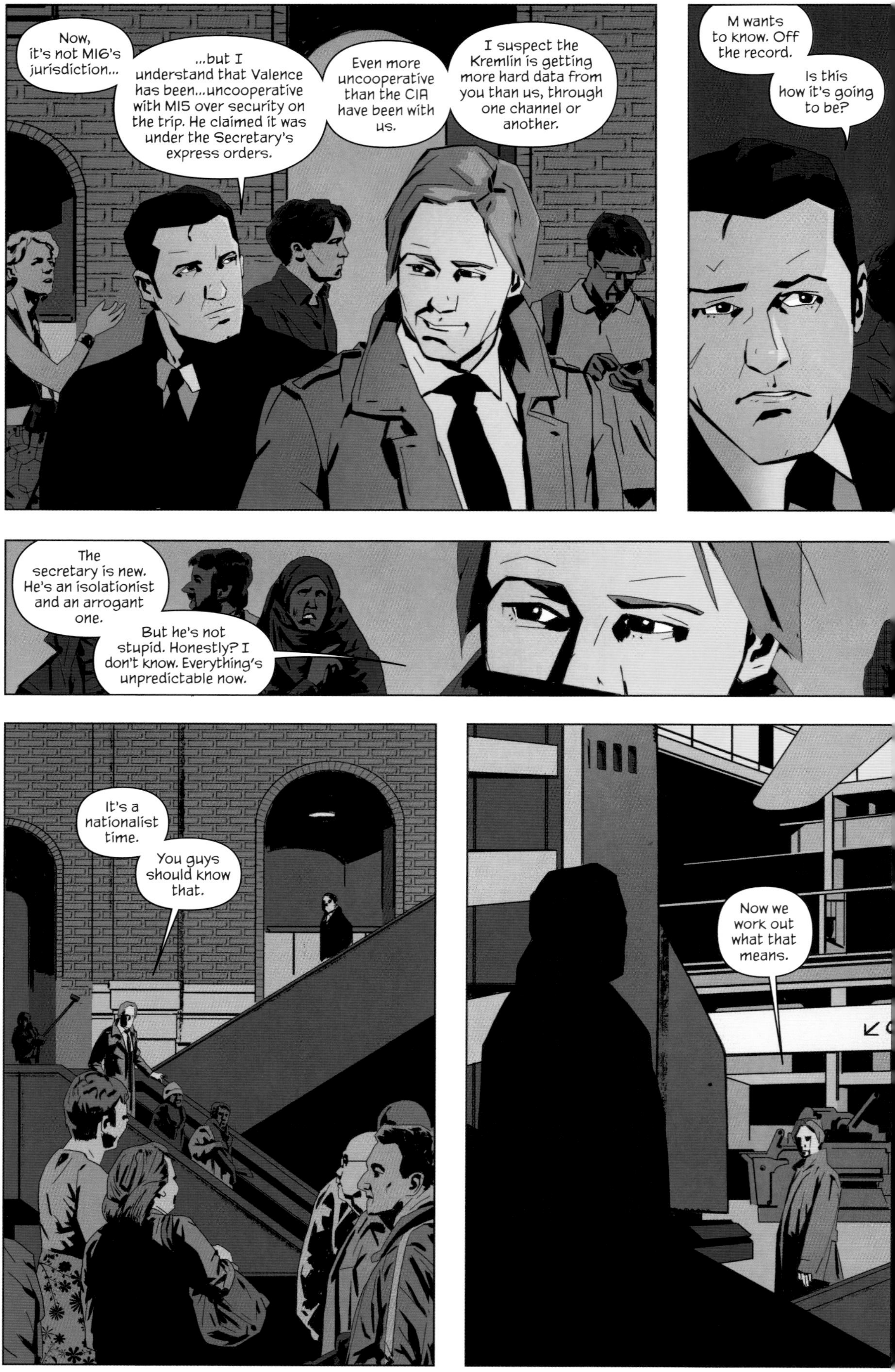
Now, it's not MI6's jurisdiction...
...but I understand that Valence has been...uncooperative with MI5 over security on the trip. He claimed it was under the Secretary's express orders.
Even more uncooperative than the CIA have been with us.
I suspect the Kremlin is getting more hard data from you than us, through one channel or another.
M wants to know. Off the record.
Is this how it's going to be?
The secretary is new. He's an isolationist and an arrogant one.
But he's not stupid. Honestly? I don't know. Everything's unpredictable now.
It's a nationalist time.
You guys should know that.
Now we work out what that means.

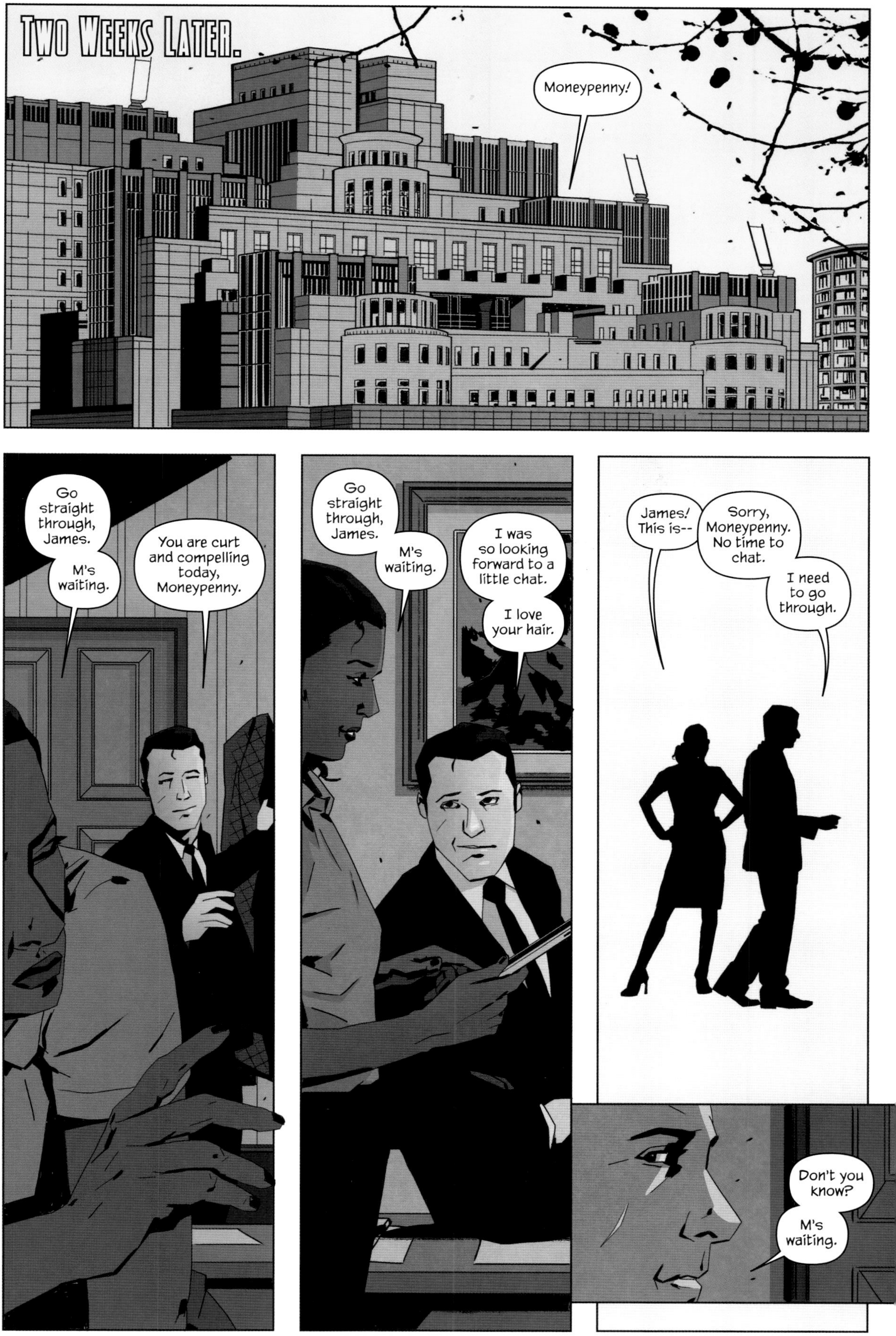
TWO WEEKS LATER.
Moneypenny!
Go straight through, James.
M's waiting.
You are curt and compelling today, Moneypenny.
Go straight through, James.
M's waiting.
I was so looking forward to a little chat.
I love your hair.
James! This is--
Sorry, Moneypenny. No time to chat.
I need to go through.
Don't you know?
M's waiting.

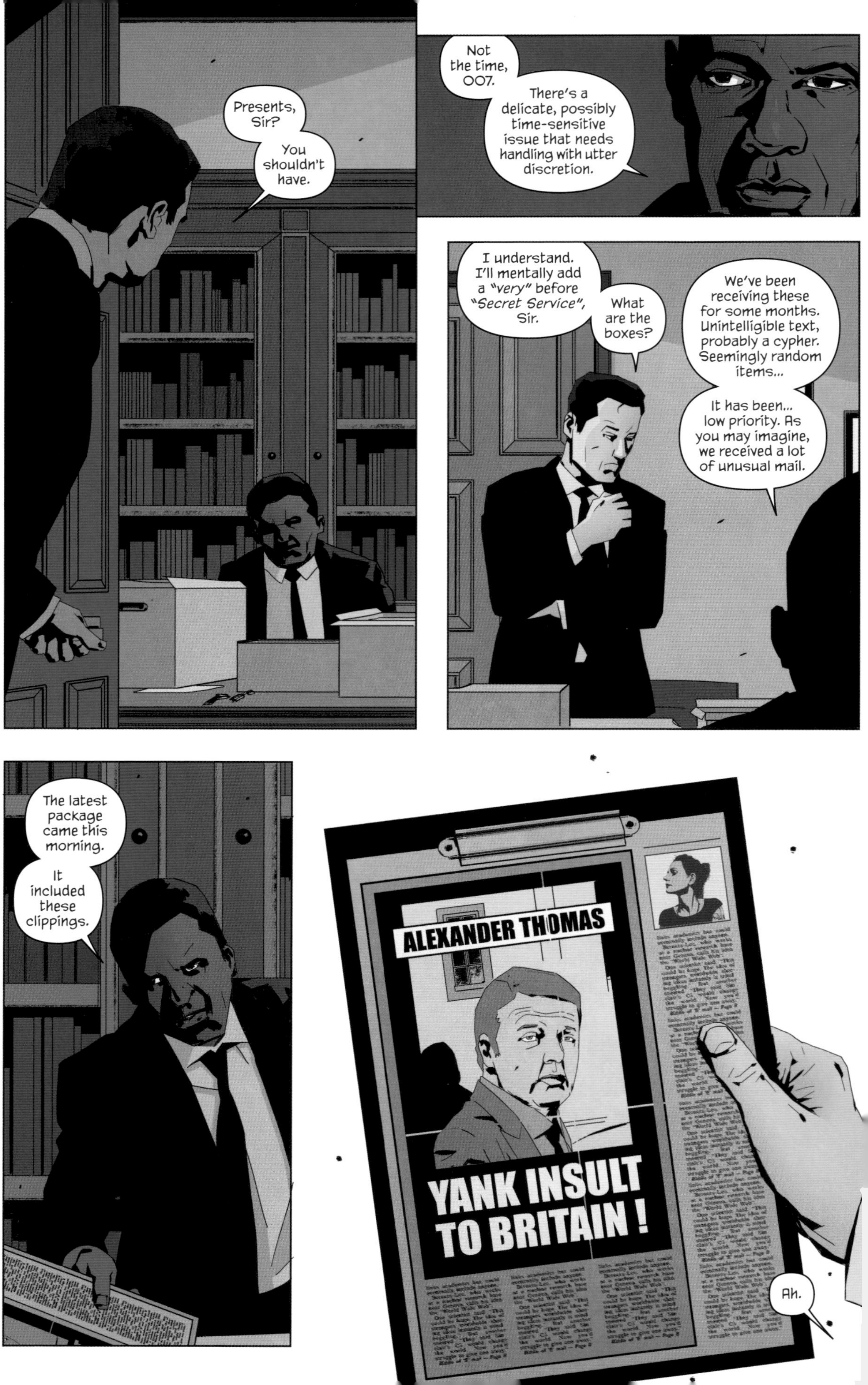
Presents, Sir?
You shouldn't have.
Not the time, 007.
There's a delicate, possibly time-sensitive issue that needs handling with utter discretion.
I understand. I'll mentally add a "very" before "Secret Service", Sir.
What are the boxes?
We've been receiving these for some months. Unintelligible text, probably a cypher. Seemingly random items...
It has been... low priority. As you may imagine, we received a lot of unusual mail.
The latest package came this morning.
It included these clippings.
ALEXANDER THOMAS
YANK INSULT TO BRITAIN !
Ah.

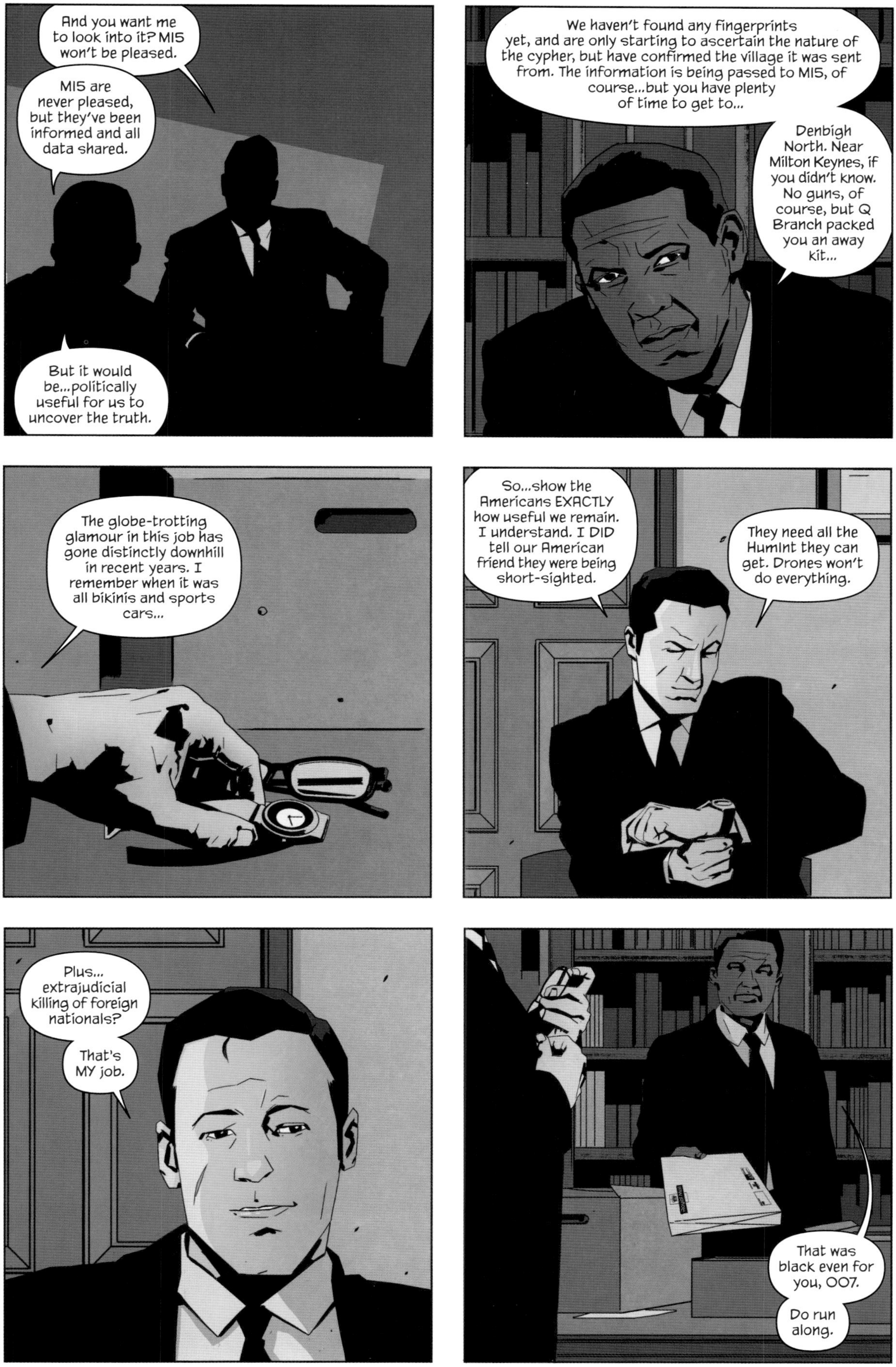
And you want me to look into it? MI5 won't be pleased.
MI5 are never pleased, but they've been informed and all data shared.
But it would be...politically useful for us to uncover the truth.
We haven't found any fingerprints yet, and are only starting to ascertain the nature of the cypher, but have confirmed the village it was sent from. The information is being passed to MI5, of course...but you have plenty of time to get to...
Denbigh North. Near Milton Keynes, if you didn't know. No guns, of course, but Q Branch packed you an away kit...
The globe-trotting glamour in this job has gone distinctly downhill in recent years. I remember when it was all bikinis and sports cars...
So...show the Americans EXACTLY how useful we remain. I understand. I DID tell our American friend they were being short-sighted.
They need all the HumInt they can get. Drones won't do everything.
Plus... extrajudicial killing of foreign nationals?
That's MY job.
That was black even for you, 007.
Do run along.

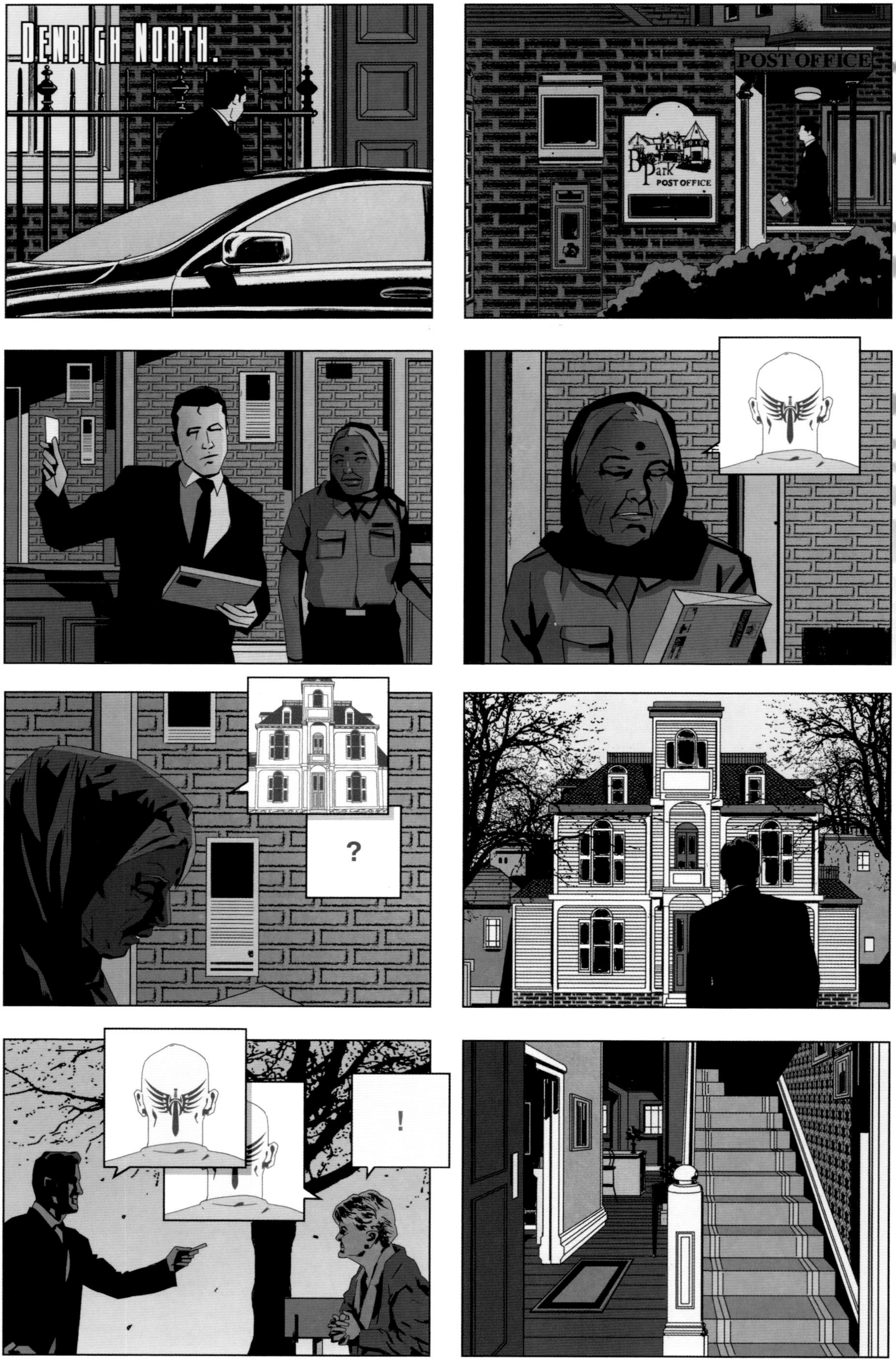
DENBIGH NORTH.
POST OFFICE
POST OFFICE
?
!

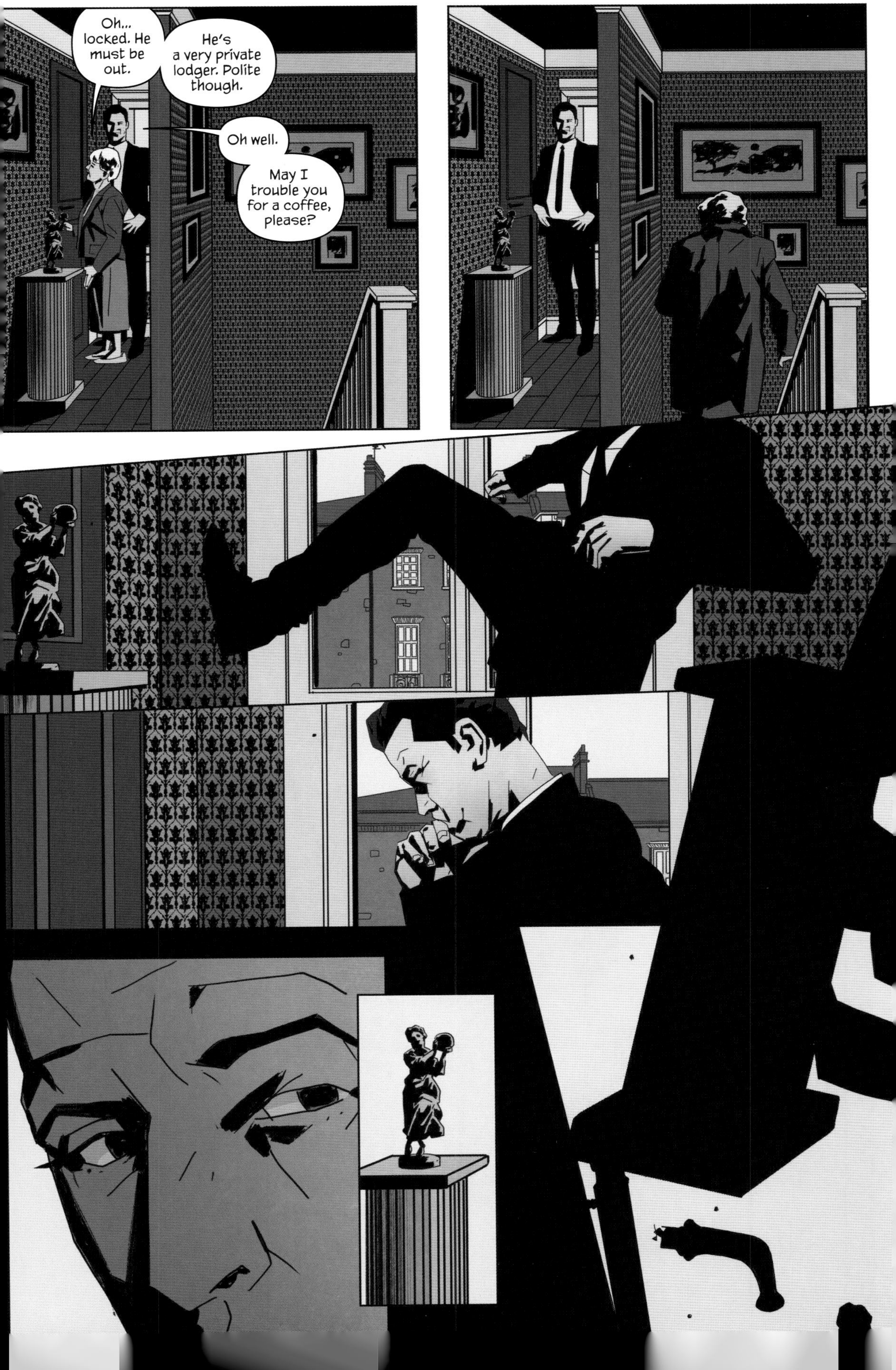
Oh... locked. He must be out.
He's a very private lodger. Polite though.
Oh well.
May I trouble you for a coffee, please?

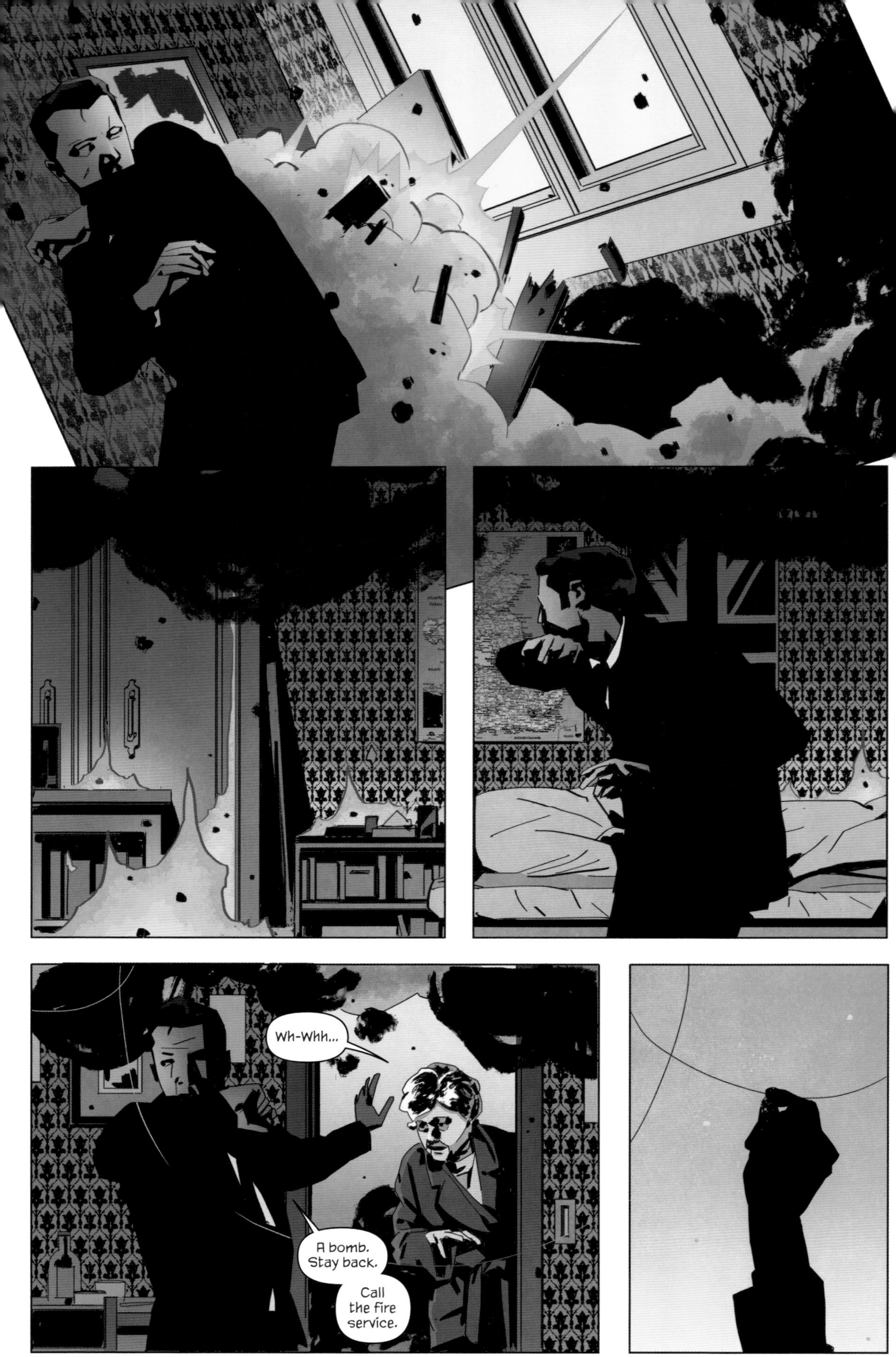
Wh-Whh...
A bomb. Stay back.
Call the fire service.

Hmm. Pin from a Mills, if I'm not mistaken.

An antique.

Call M, please.

Calling M.

There's been a little bother, M. WW period booby trap. Set to torch the room if disturbed.

But if I can check the windowsill for a second...

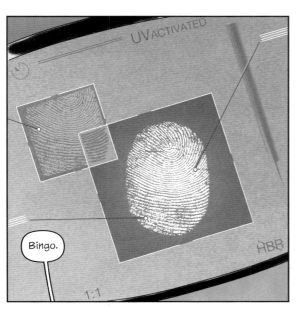

UV ACTIVATED

1:1

HBR

Bingo.

KLKK

Taking a photo and sending it through.

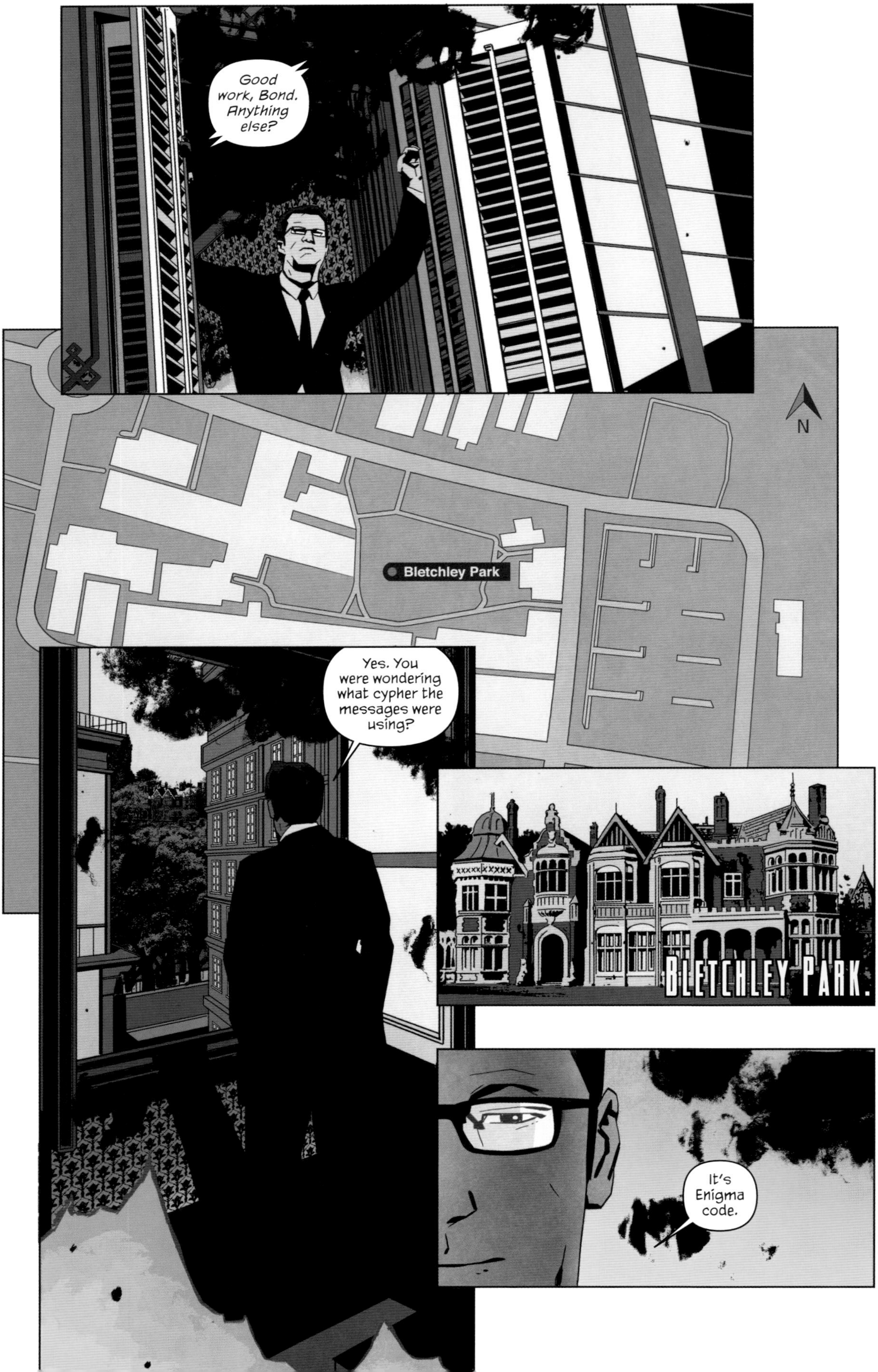
Good work, Bond. Anything else?
N
Bletchley Park
Yes. You were wondering what cypher the messages were using?
BLETCHLEY PARK.
It's Enigma code.

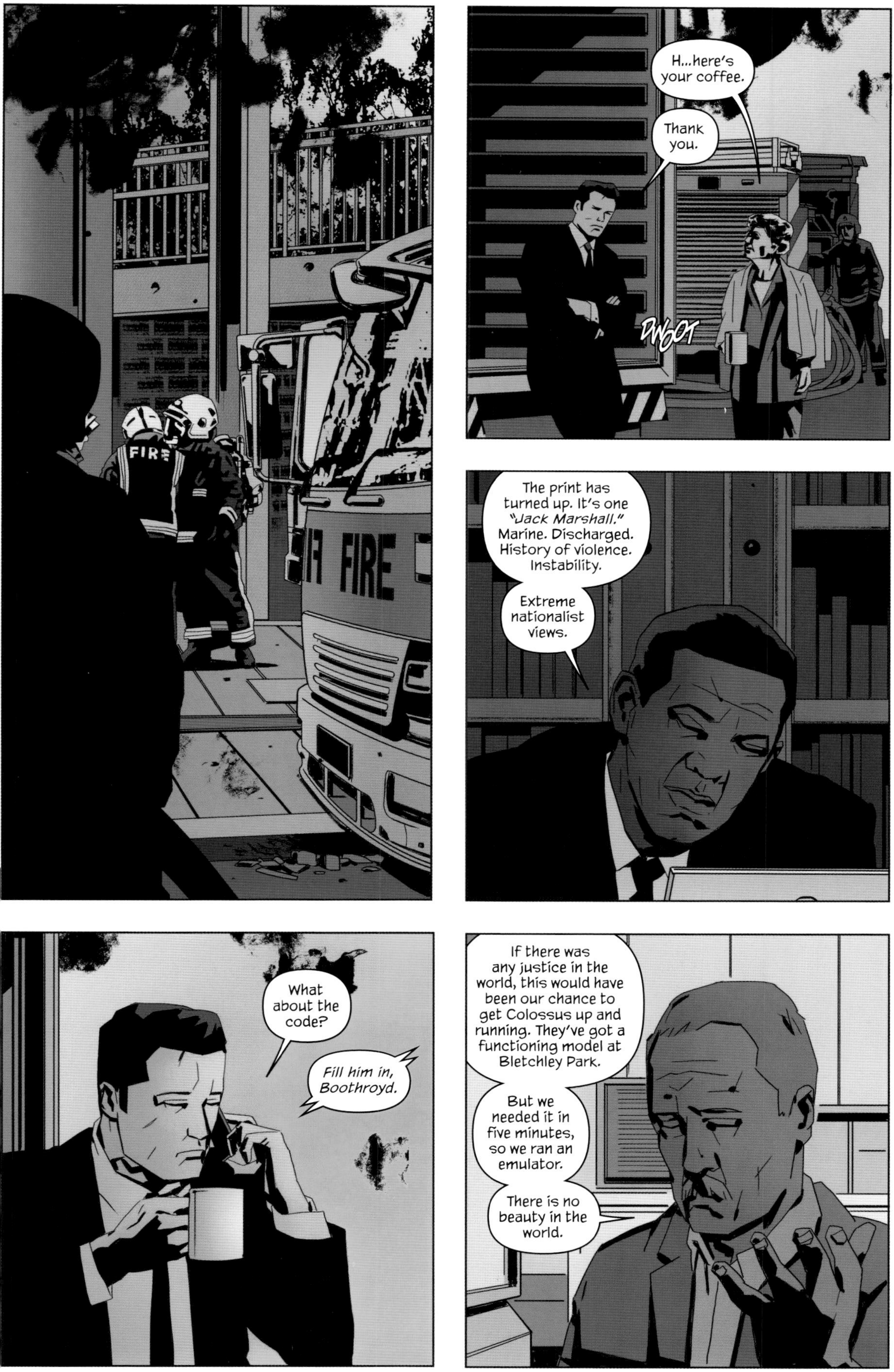
H...here's your coffee.
Thank you.
DWOOT
The print has turned up. It's one *"Jack Marshall."* Marine. Discharged. History of violence. Instability.
Extreme nationalist views.
What about the code?
Fill him in, Boothroyd.
If there was any justice in the world, this would have been our chance to get Colossus up and running. They've got a functioning model at Bletchley Park.
But we needed it in five minutes, so we ran an emulator.
There is no beauty in the world.

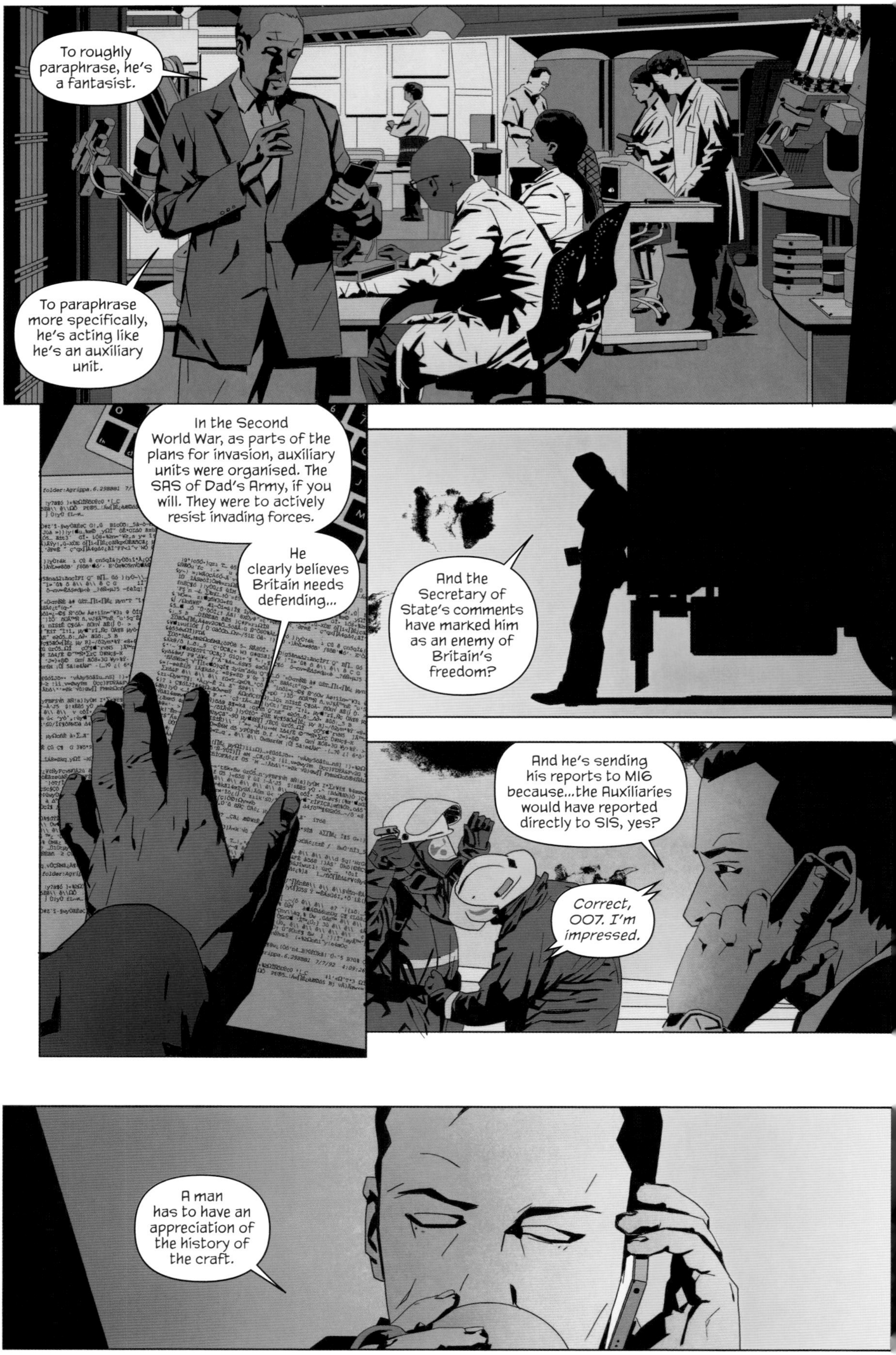

To roughly paraphrase, he's a fantasist.
To paraphrase more specifically, he's acting like he's an auxiliary unit.
In the Second World War, as parts of the plans for invasion, auxiliary units were organised. The SAS of Dad's Army, if you will. They were to actively resist invading forces.
He clearly believes Britain needs defending...
And the Secretary of State's comments have marked him as an enemy of Britain's freedom?
And he's sending his reports to MI6 because...the Auxiliaries would have reported directly to SIS, yes?
Correct, 007. I'm impressed.
A man has to have an appreciation of the history of the craft.

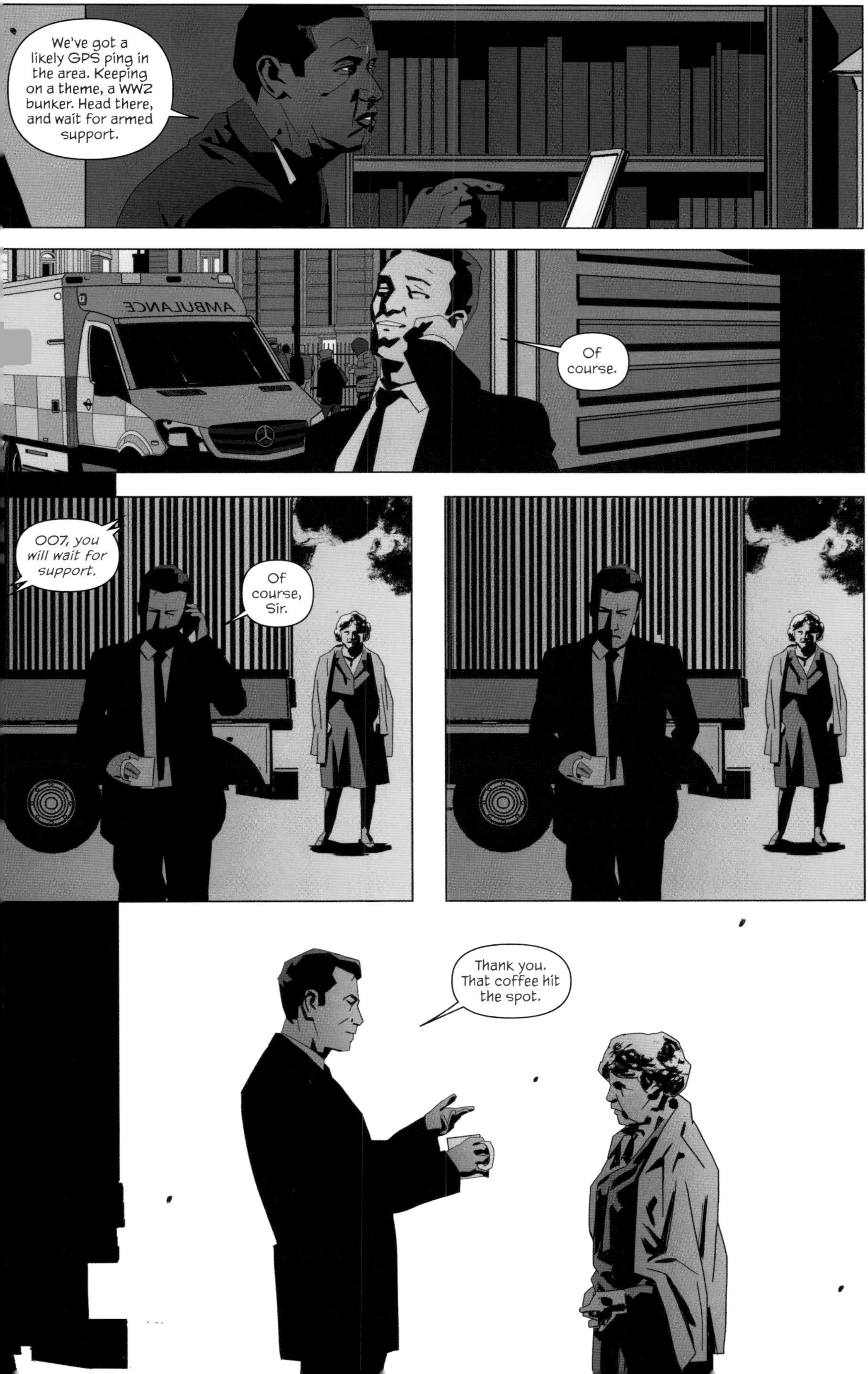
We've got a likely GPS ping in the area. Keeping on a theme, a WW2 bunker. Head there, and wait for armed support.
AMBULANCE
Of course.
007, you will wait for support.
Of course, Sir.
Thank you. That coffee hit the spot.

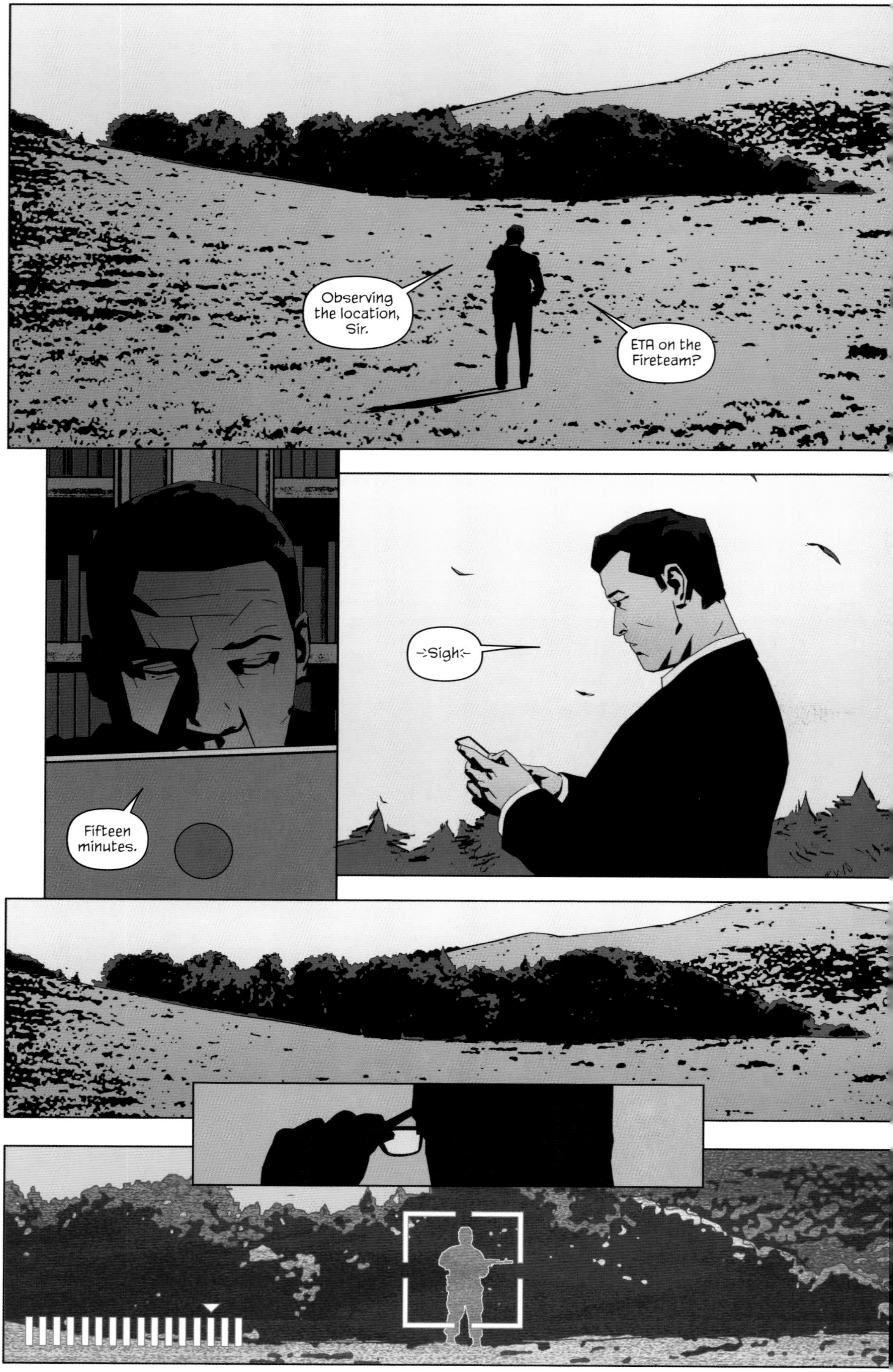
Observing the location, Sir.
ETA on the Fireteam?
Fifteen minutes.
-Sigh-

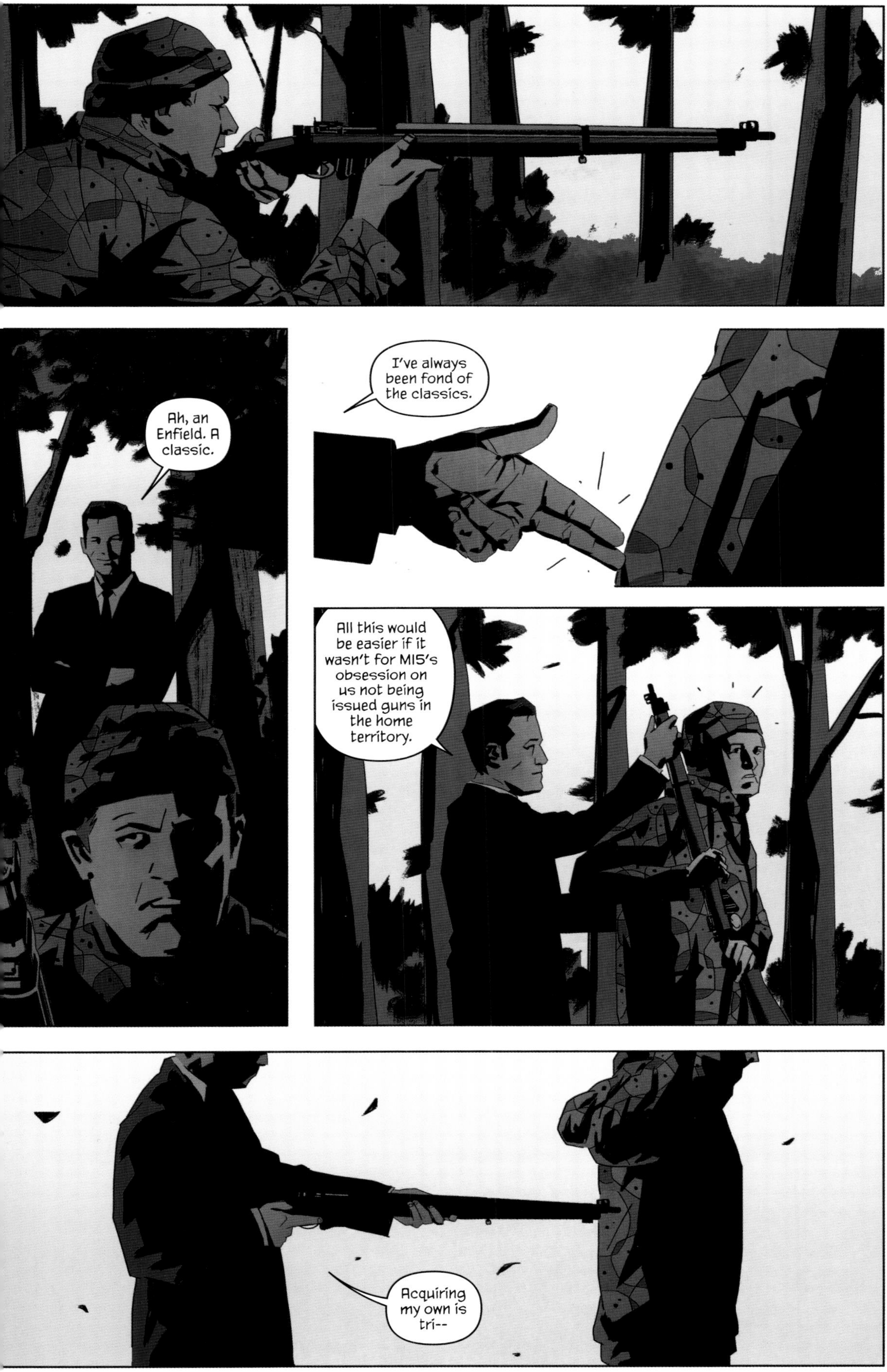
Ah, an Enfield. A classic.
I've always been fond of the classics.
All this would be easier if it wasn't for MI5's obsession on us not being issued guns in the home territory.
Acquiring my own is tri--

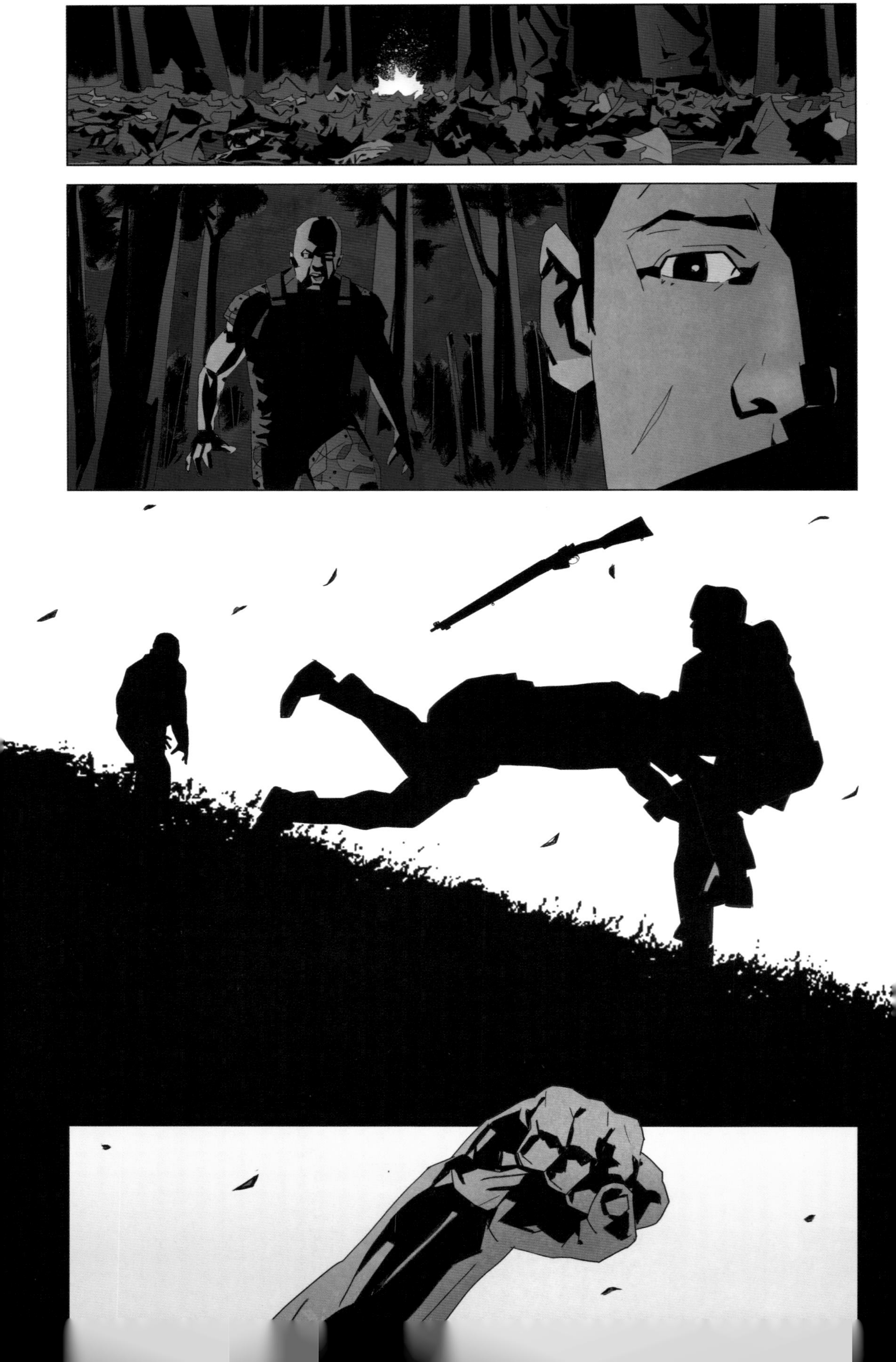

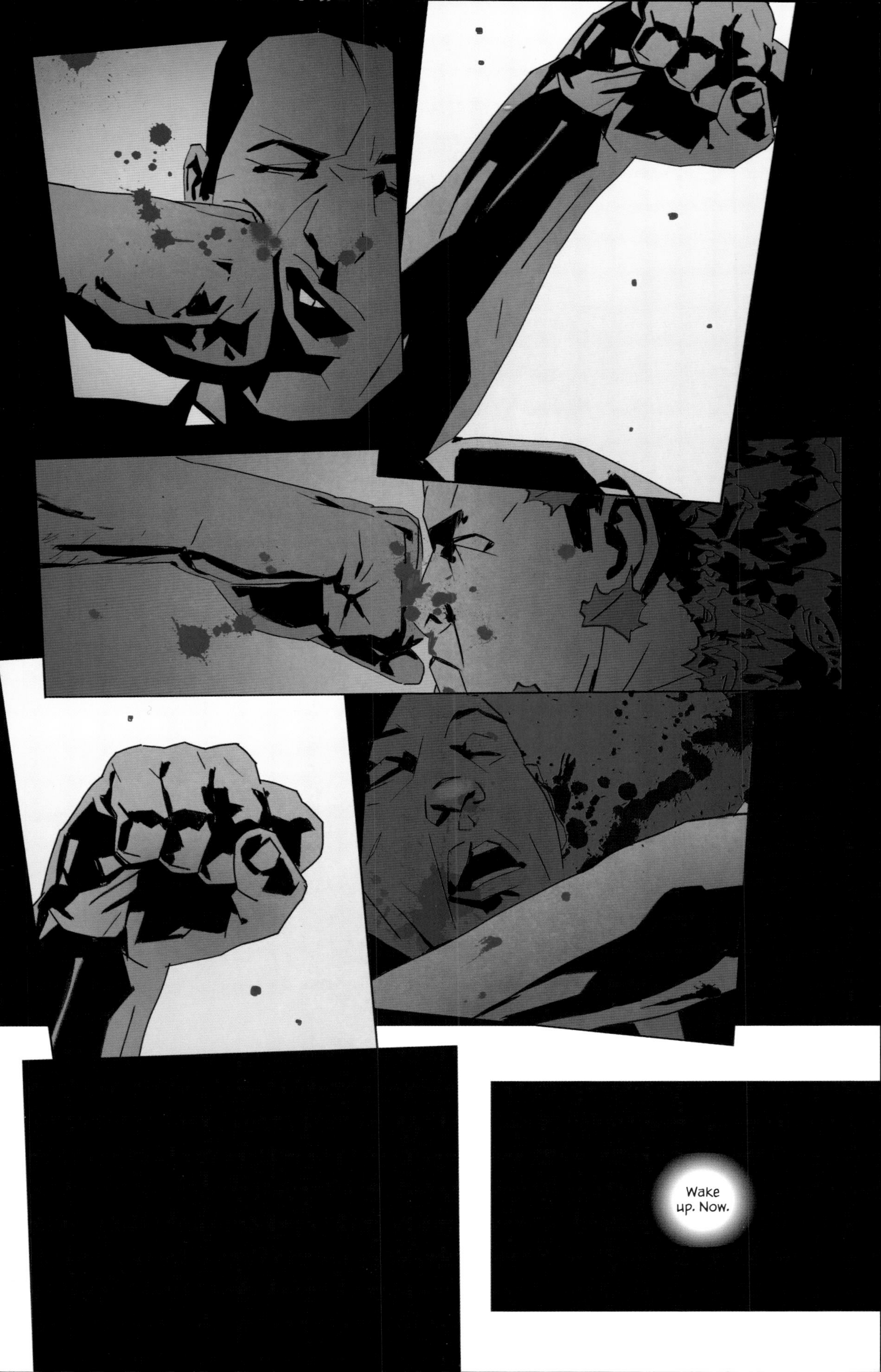
Wake up. Now.

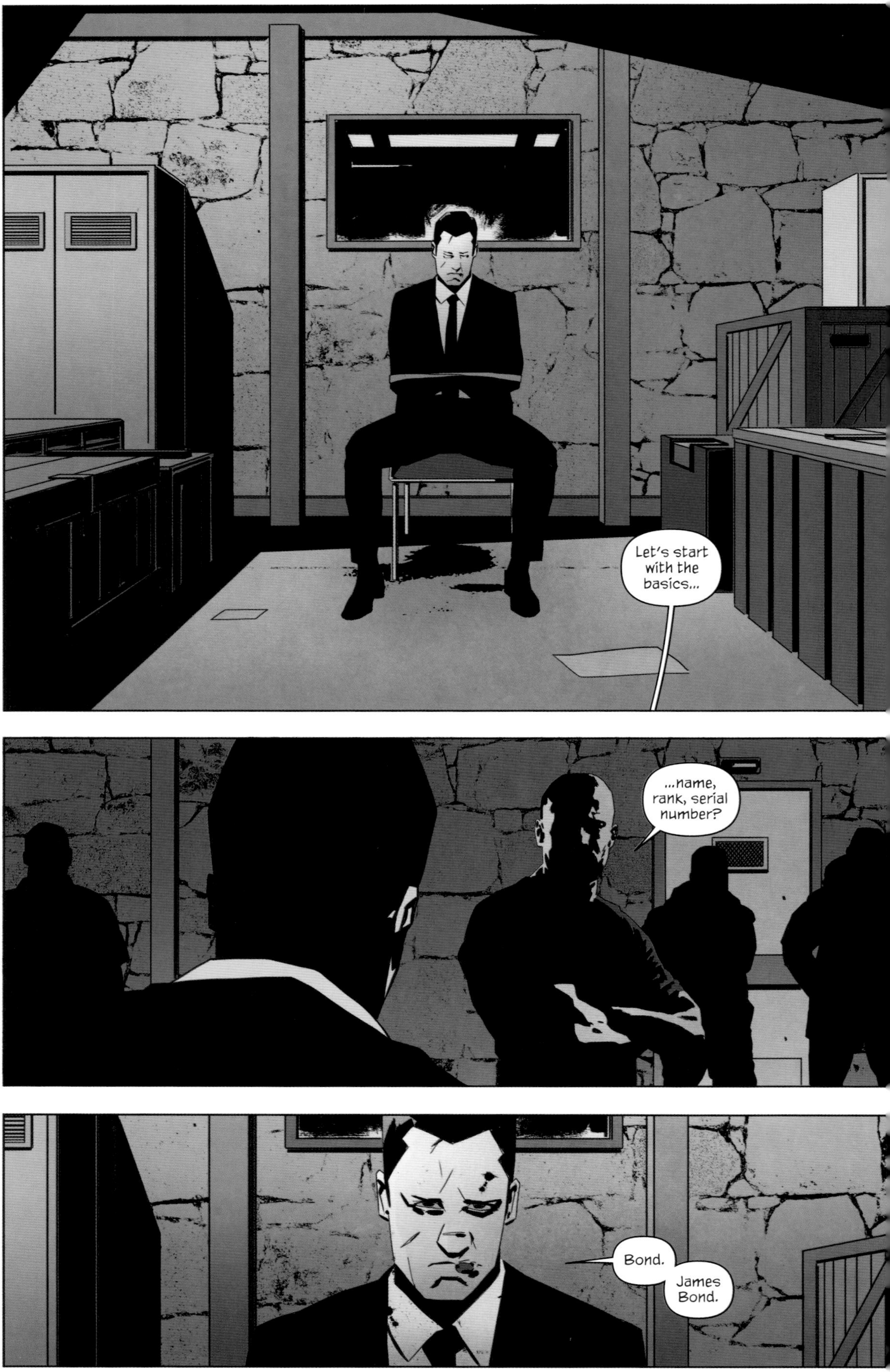
Let's start with the basics...
...name, rank, serial number?
Bond.
James Bond.

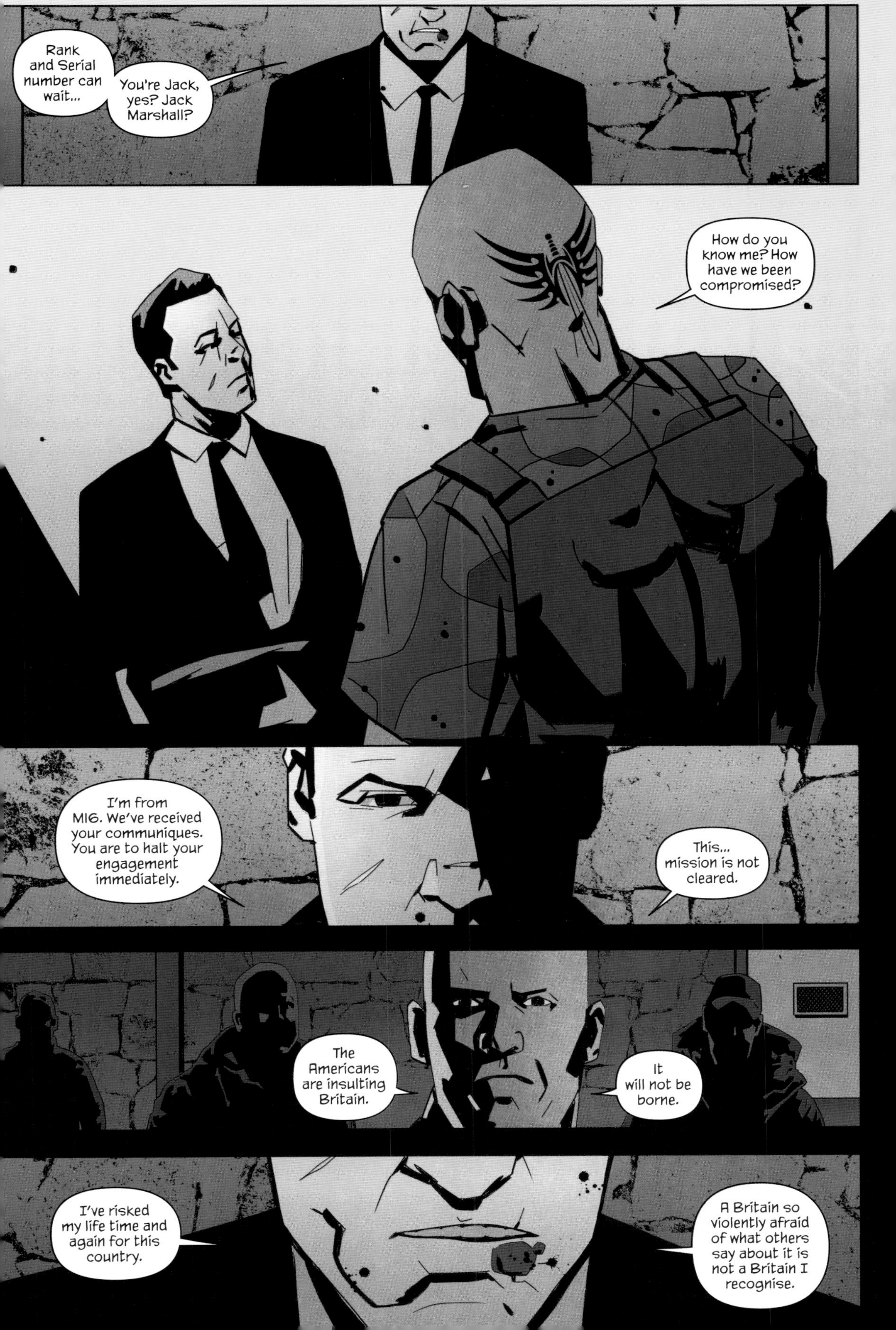

Rank and Serial number can wait...
You're Jack, yes? Jack Marshall?
How do you know me? How have we been compromised?
I'm from MI6. We've received your communiques. You are to halt your engagement immediately.
This... mission is not cleared.
The Americans are insulting Britain.
It will not be borne.
I've risked my life time and again for this country.
A Britain so violently afraid of what others say about it is not a Britain I recognise.

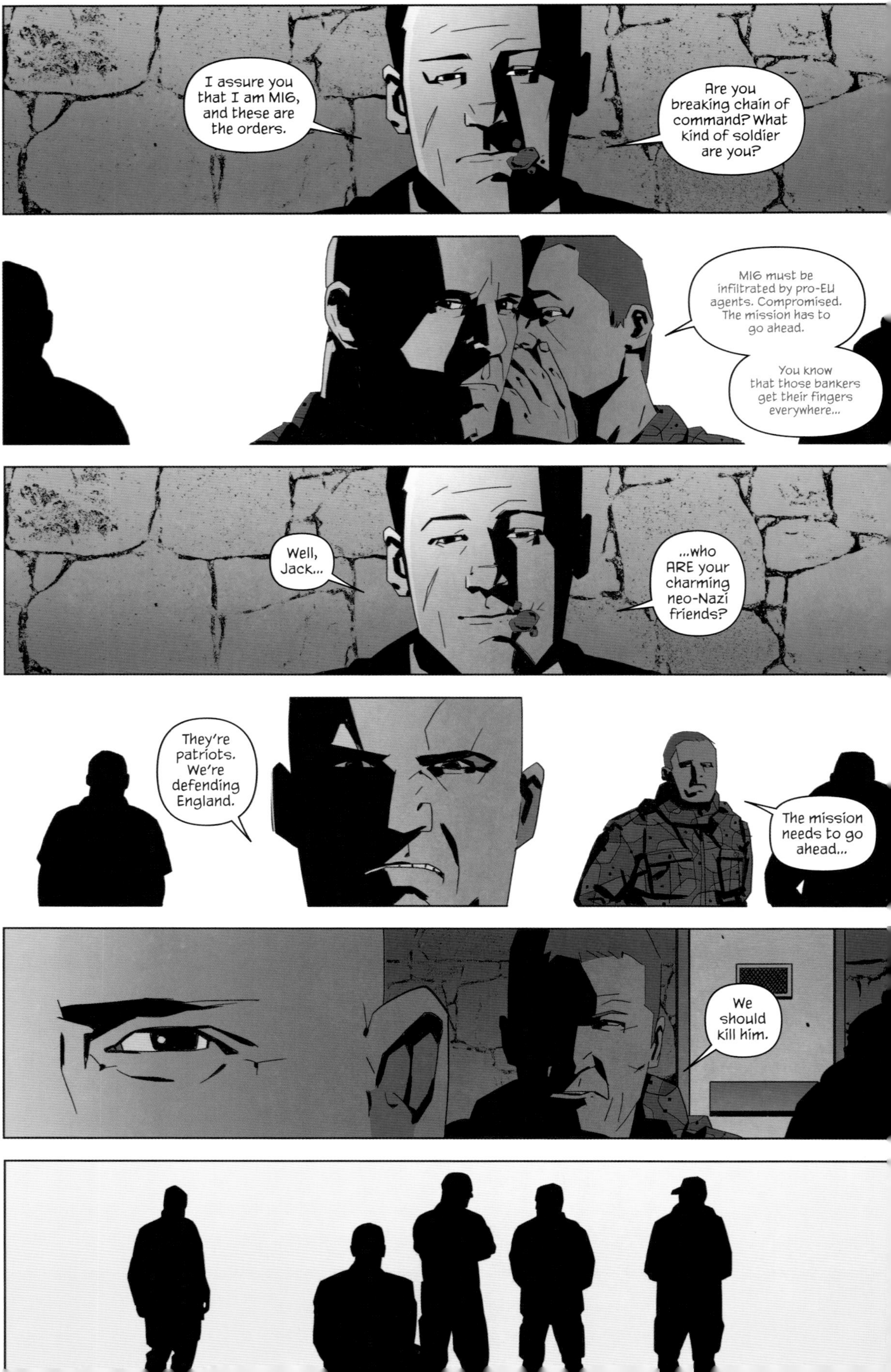
I assure you that I am MI6, and these are the orders.
Are you breaking chain of command? What kind of soldier are you?
MI6 must be infiltrated by pro-EU agents. Compromised. The mission has to go ahead.
You know that those bankers get their fingers everywhere...
Well, Jack...
...who ARE your charming neo-Nazi friends?
They're patriots. We're defending England.
The mission needs to go ahead...
We should kill him.

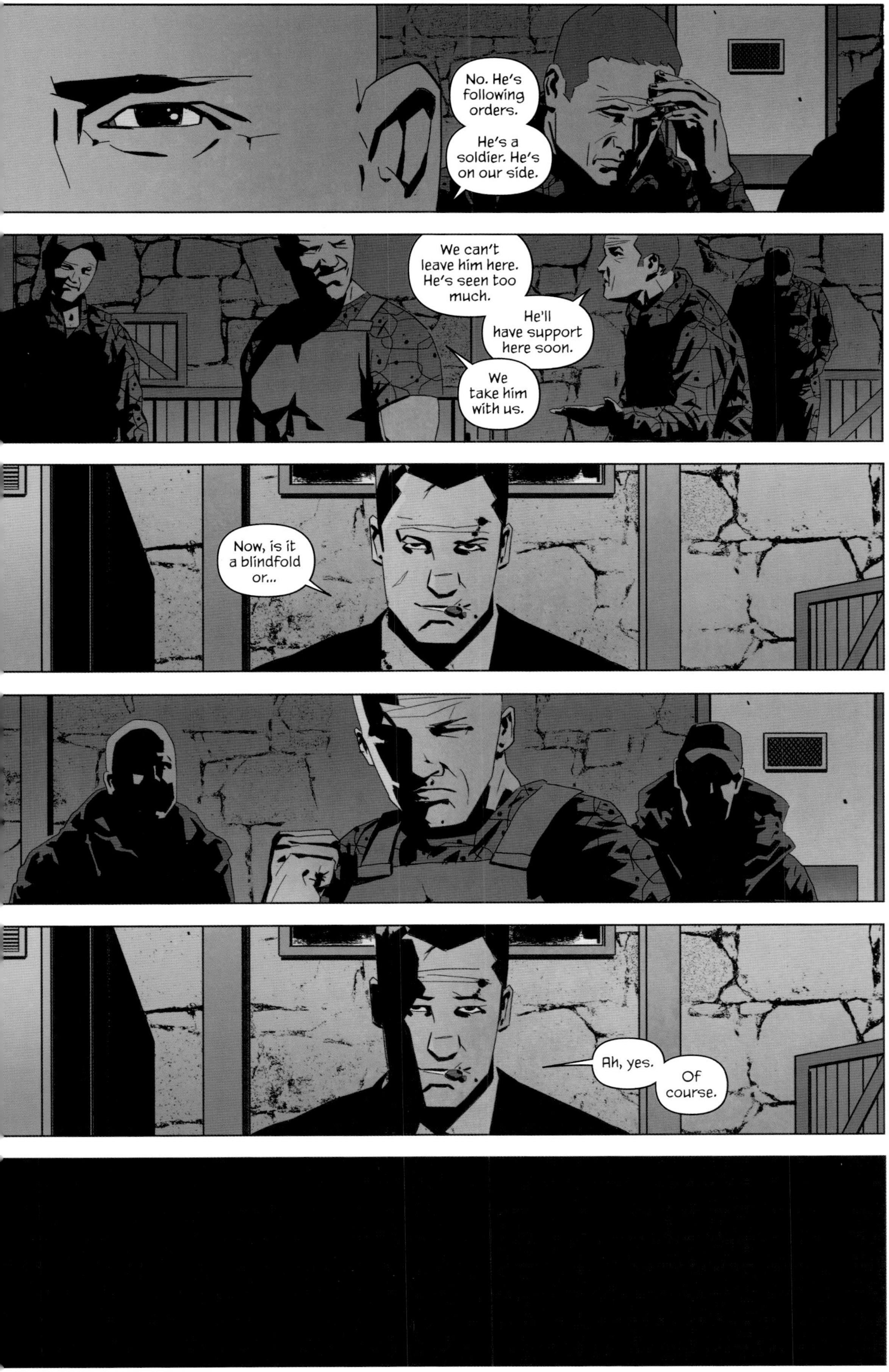
No. He's following orders.
He's a soldier. He's on our side.
We can't leave him here. He's seen too much.
He'll have support here soon.
We take him with us.
Now, is it a blindfold or...
Ah, yes.
Of course.

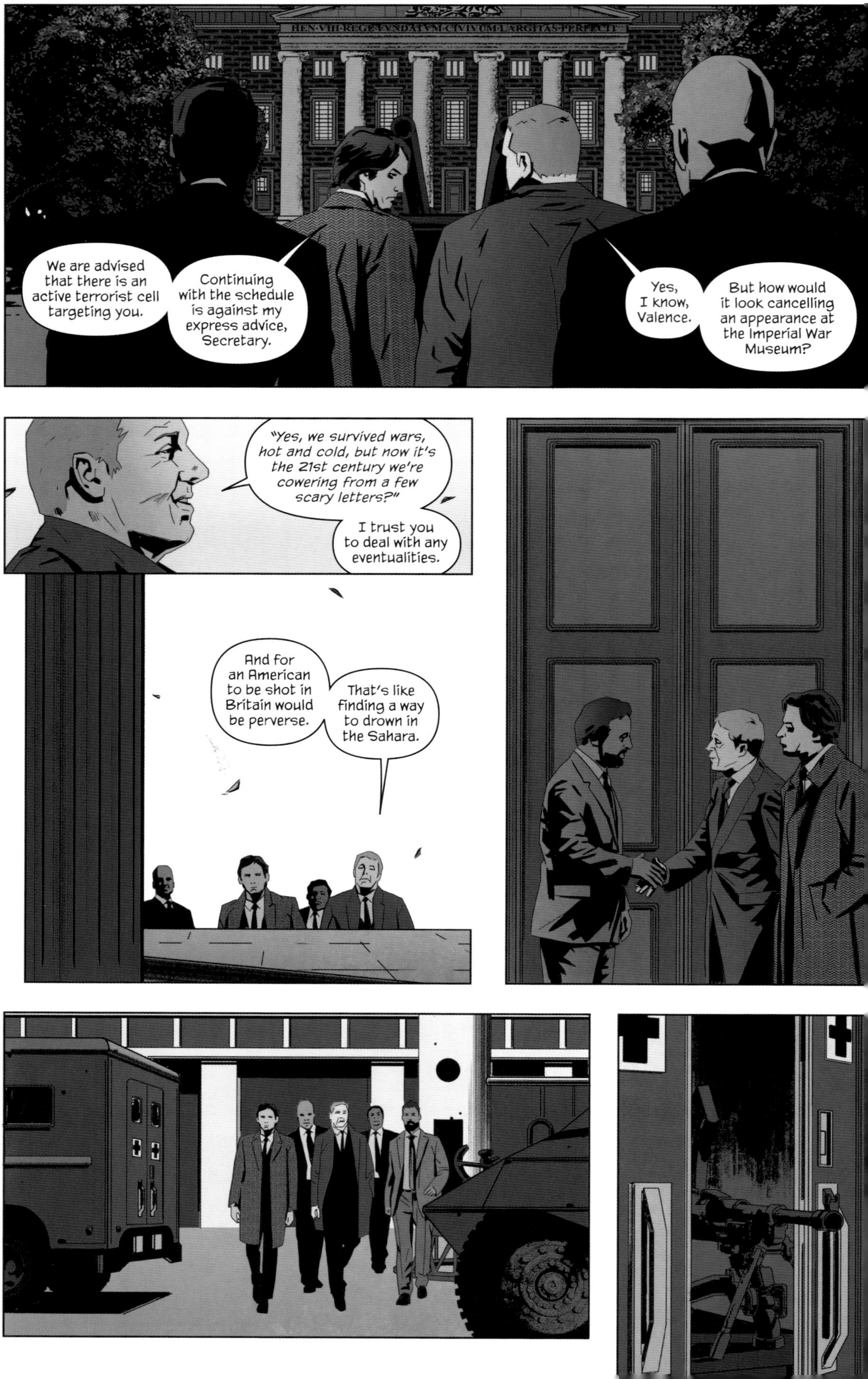

HEN·VIII·REGE·FVNDATVM·CIVIVM·LARGITAS·PERFECIT
We are advised that there is an active terrorist cell targeting you.
Continuing with the schedule is against my express advice, Secretary.
Yes, I know, Valence.
But how would it look cancelling an appearance at the Imperial War Museum?
"Yes, we survived wars, hot and cold, but now it's the 21st century we're cowering from a few scary letters?"
I trust you to deal with any eventualities.
And for an American to be shot in Britain would be perverse.
That's like finding a way to drown in the Sahara.

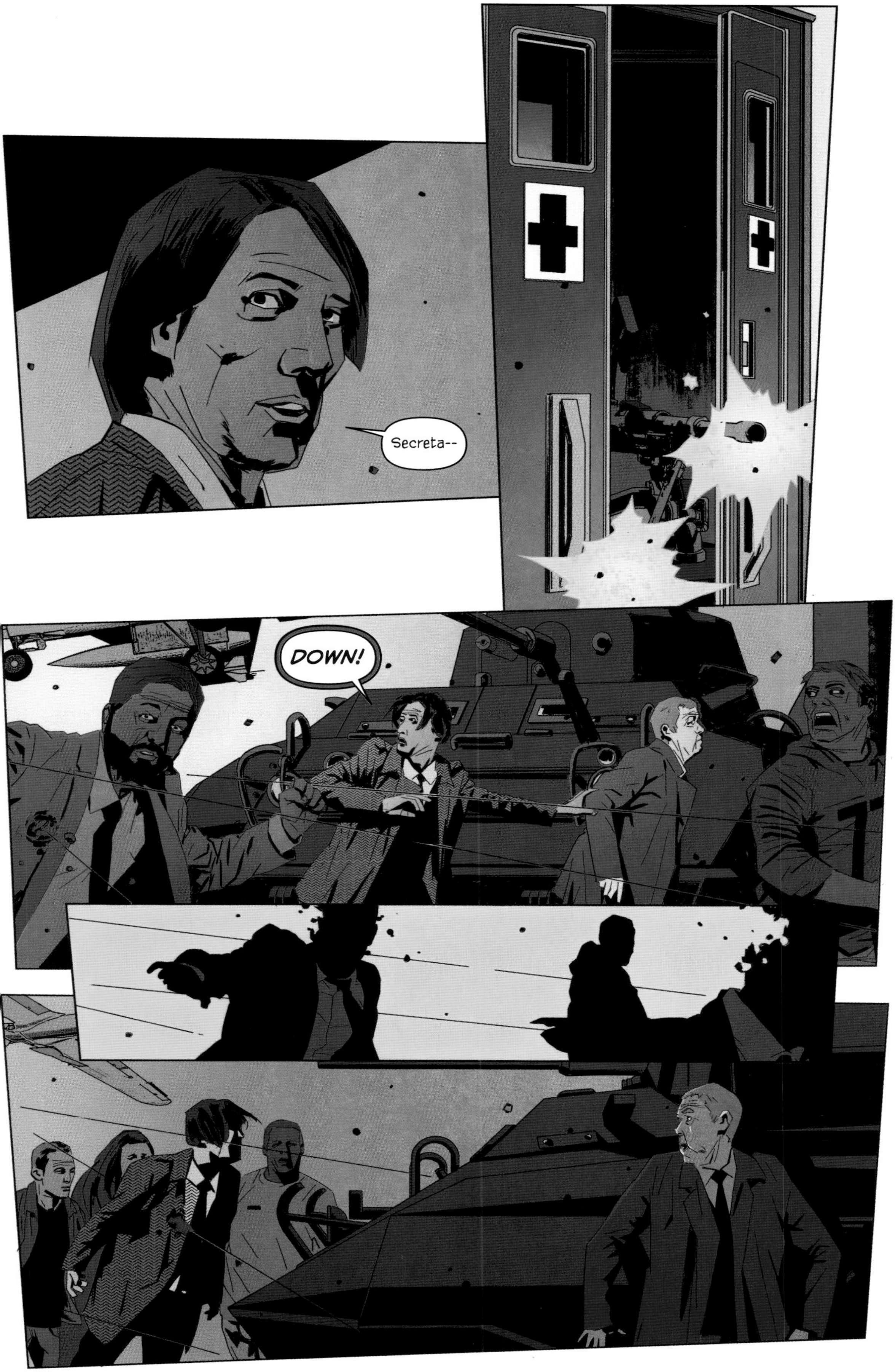
Secreta--
DOWN!

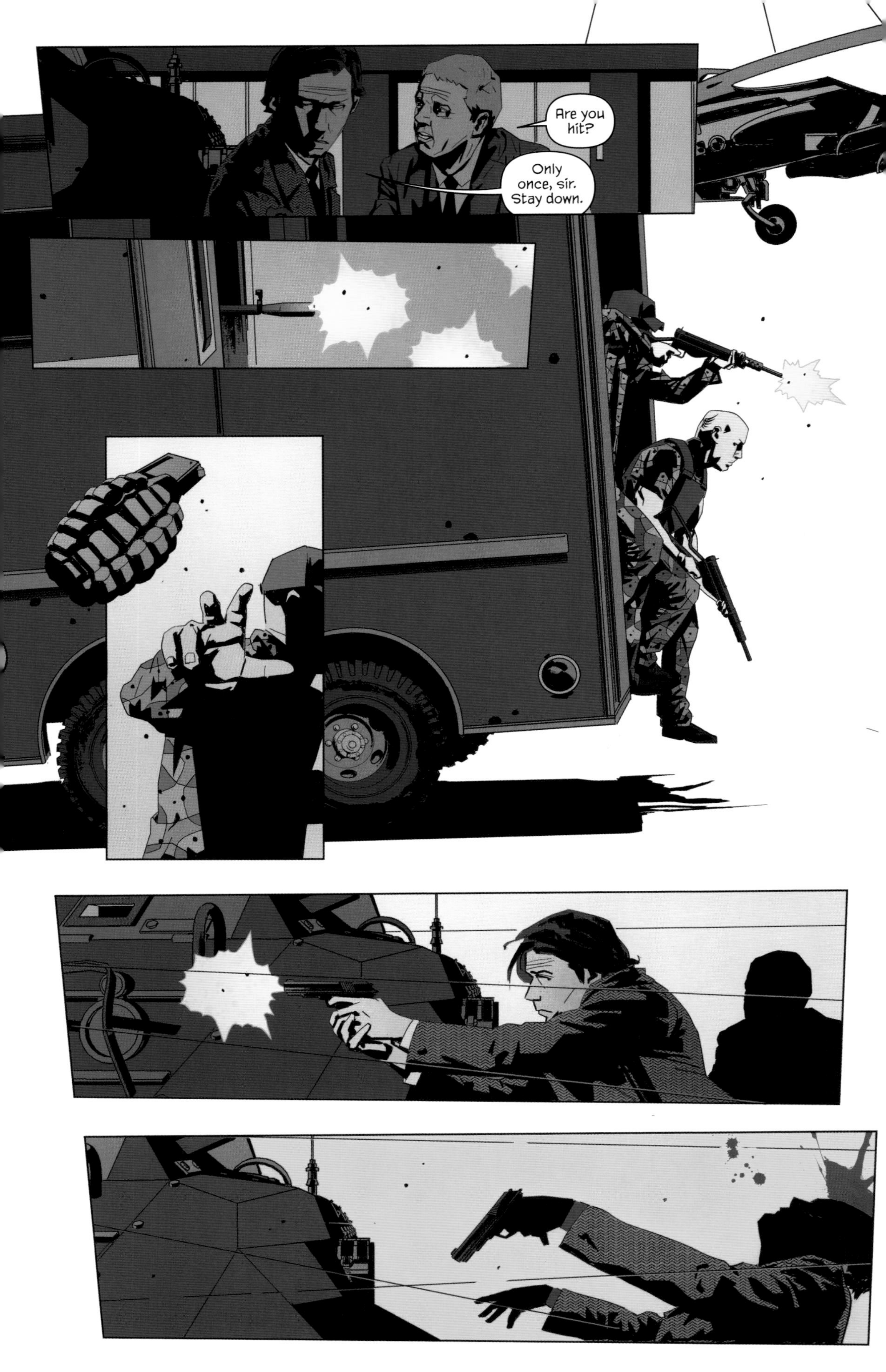
Are you hit?
Only once, sir. Stay down.

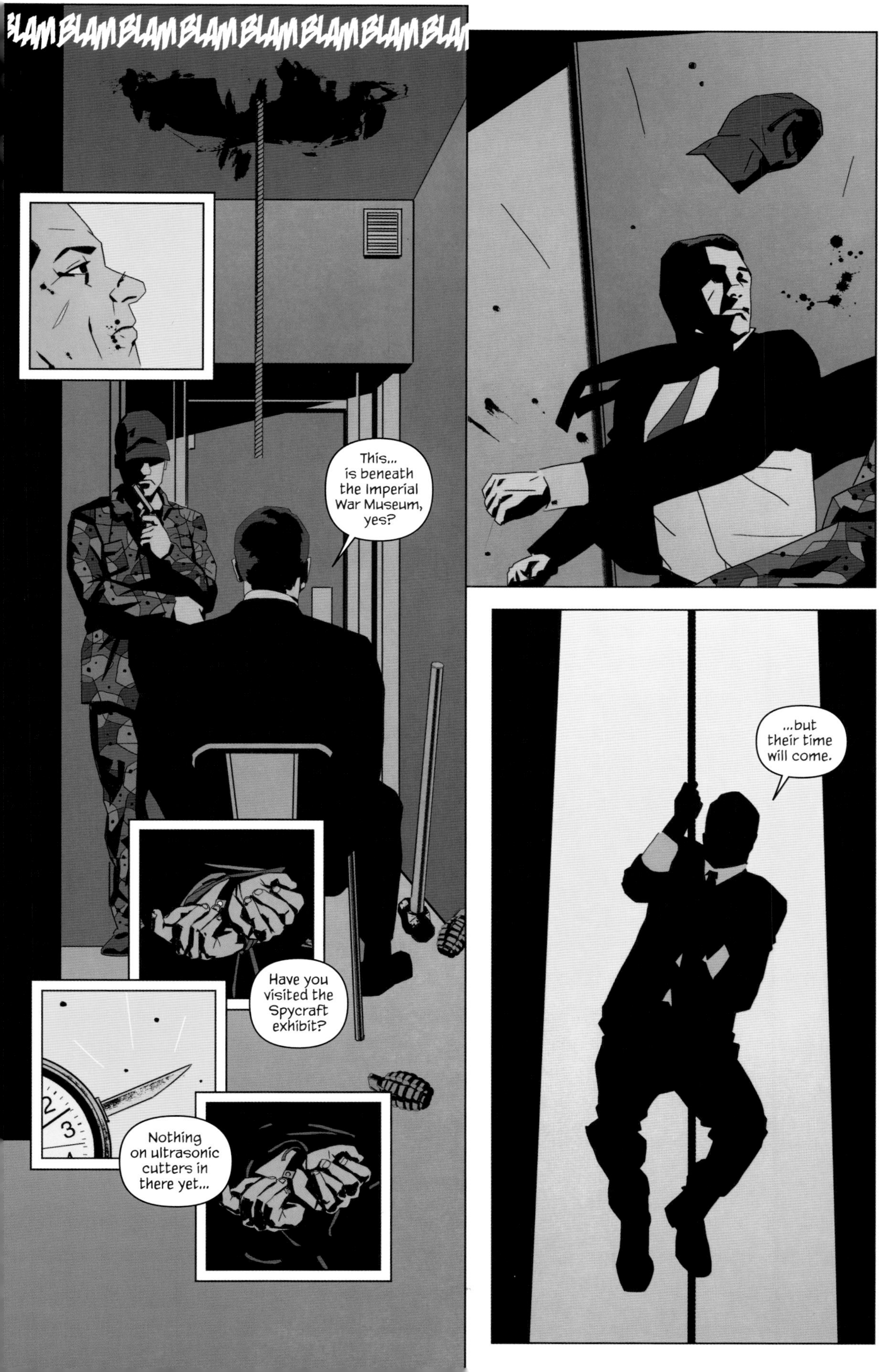
BLAM BLAM BLAM BLAM BLAM BLAM BLAM BLAM
This... is beneath the Imperial War Museum, yes?
Have you visited the Spycraft exhibit?
Nothing on ultrasonic cutters in there yet...
...but their time will come.

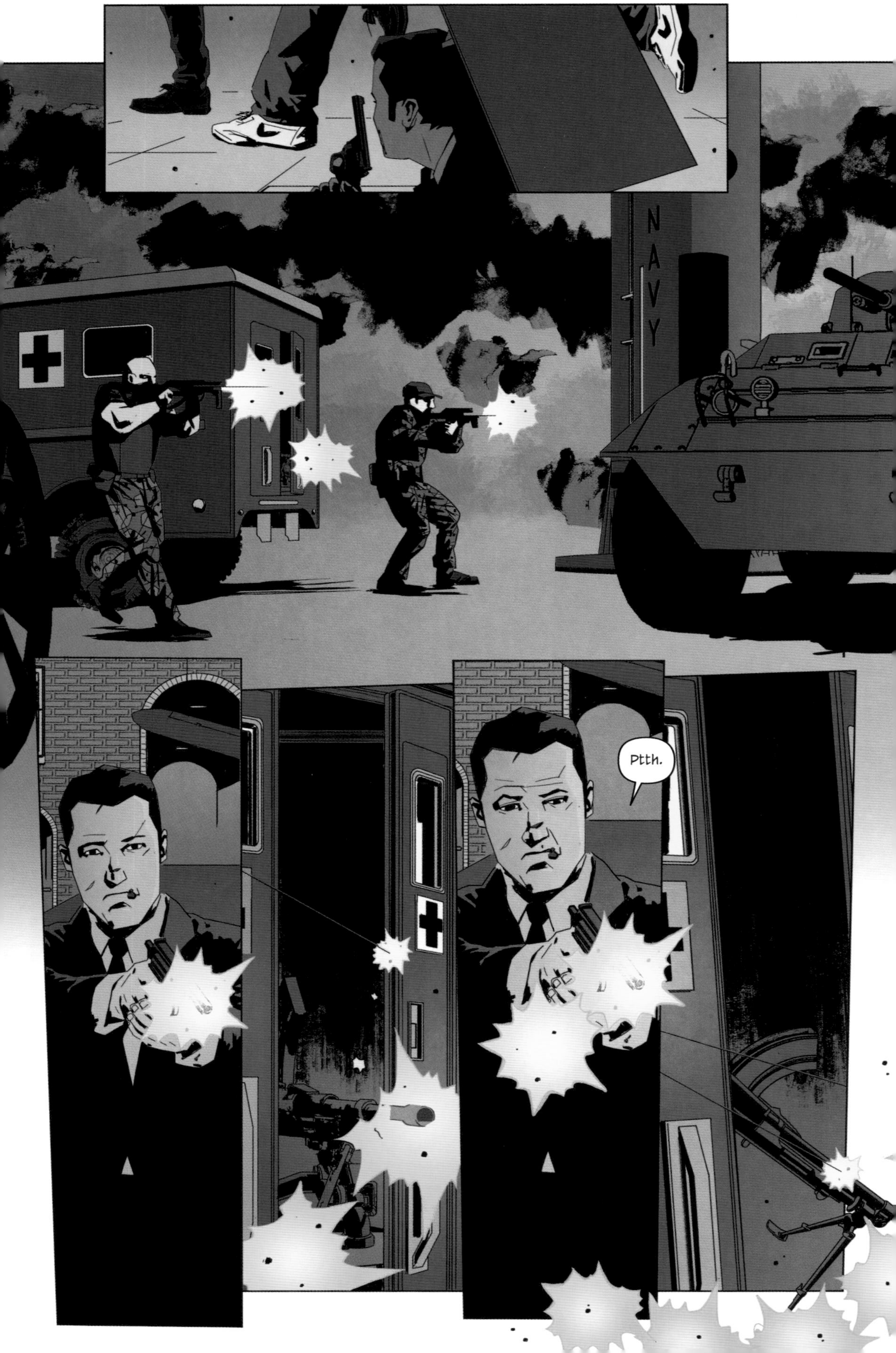
NAVY
Ptth.

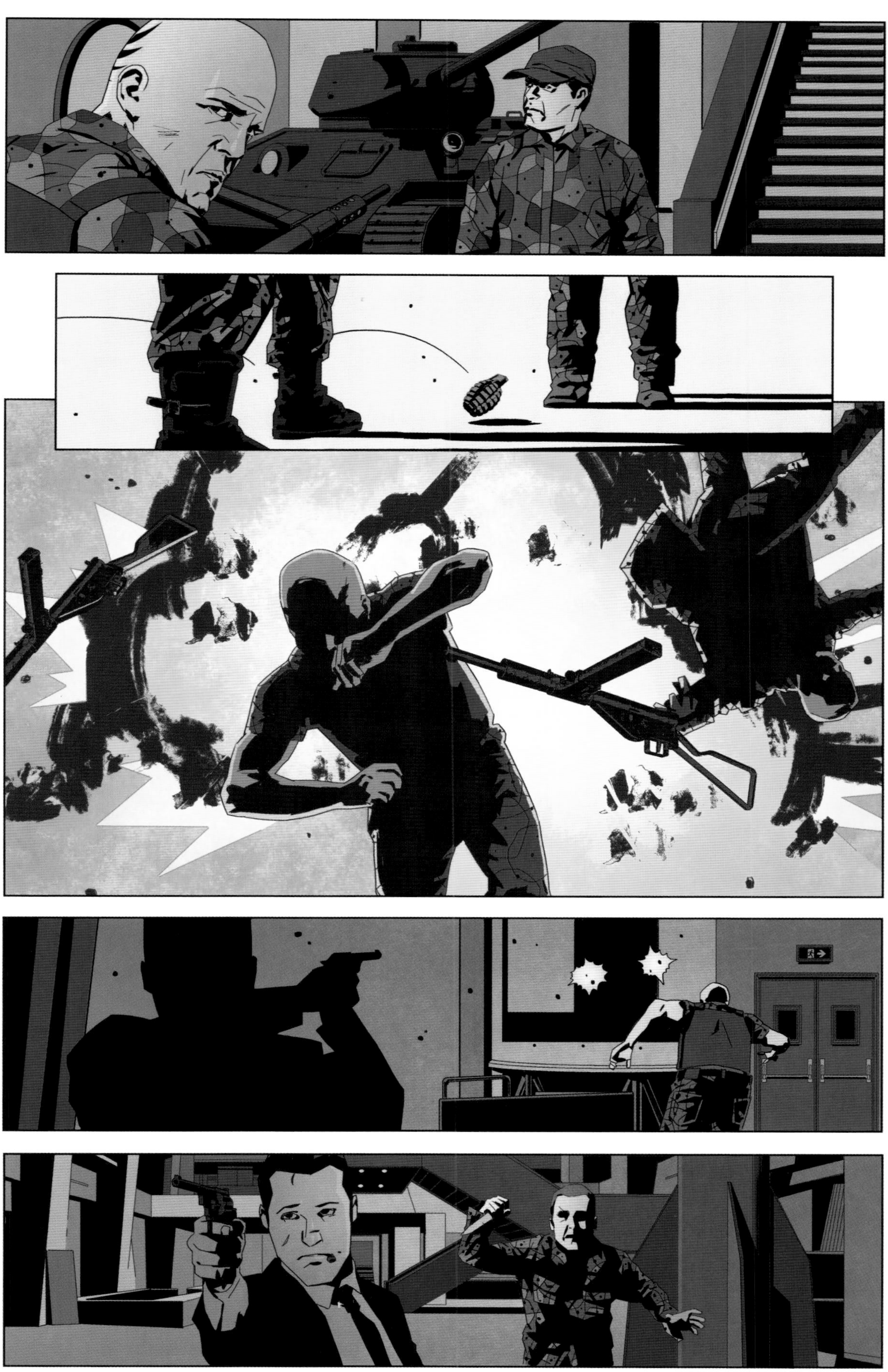

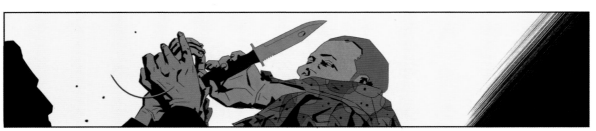

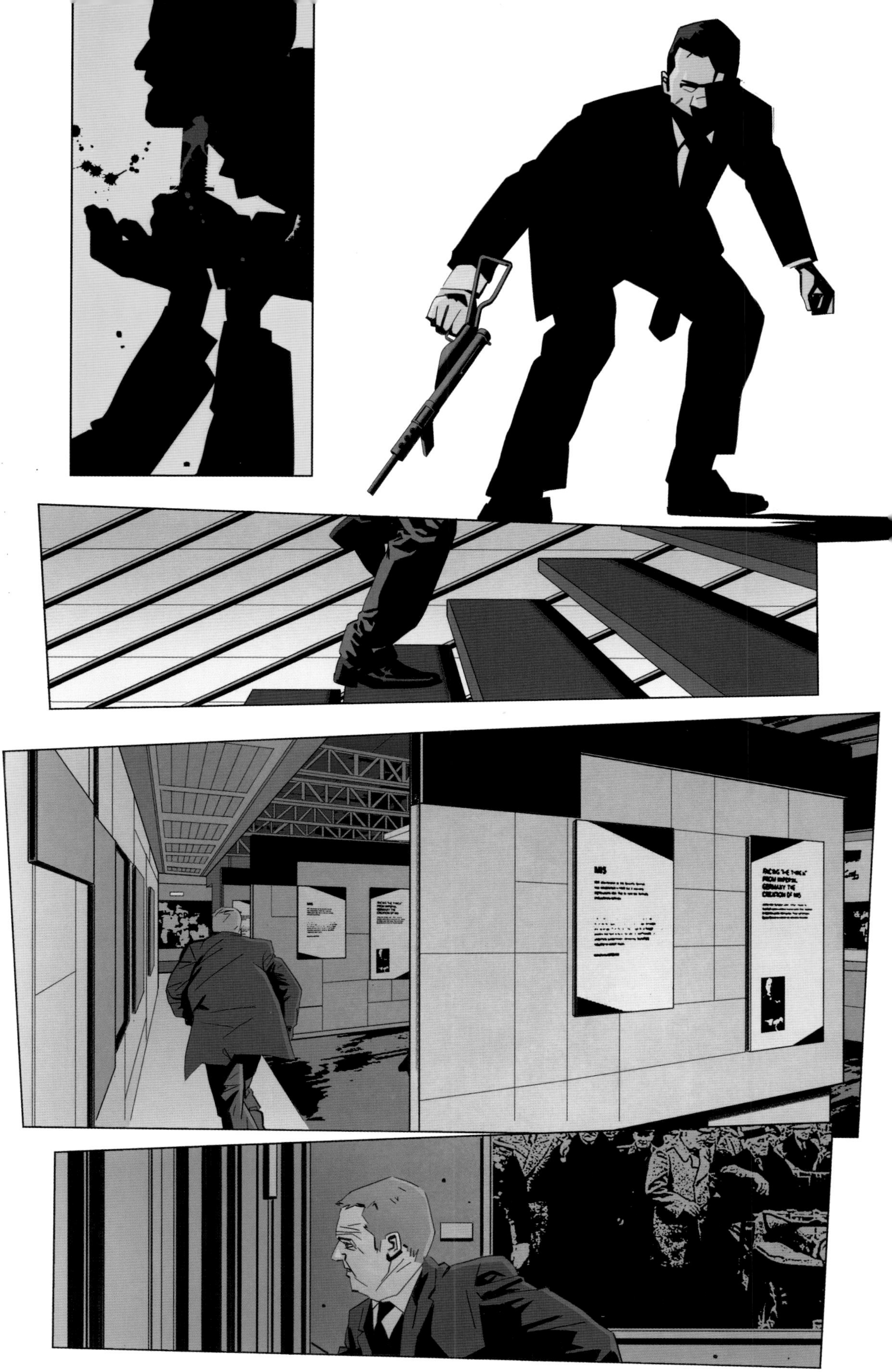
MI5
FACING THE THREAT FROM IMPERIAL GERMANY THE CREATION OF MI5

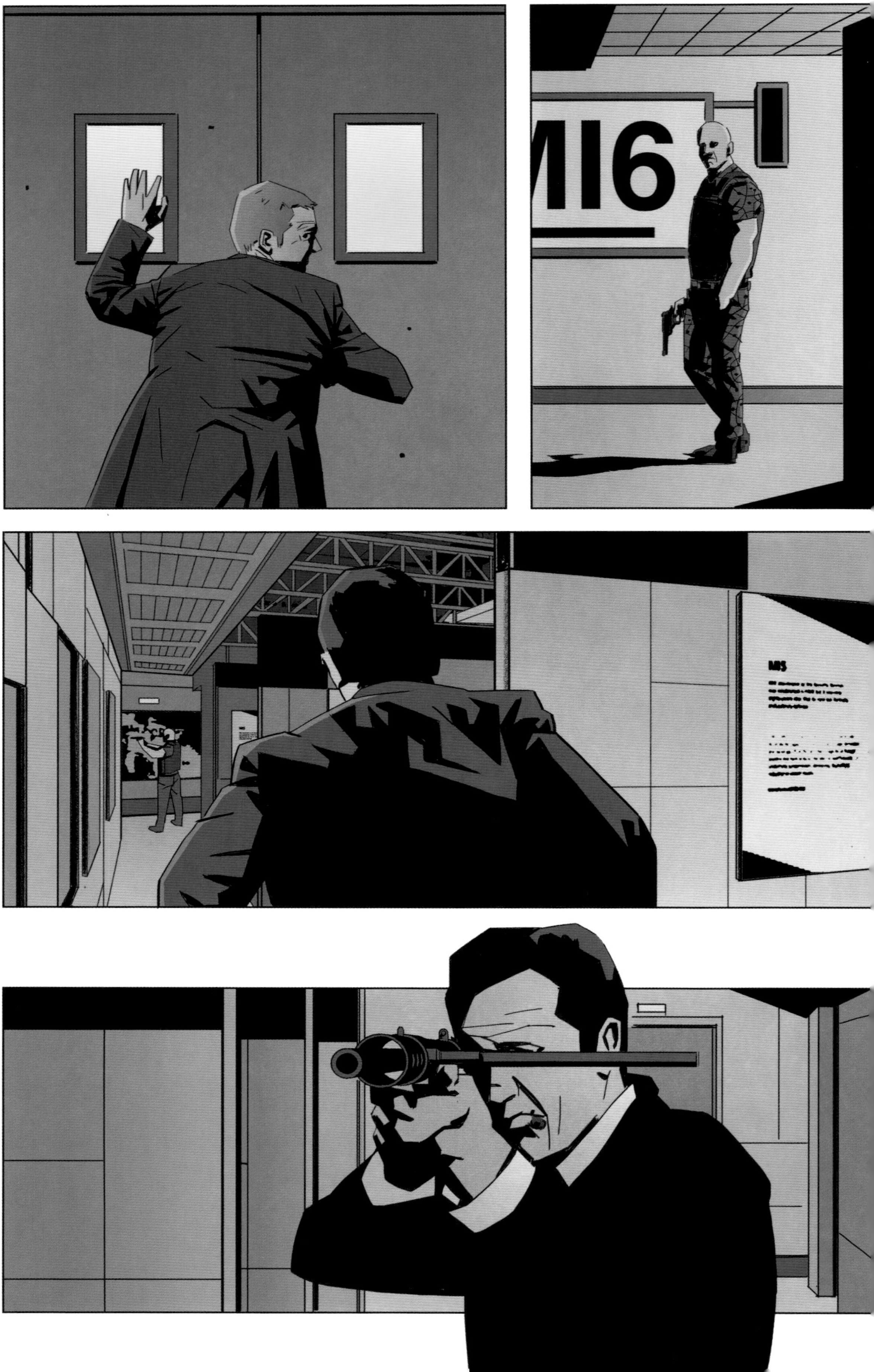
MI6

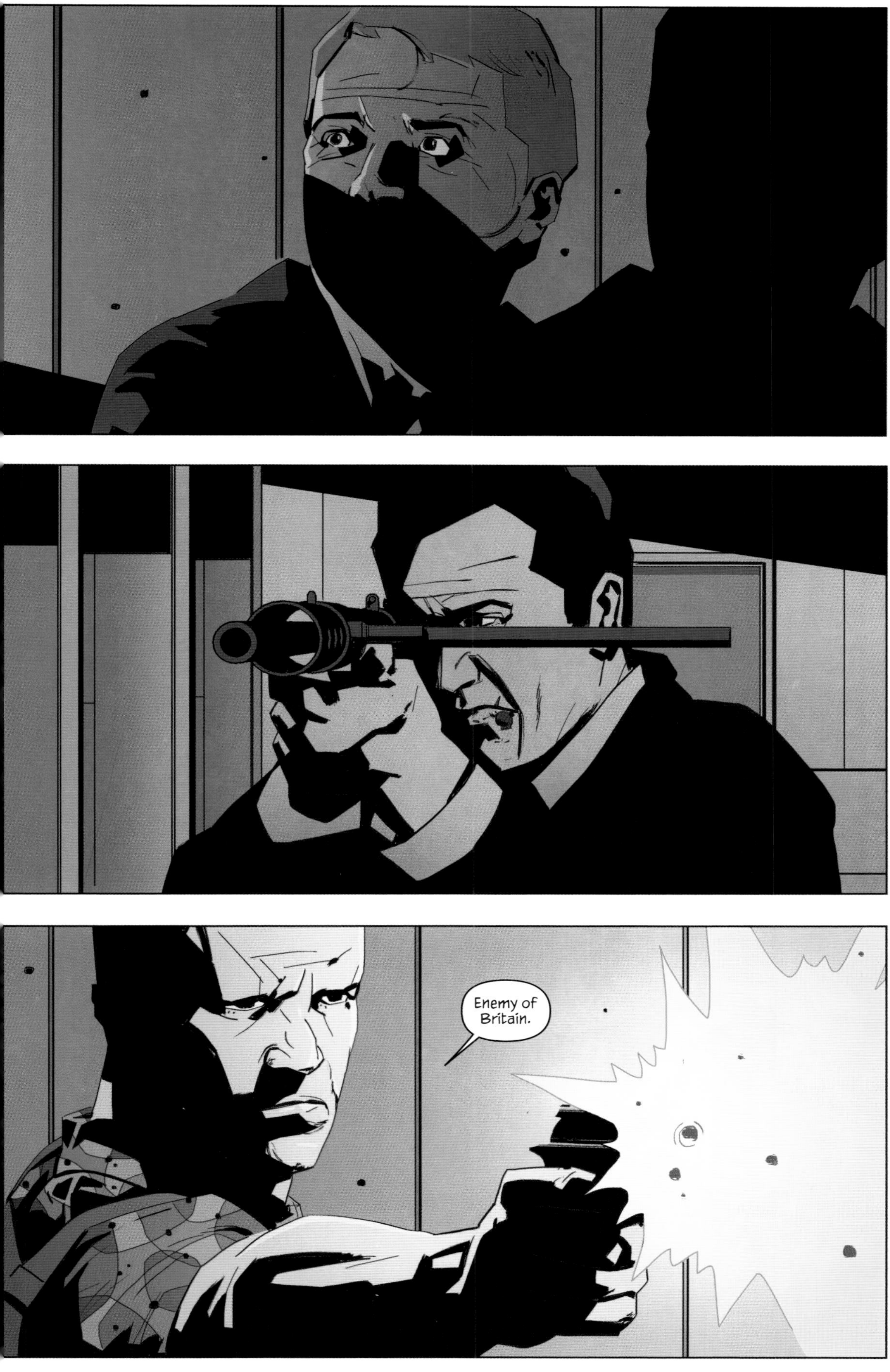
Enemy of Britain.

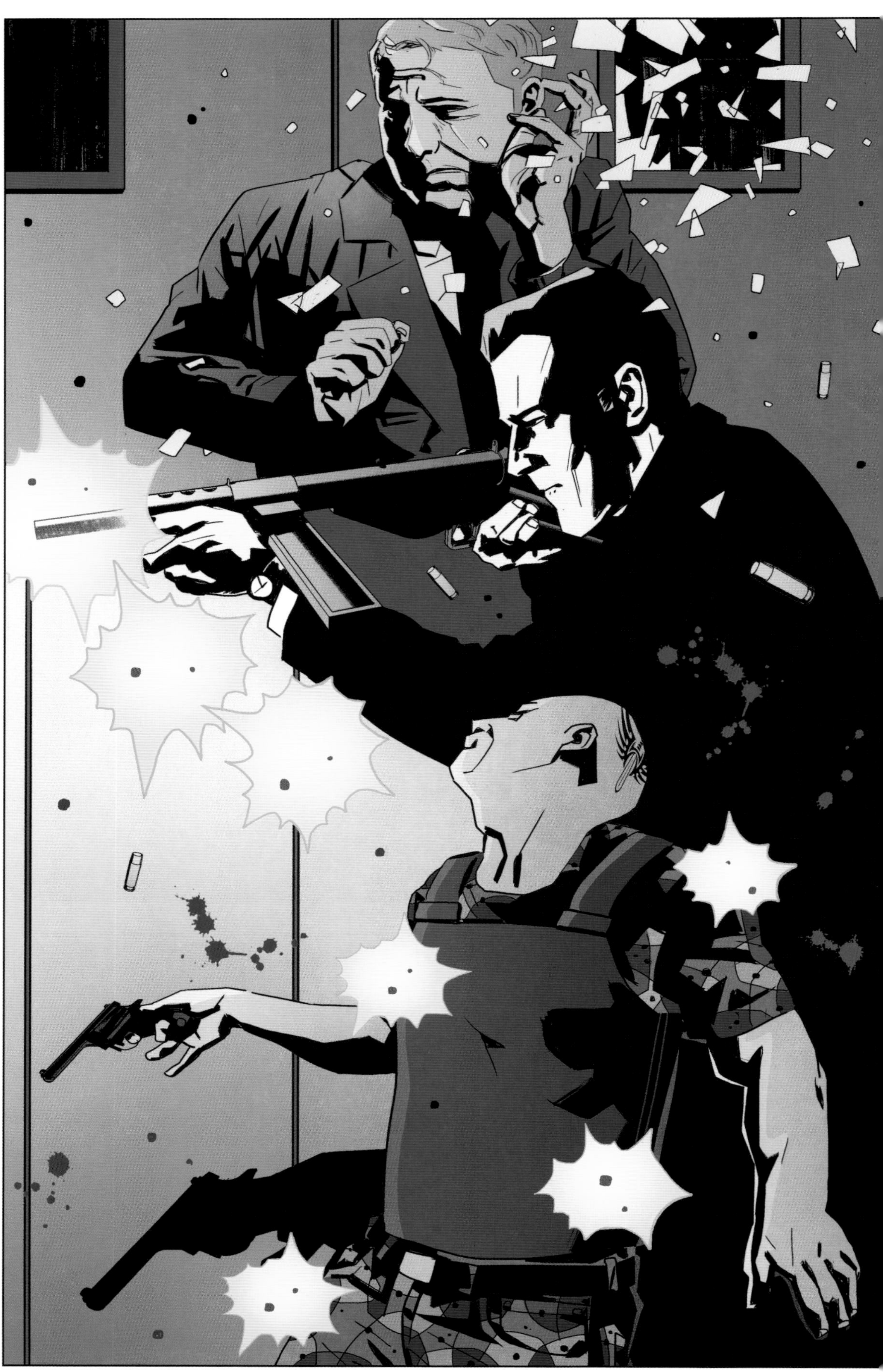

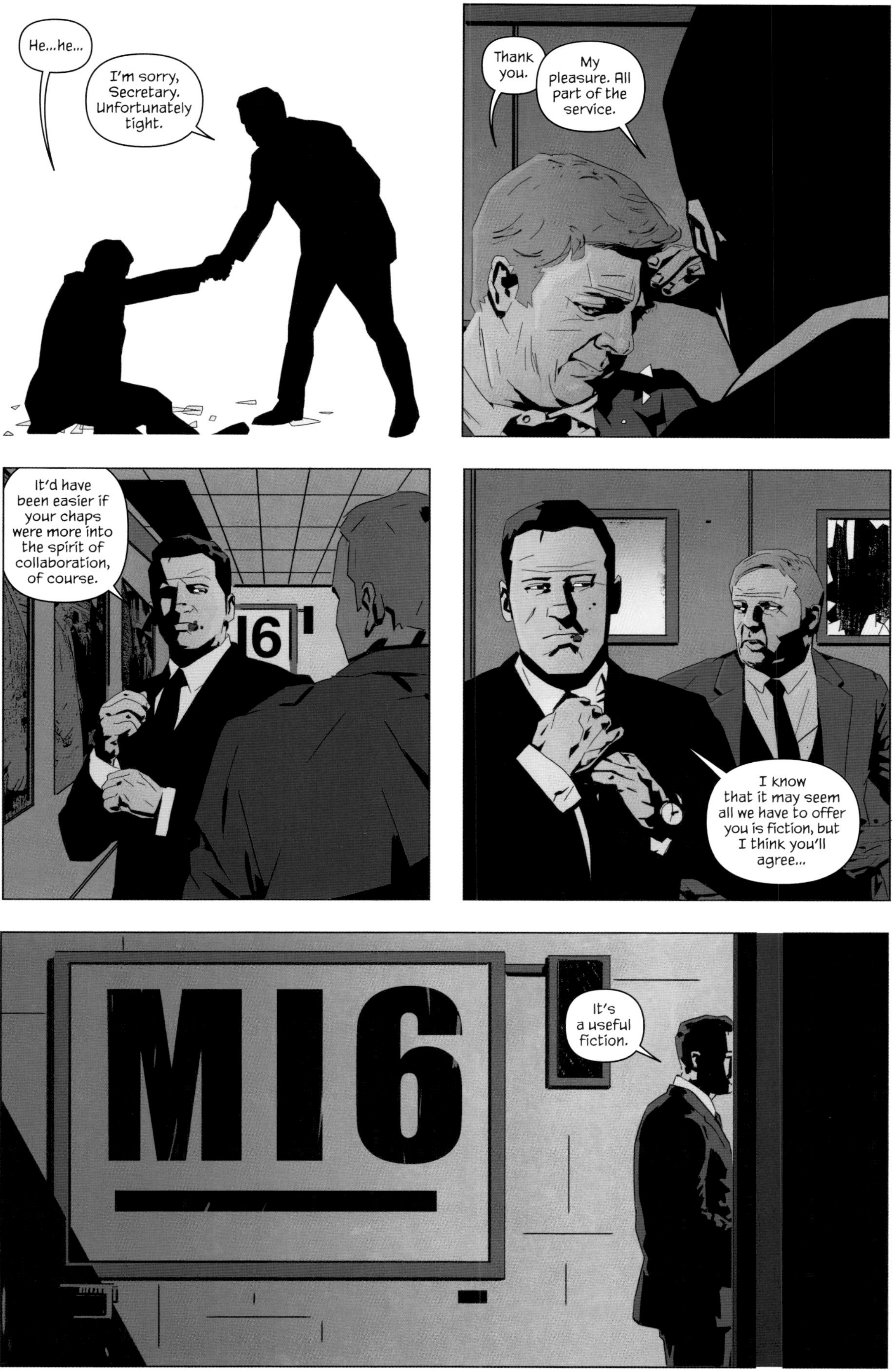
He...he...
I'm sorry, Secretary. Unfortunately tight.
Thank you.
My pleasure. All part of the service.
It'd have been easier if your chaps were more into the spirit of collaboration, of course.
MI6
I know that it may seem all we have to offer you is fiction, but I think you'll agree...
MI6
It's a useful fiction.

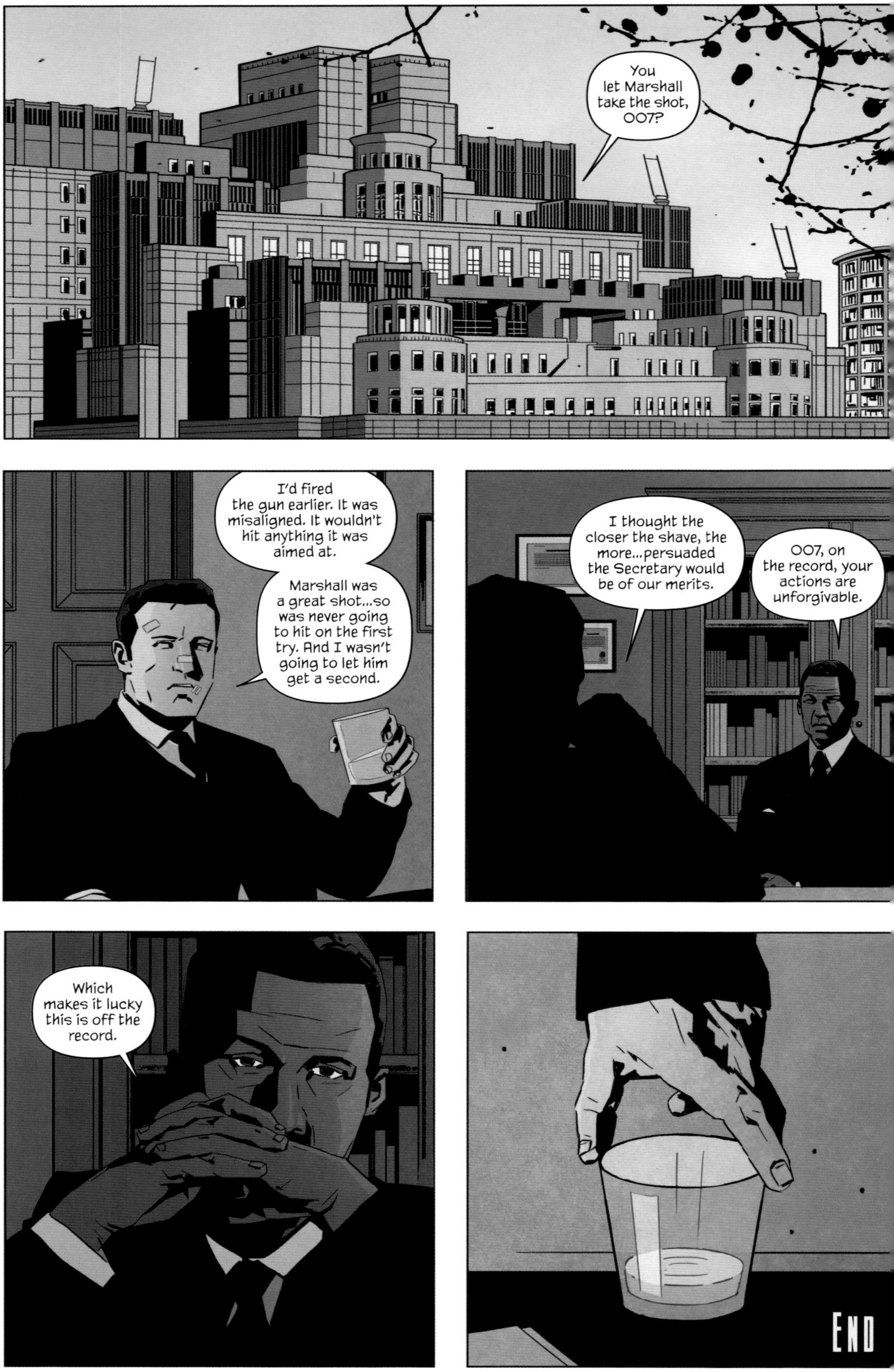
You let Marshall take the shot, 007?
I'd fired the gun earlier. It was misaligned. It wouldn't hit anything it was aimed at.
Marshall was a great shot...so was never going to hit on the first try. And I wasn't going to let him get a second.
I thought the closer the shave, the more...persuaded the Secretary would be of our merits.
007, on the record, your actions are unforgivable.
Which makes it lucky this is off the record.
END

MONEYPENNY

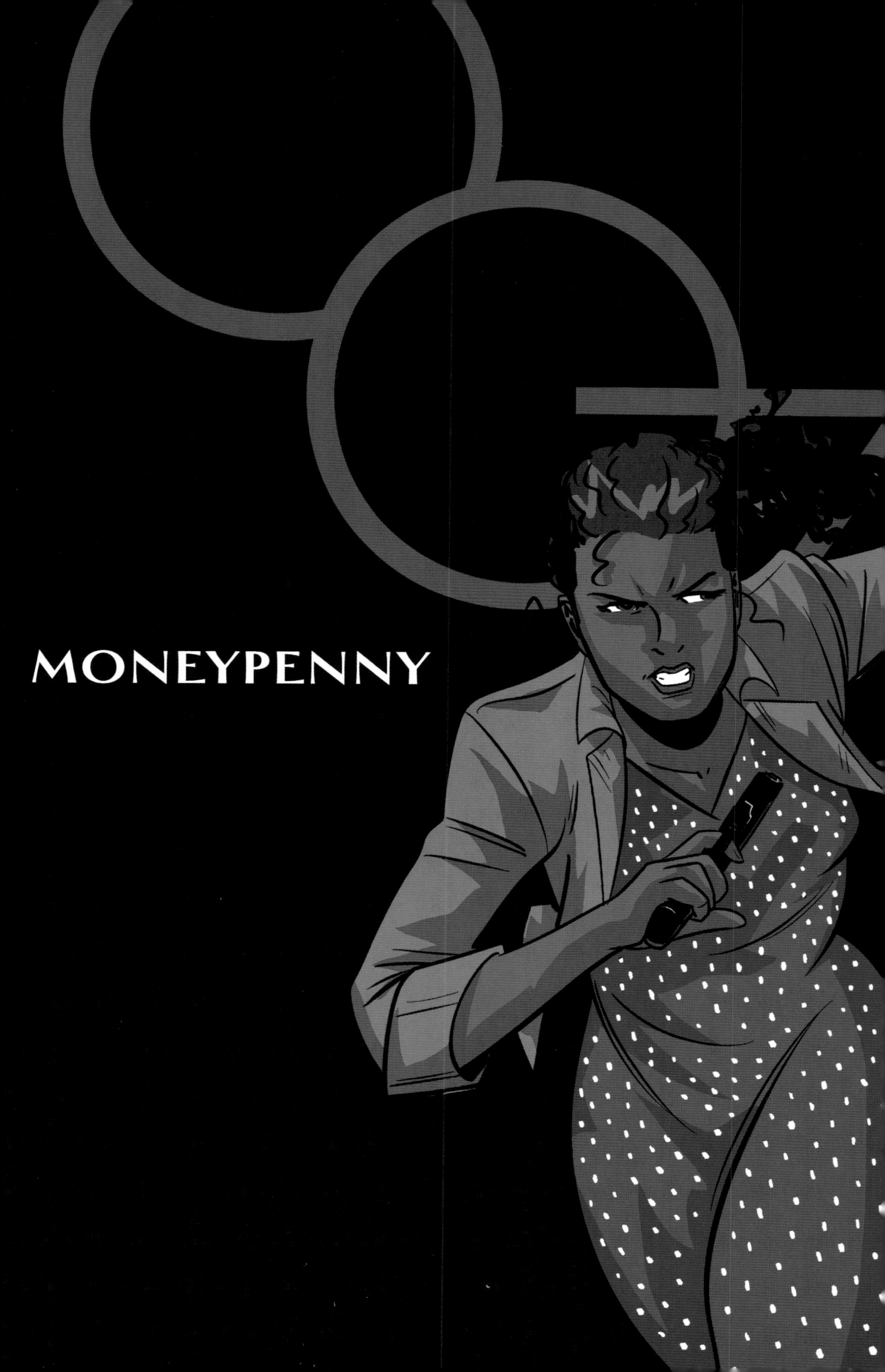
007

JAMES BOND: MONEYPENNY
COVER BY TULA LOTAY

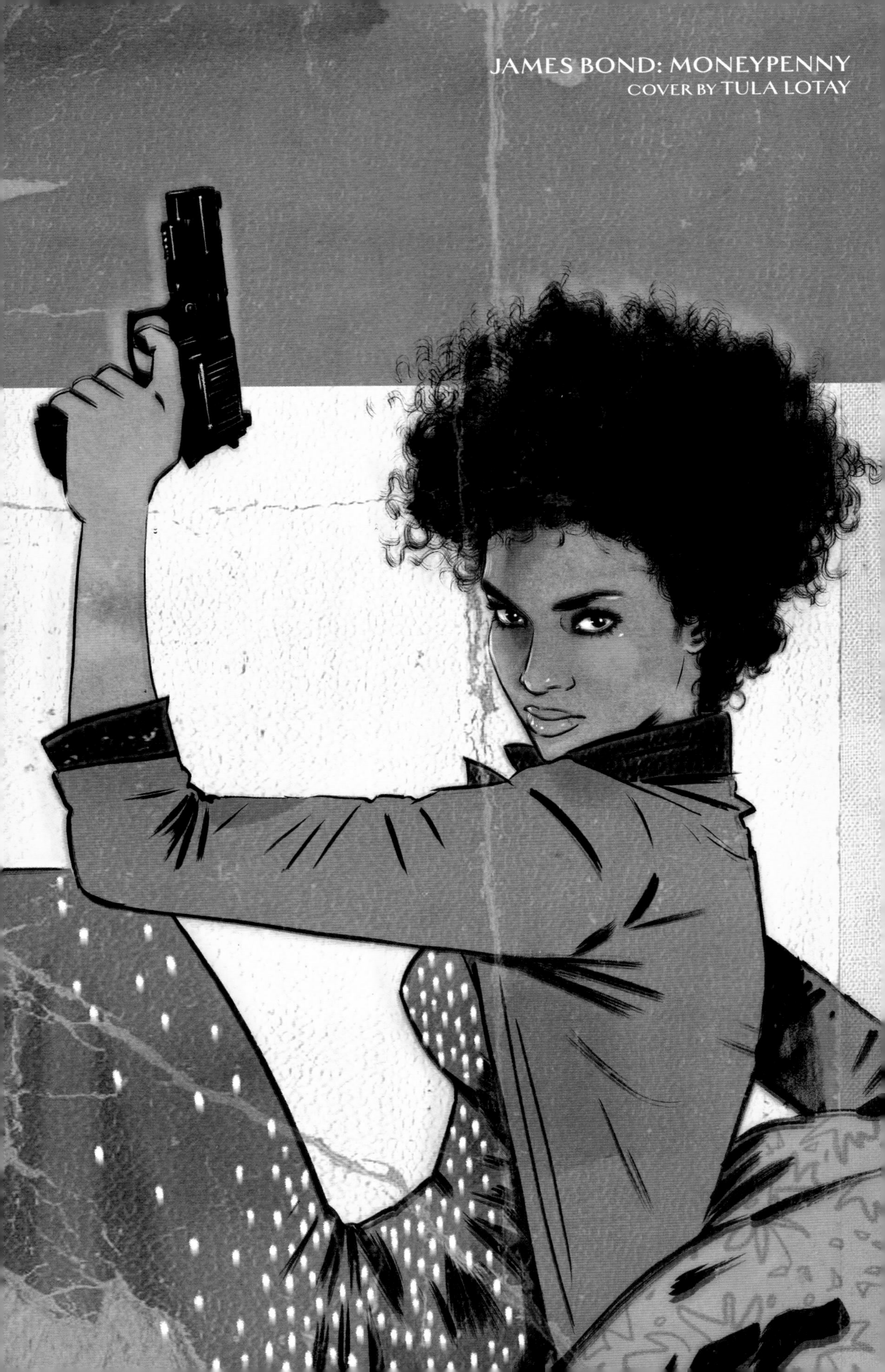

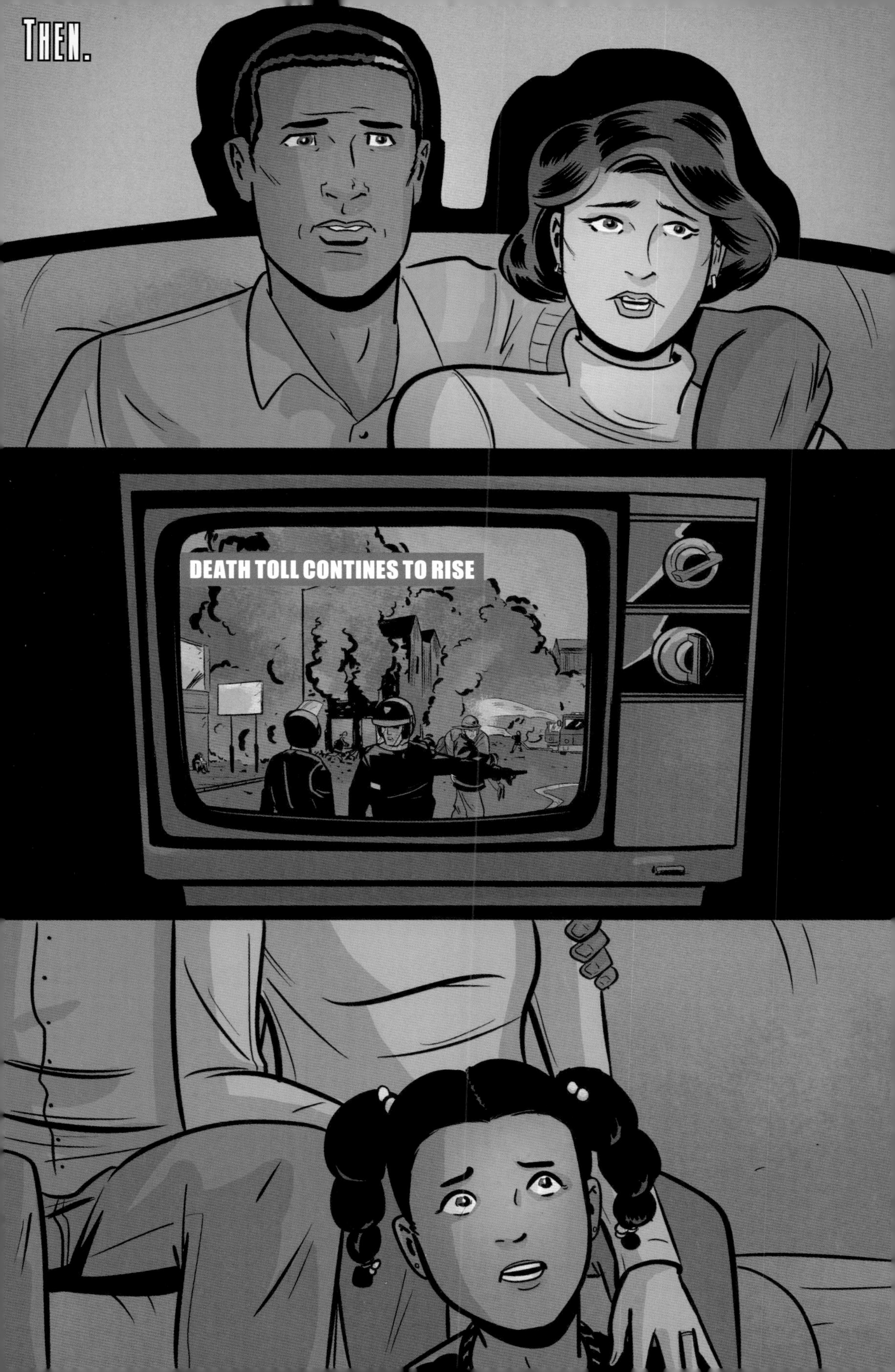
THEN.
DEATH TOLL CONTINES TO RISE

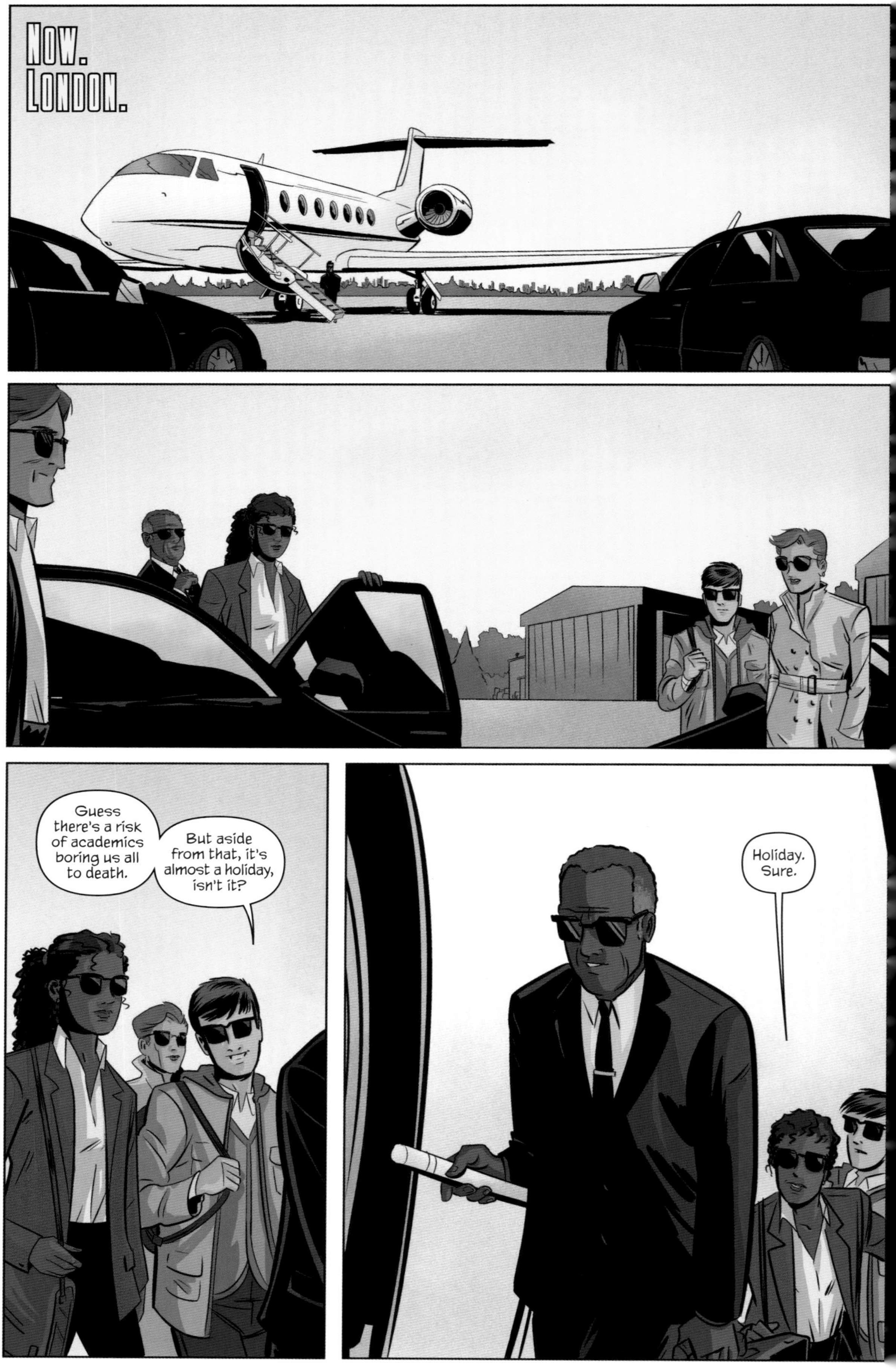
NOW.
LONDON.
Guess there's a risk of academics boring us all to death.
But aside from that, it's almost a holiday, isn't it?
Holiday. Sure.

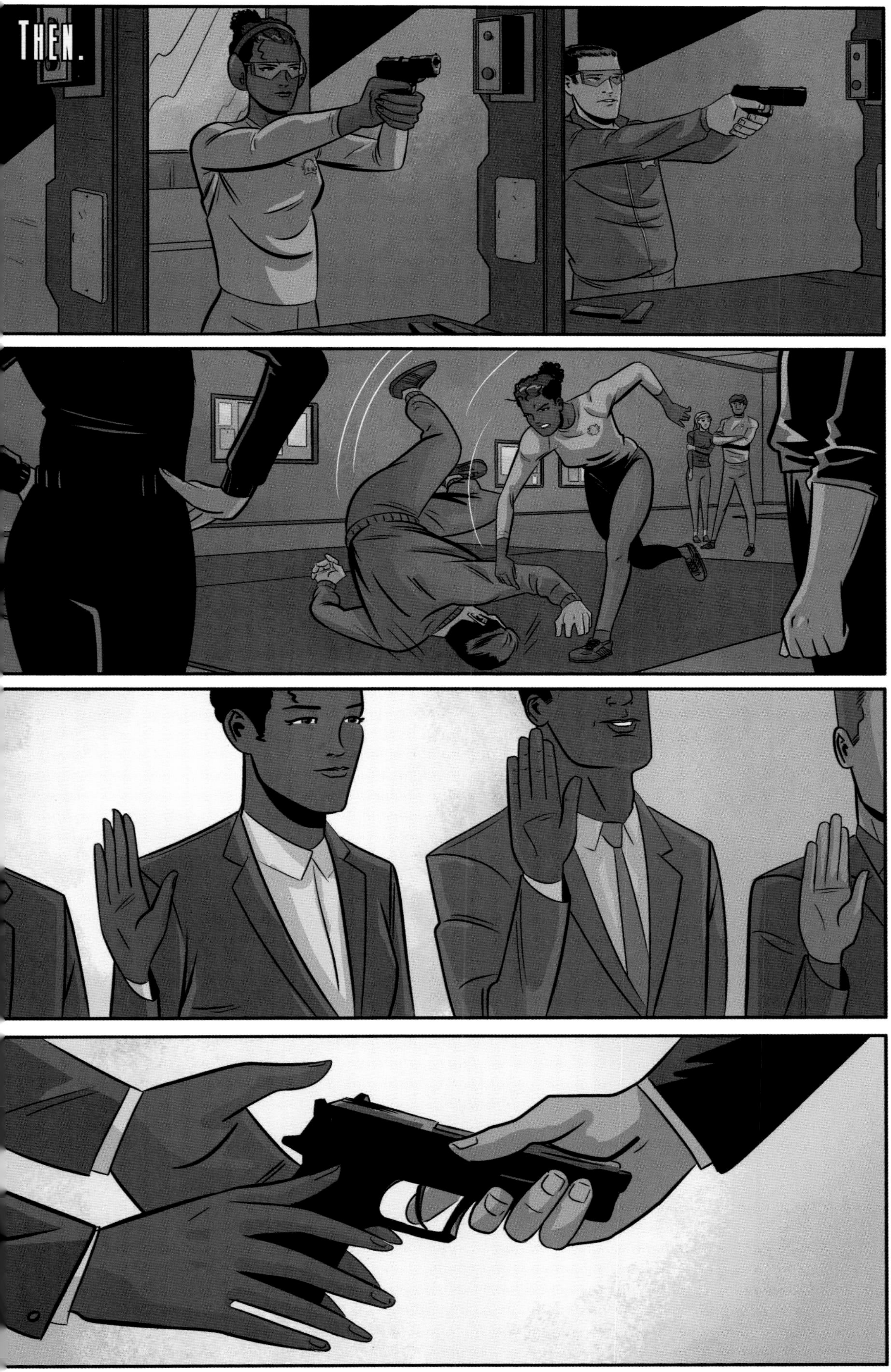
THEN.

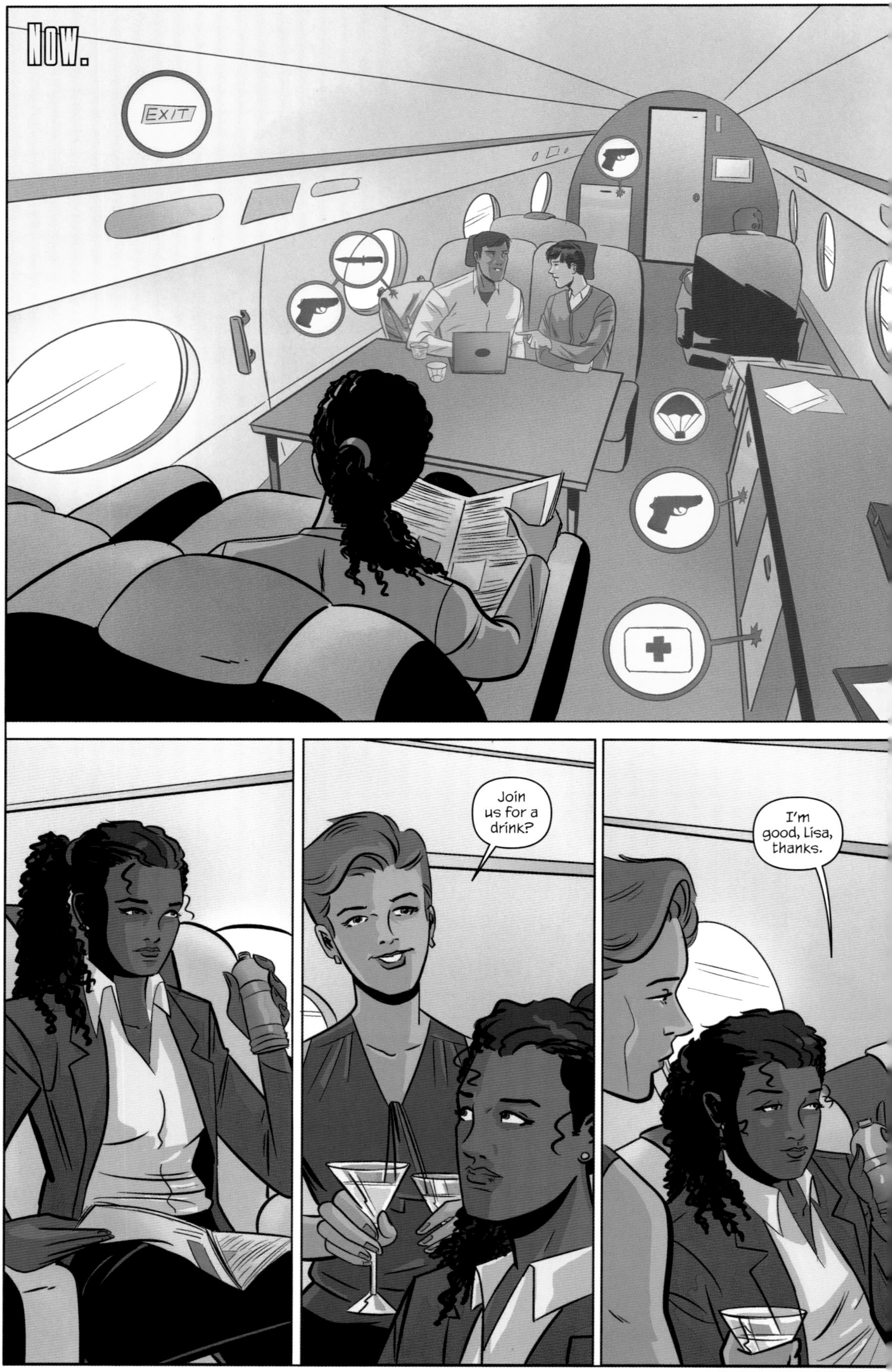
NOW.
EXIT
Join us for a drink?
I'm good, Lisa, thanks.

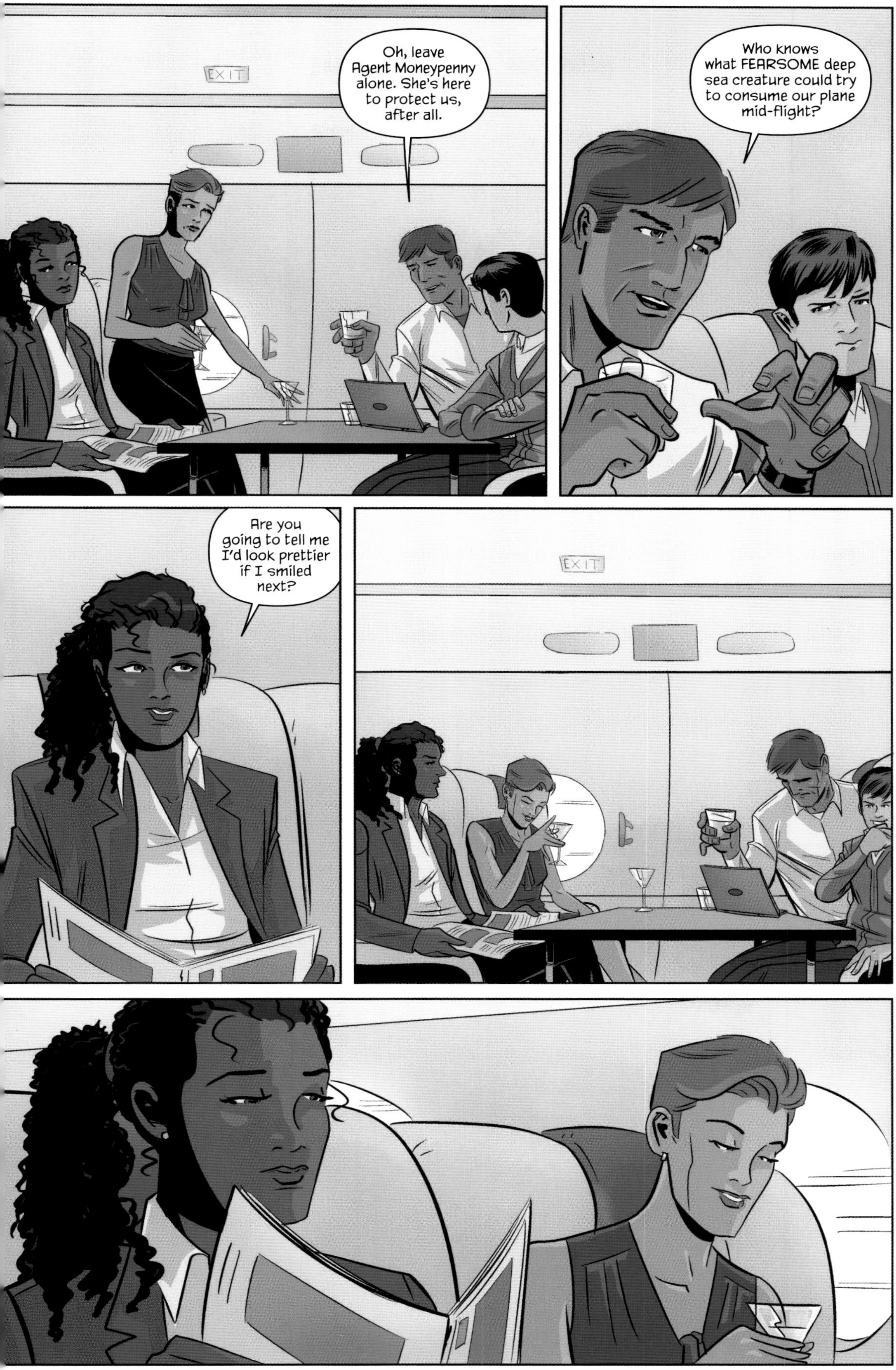
EXIT
Oh, leave Agent Moneypenny alone. She's here to protect us, after all.
Who knows what FEARSOME deep sea creature could try to consume our plane mid-flight?
Are you going to tell me I'd look prettier if I smiled next?
EXIT

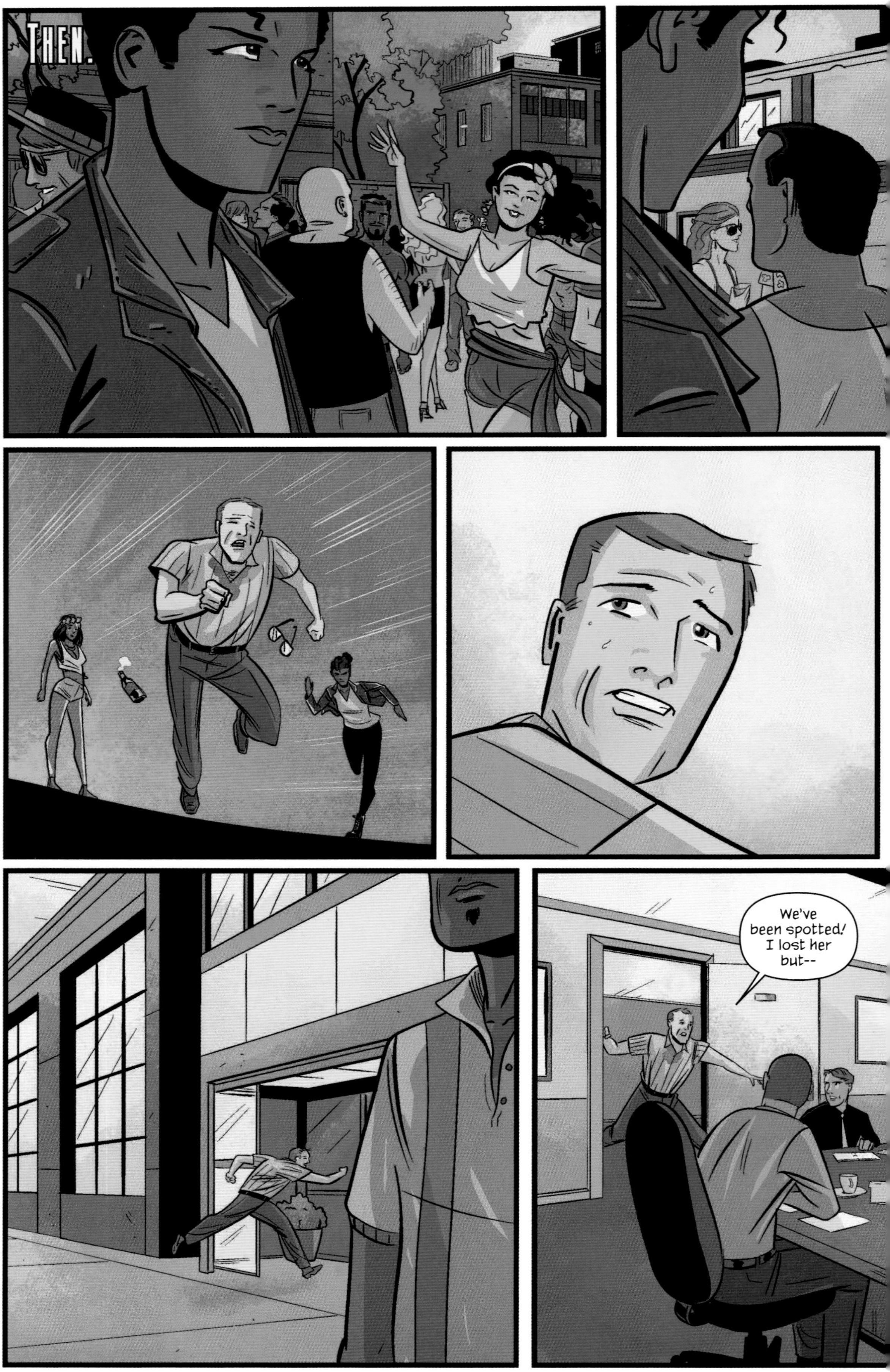
THEN.
We've been spotted! I lost her but--

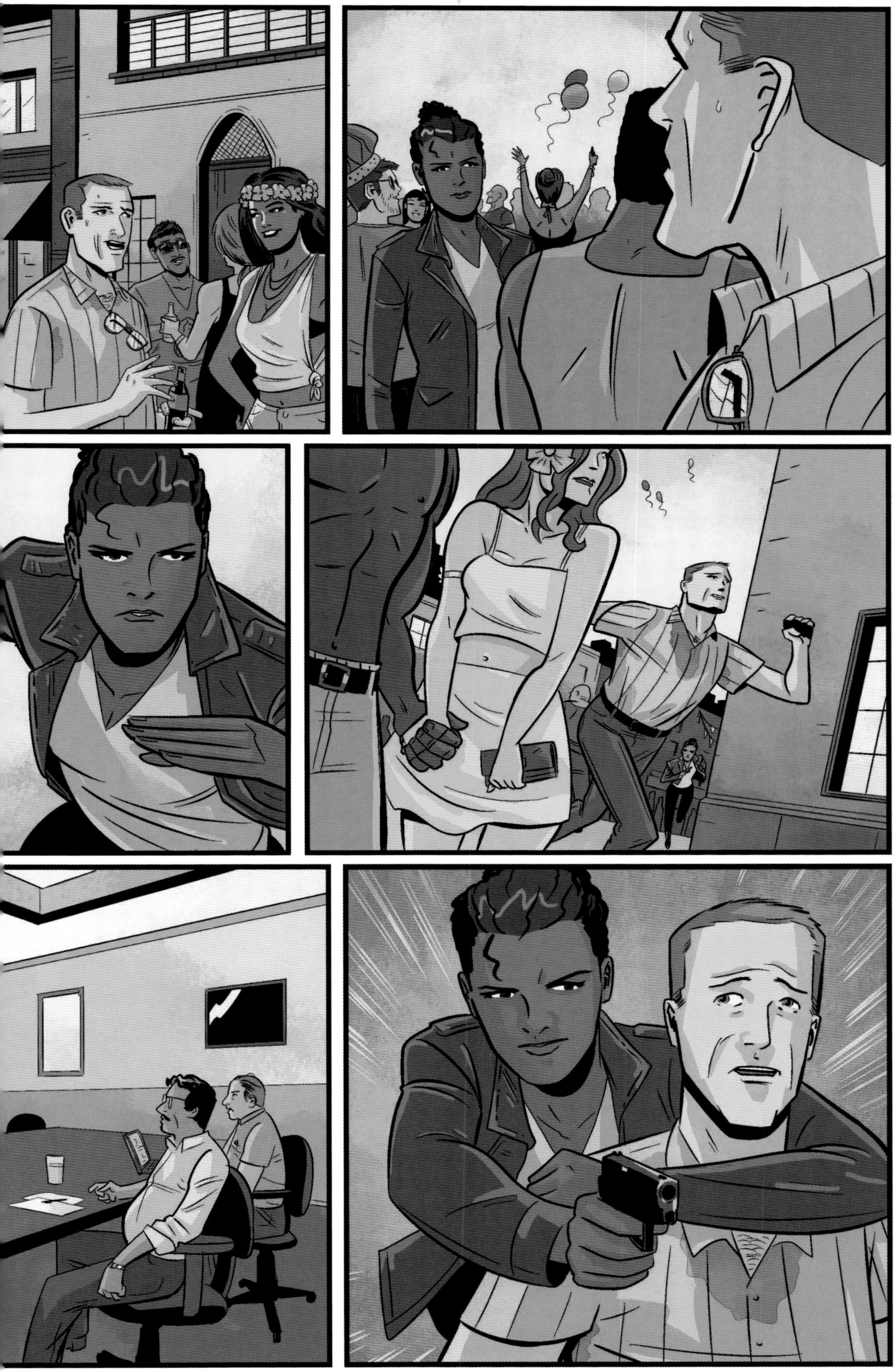

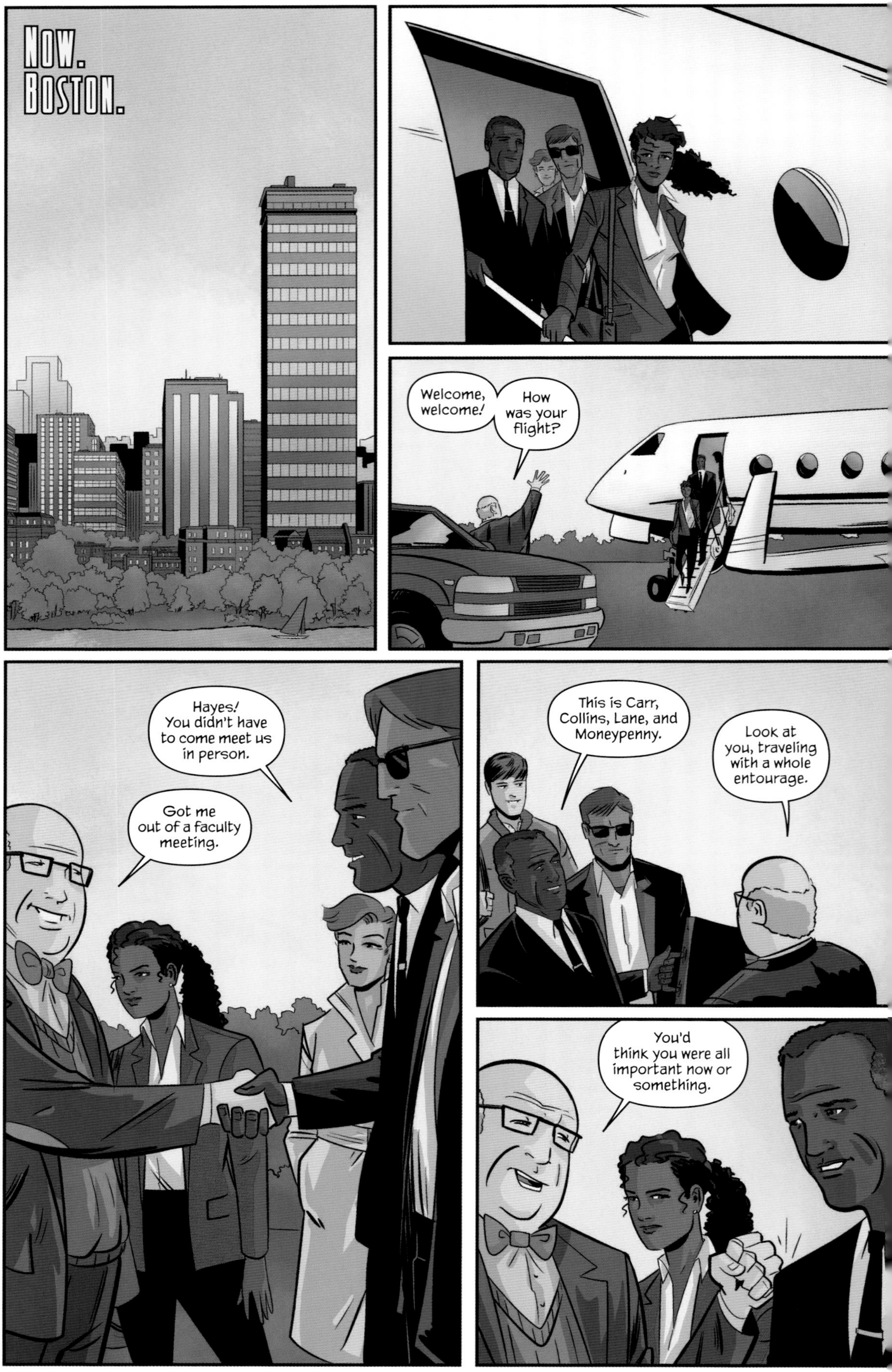

NOW. BOSTON.
Welcome, welcome!
How was your flight?
Hayes! You didn't have to come meet us in person.
Got me out of a faculty meeting.
This is Carr, Collins, Lane, and Moneypenny.
Look at you, traveling with a whole entourage.
You'd think you were all important now or something.

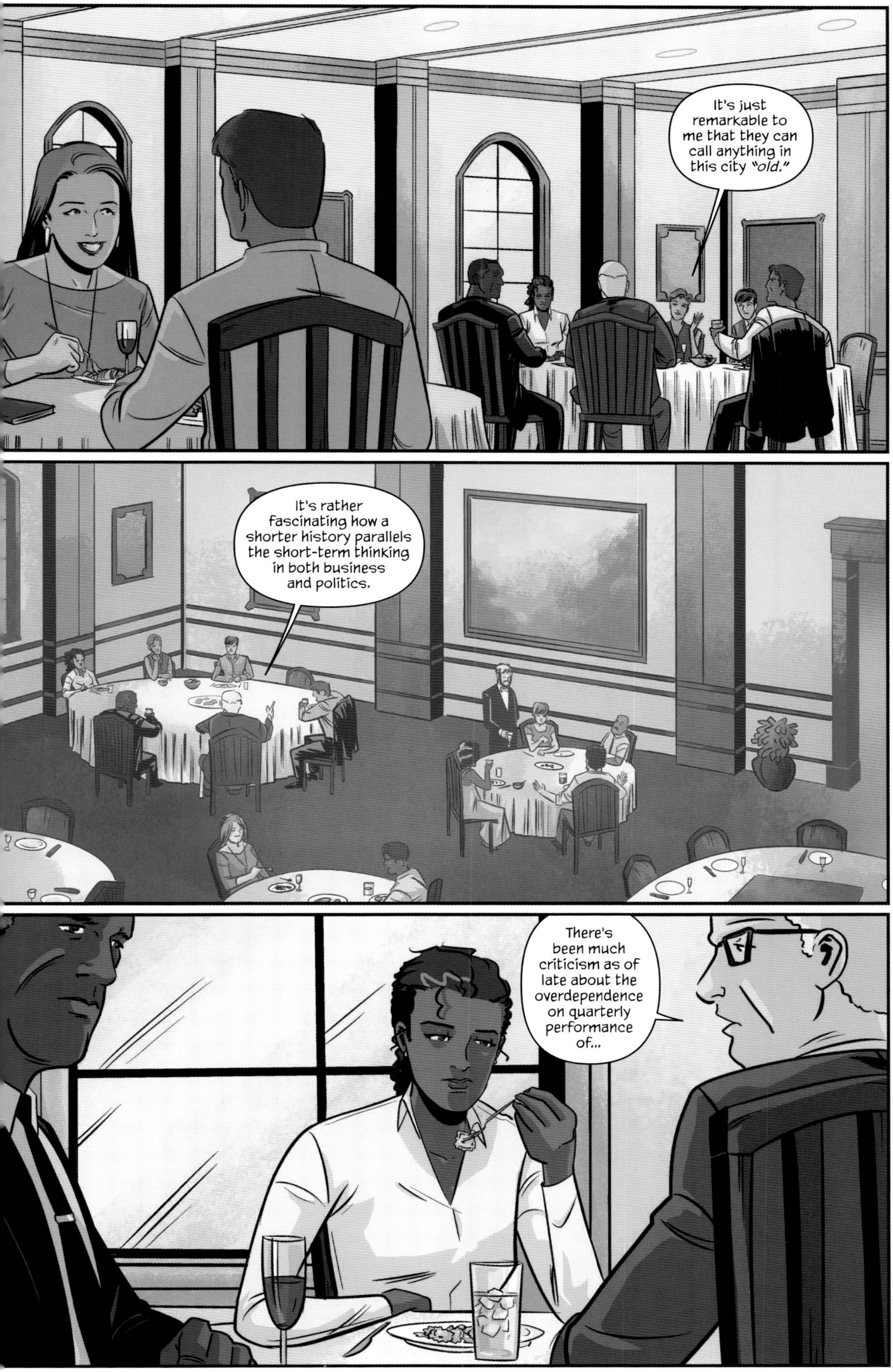
It's just remarkable to me that they can call anything in this city "old."
It's rather fascinating how a shorter history parallels the short-term thinking in both business and politics.
There's been much criticism as of late about the overdependence on quarterly performance of...

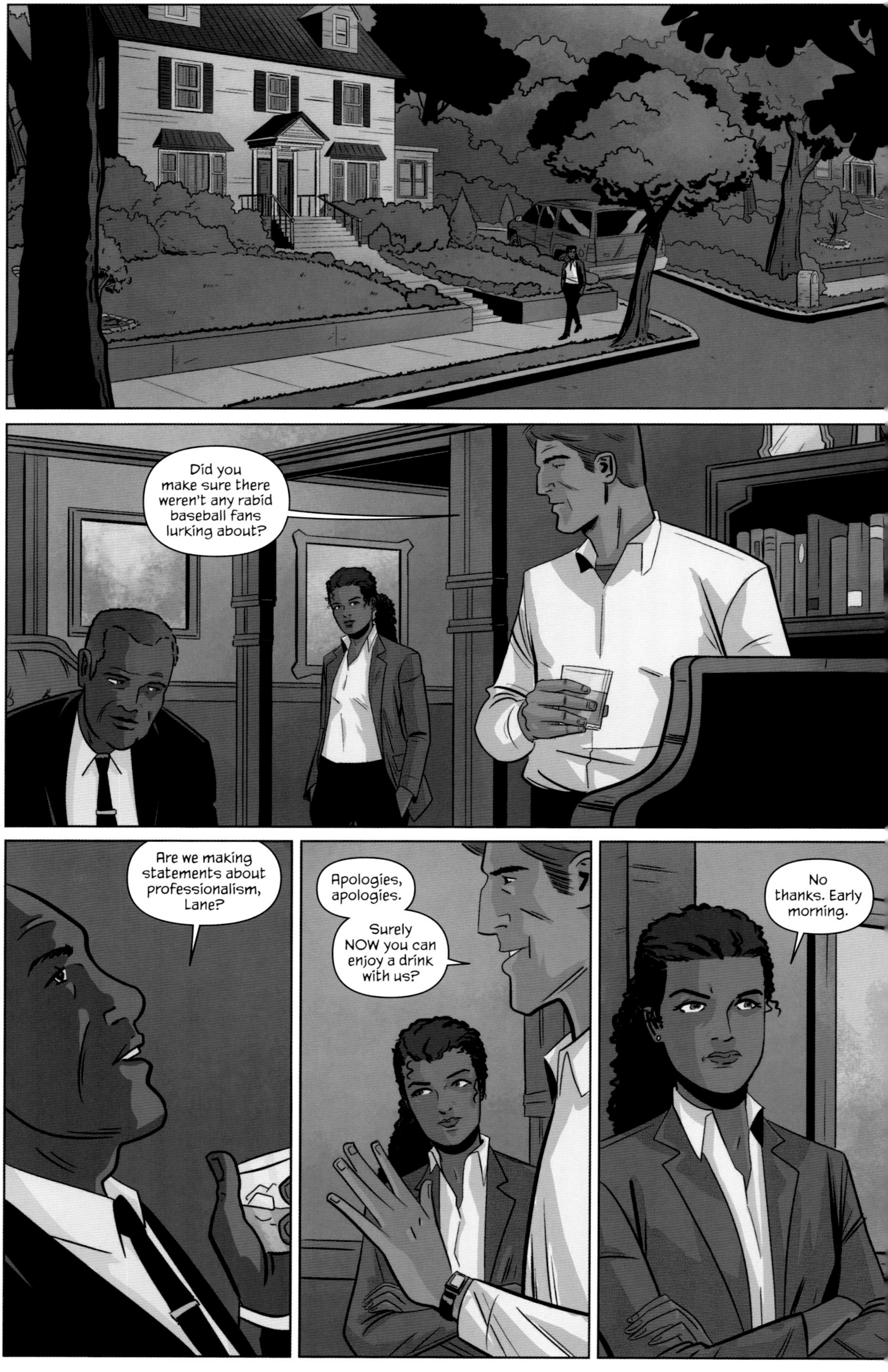
Did you make sure there weren't any rabid baseball fans lurking about?
Are we making statements about professionalism, Lane?
Apologies, apologies.
Surely NOW you can enjoy a drink with us?
No thanks. Early morning.

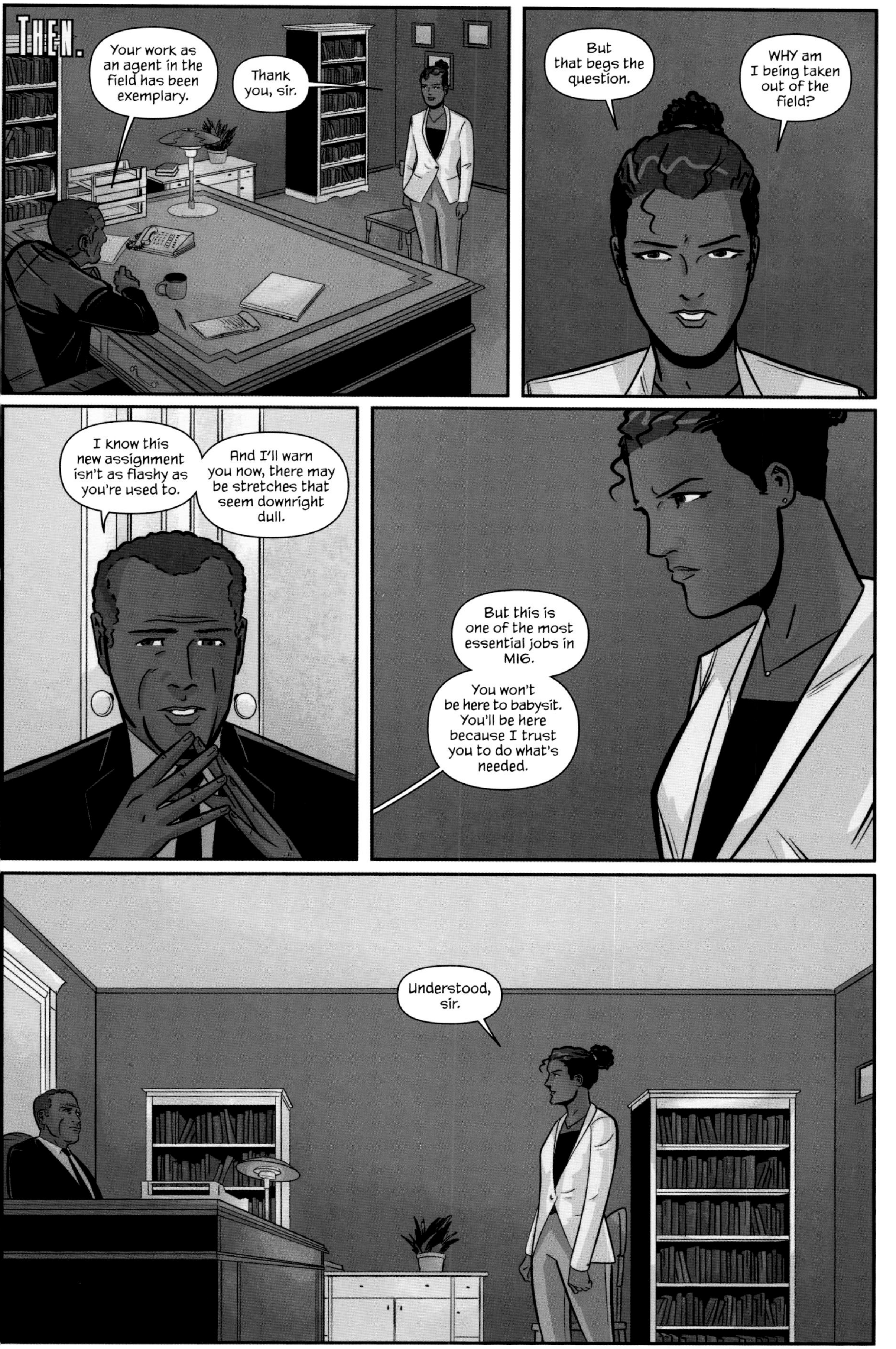
THEN.
Your work as an agent in the field has been exemplary.
Thank you, sir.
But that begs the question.
WHY am I being taken out of the field?
I know this new assignment isn't as flashy as you're used to.
And I'll warn you now, there may be stretches that seem downright dull.
But this is one of the most essential jobs in MI6.
You won't be here to babysit. You'll be here because I trust you to do what's needed.
Understood, sir.

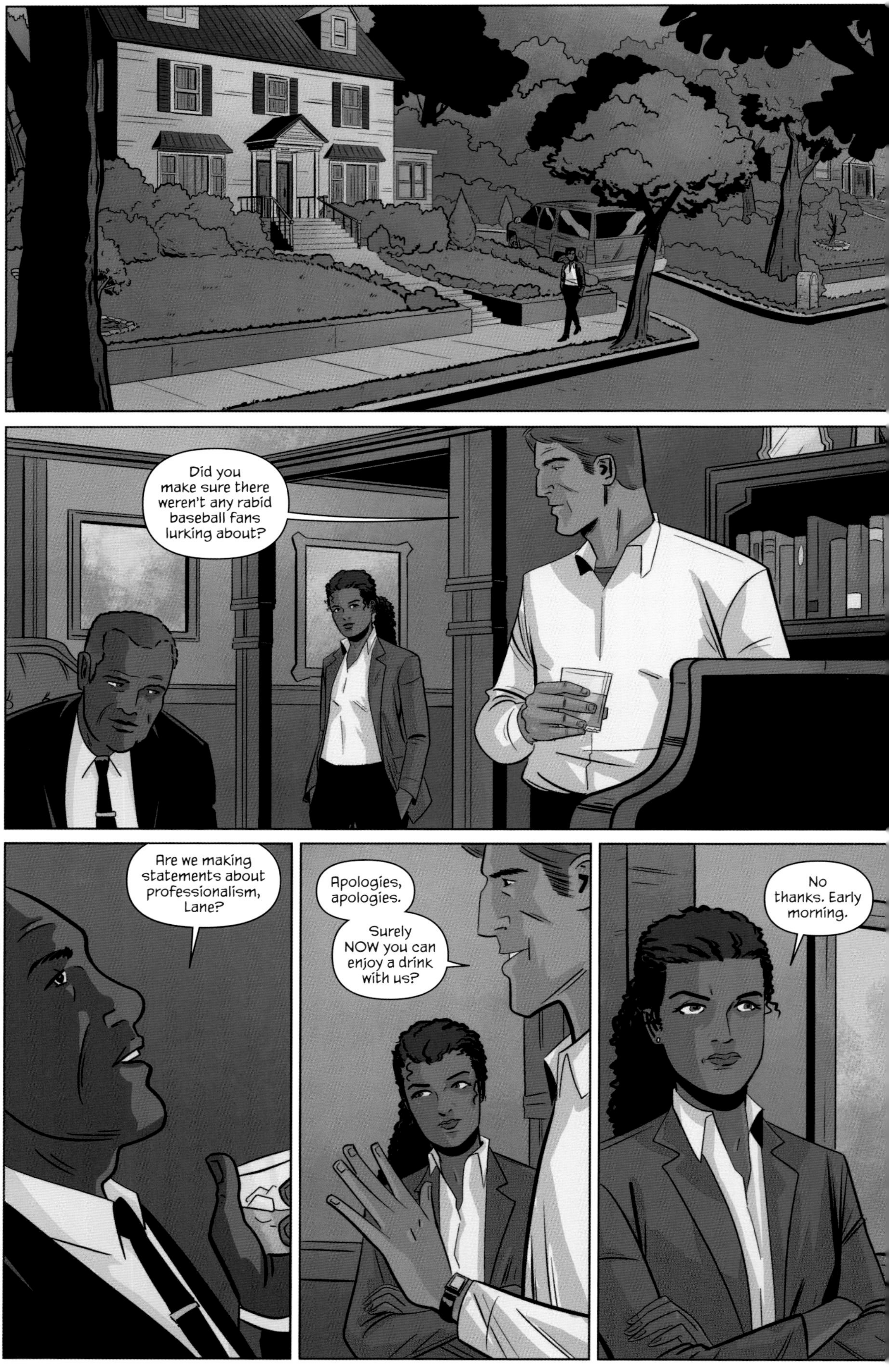
Did you make sure there weren't any rabid baseball fans lurking about?
Are we making statements about professionalism, Lane?
Apologies, apologies.
Surely NOW you can enjoy a drink with us?
No thanks. Early morning.

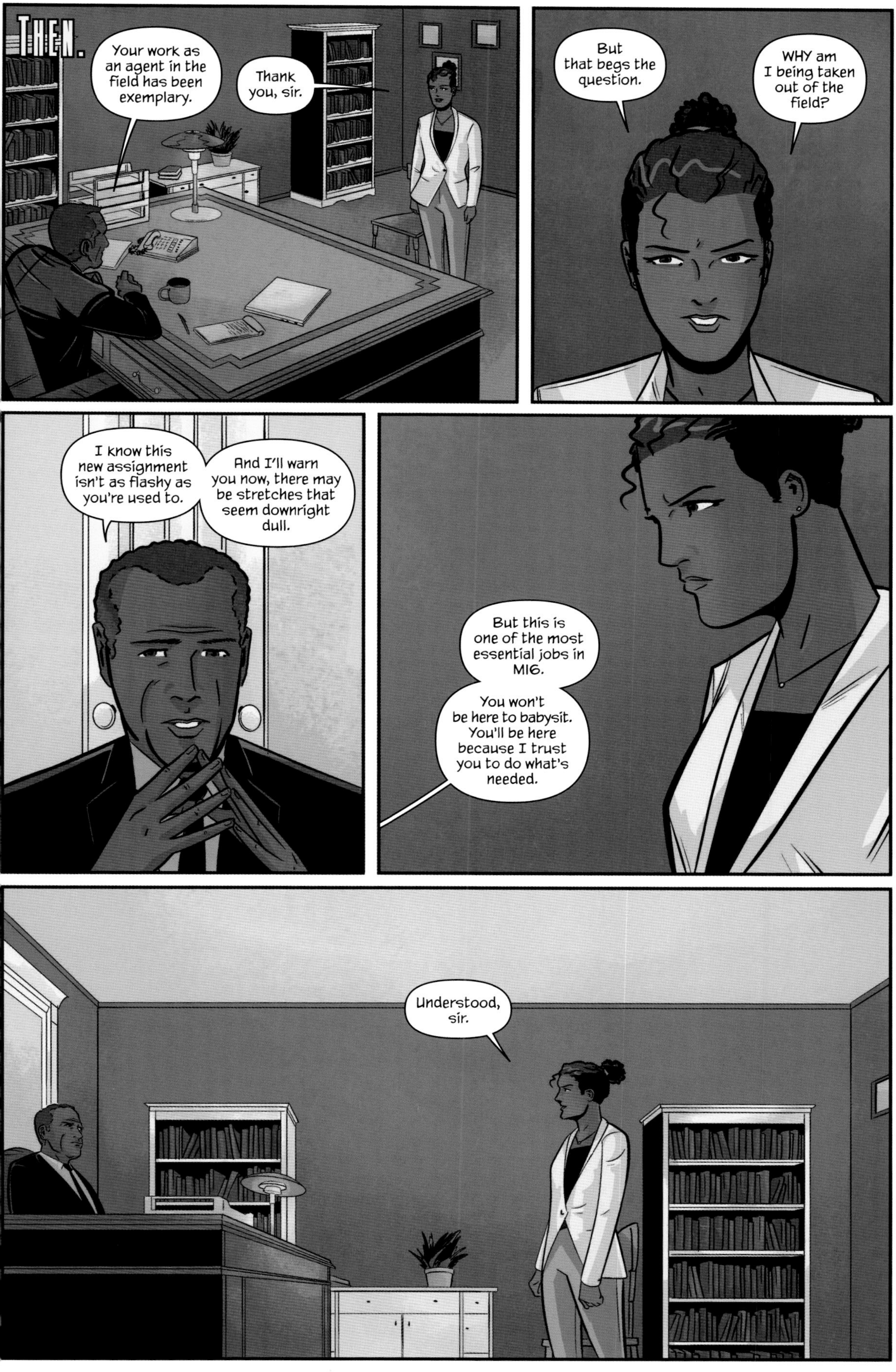
THEN.
Your work as an agent in the field has been exemplary.
Thank you, sir.
But that begs the question.
WHY am I being taken out of the field?
I know this new assignment isn't as flashy as you're used to.
And I'll warn you now, there may be stretches that seem downright dull.
But this is one of the most essential jobs in MI6.
You won't be here to babysit. You'll be here because I trust you to do what's needed.
Understood, sir.

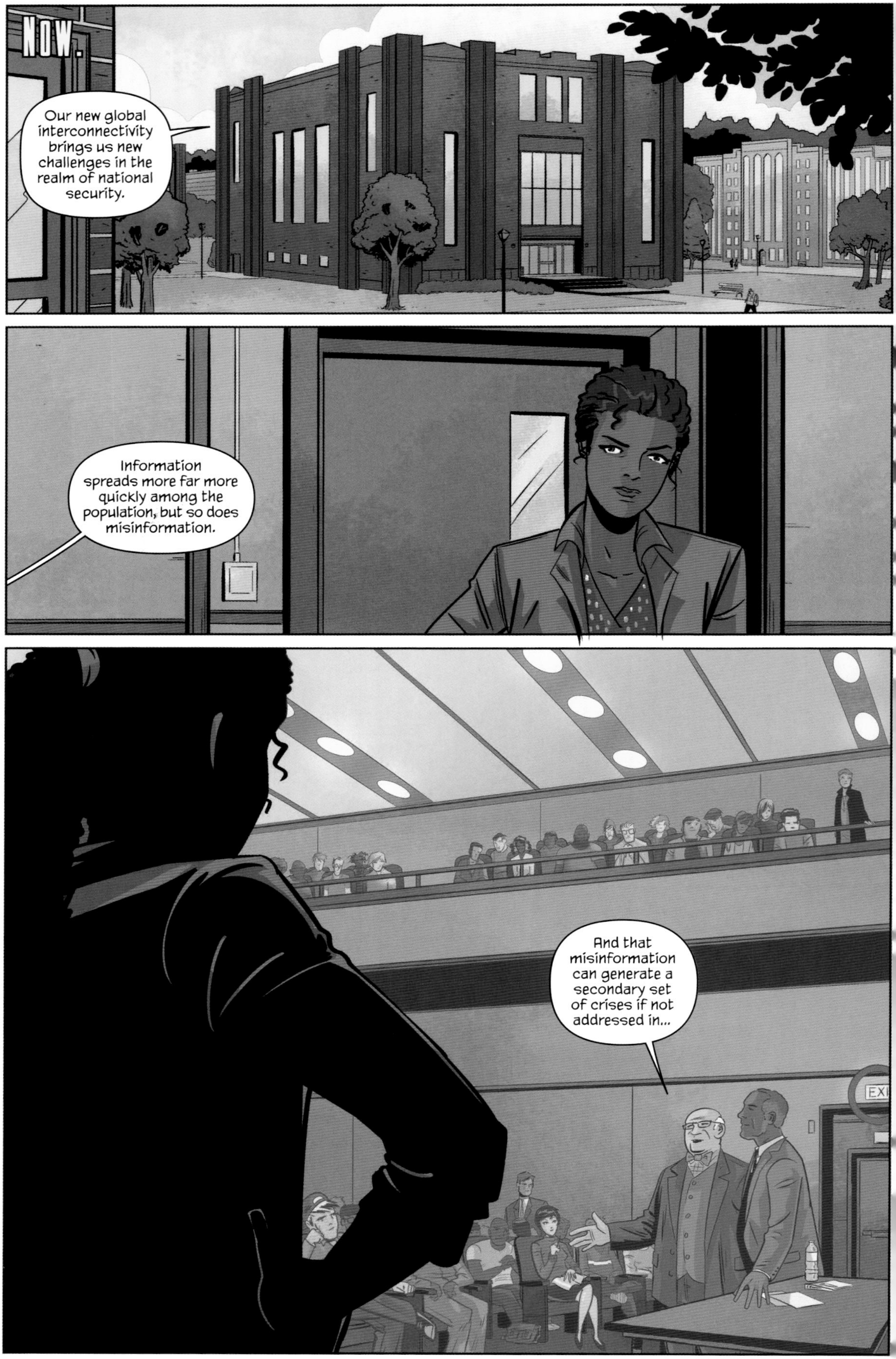
NOW.
Our new global interconnectivity brings us new challenges in the realm of national security.
Information spreads more far more quickly among the population, but so does misinformation.
And that misinformation can generate a secondary set of crises if not addressed in...

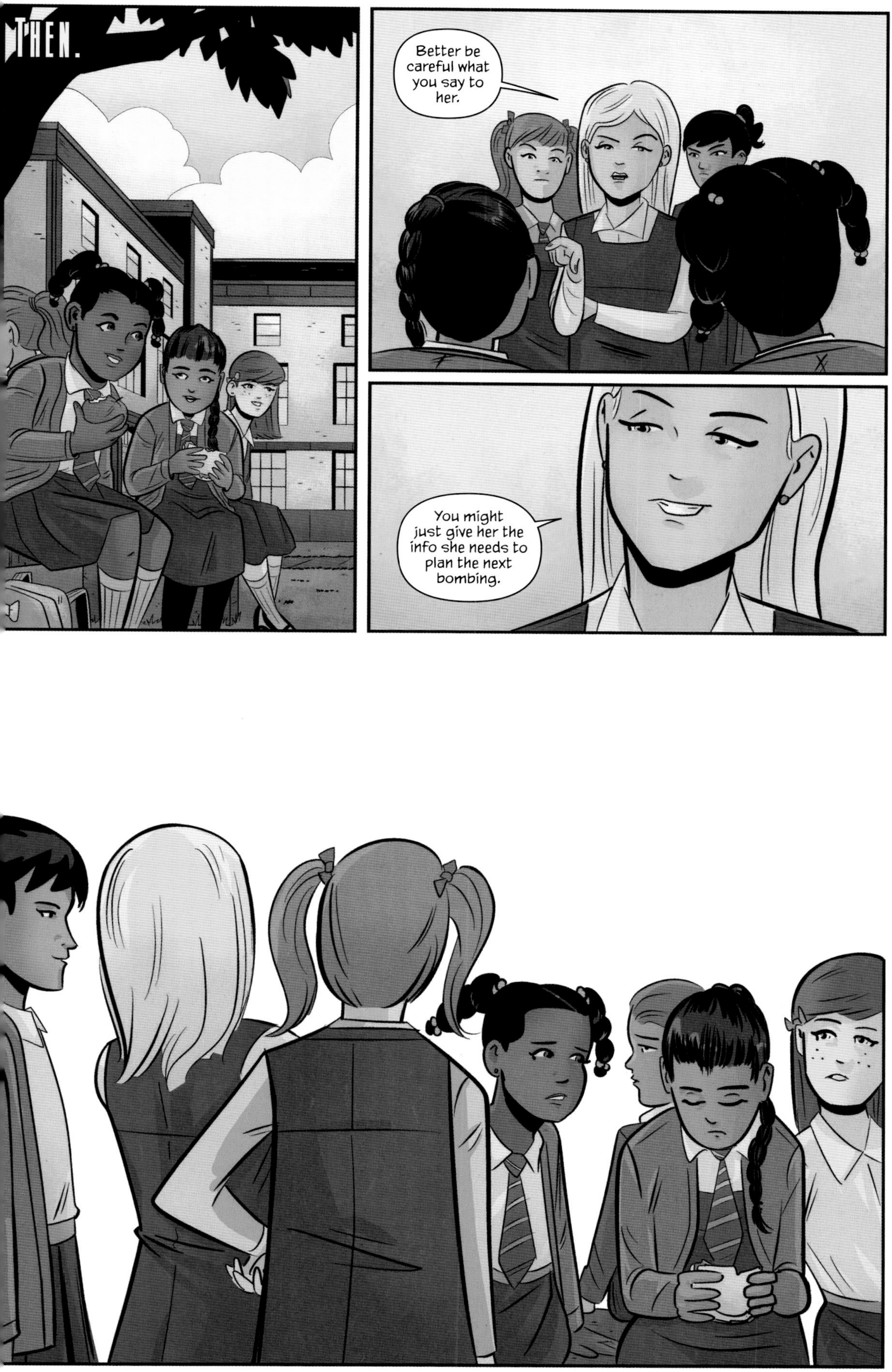
THEN.
Better be careful what you say to her.
You might just give her the info she needs to plan the next bombing.

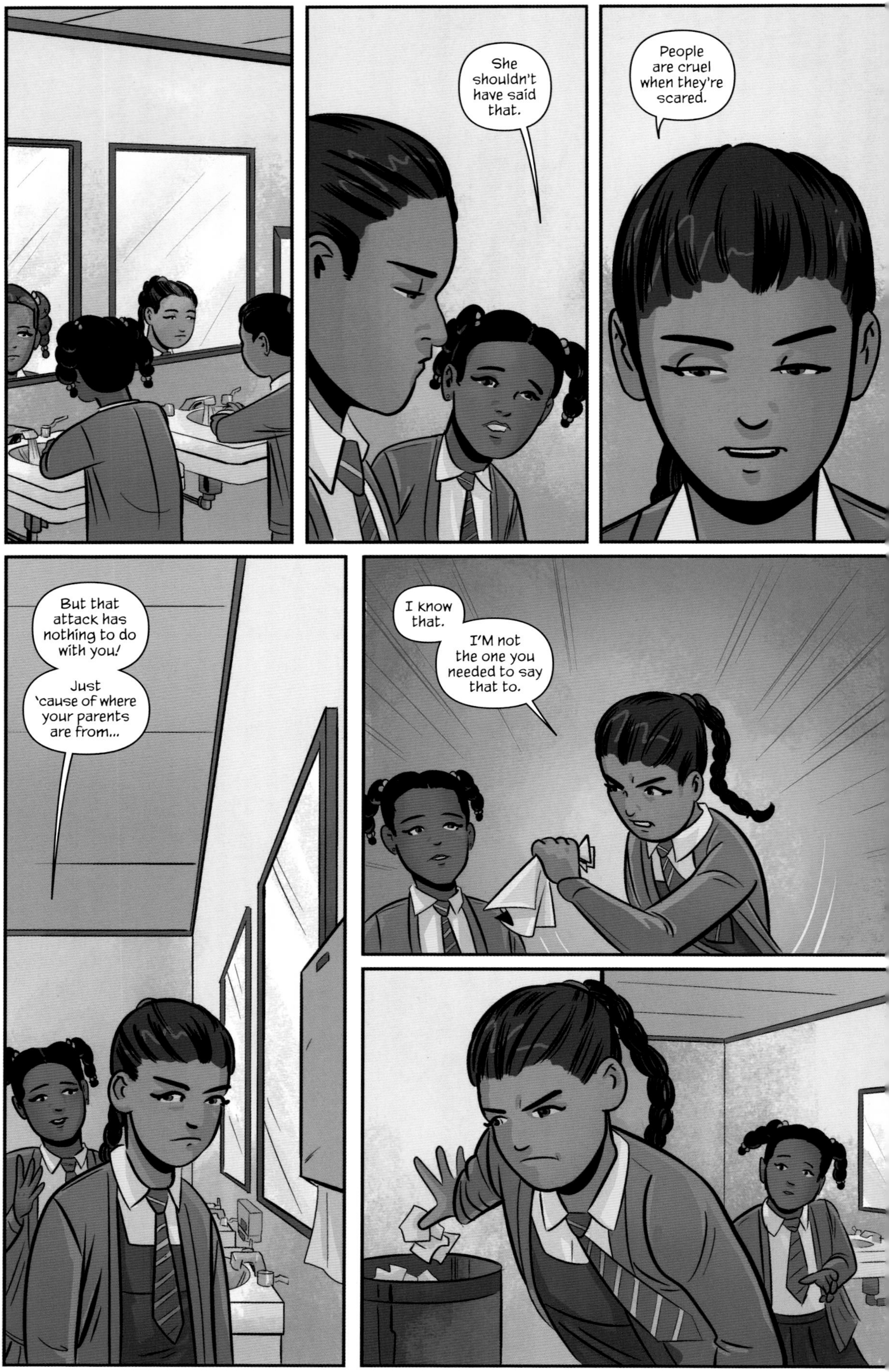
She shouldn't have said that.
People are cruel when they're scared.
But that attack has nothing to do with you!
Just 'cause of where your parents are from...
I know that.
I'M not the one you needed to say that to.

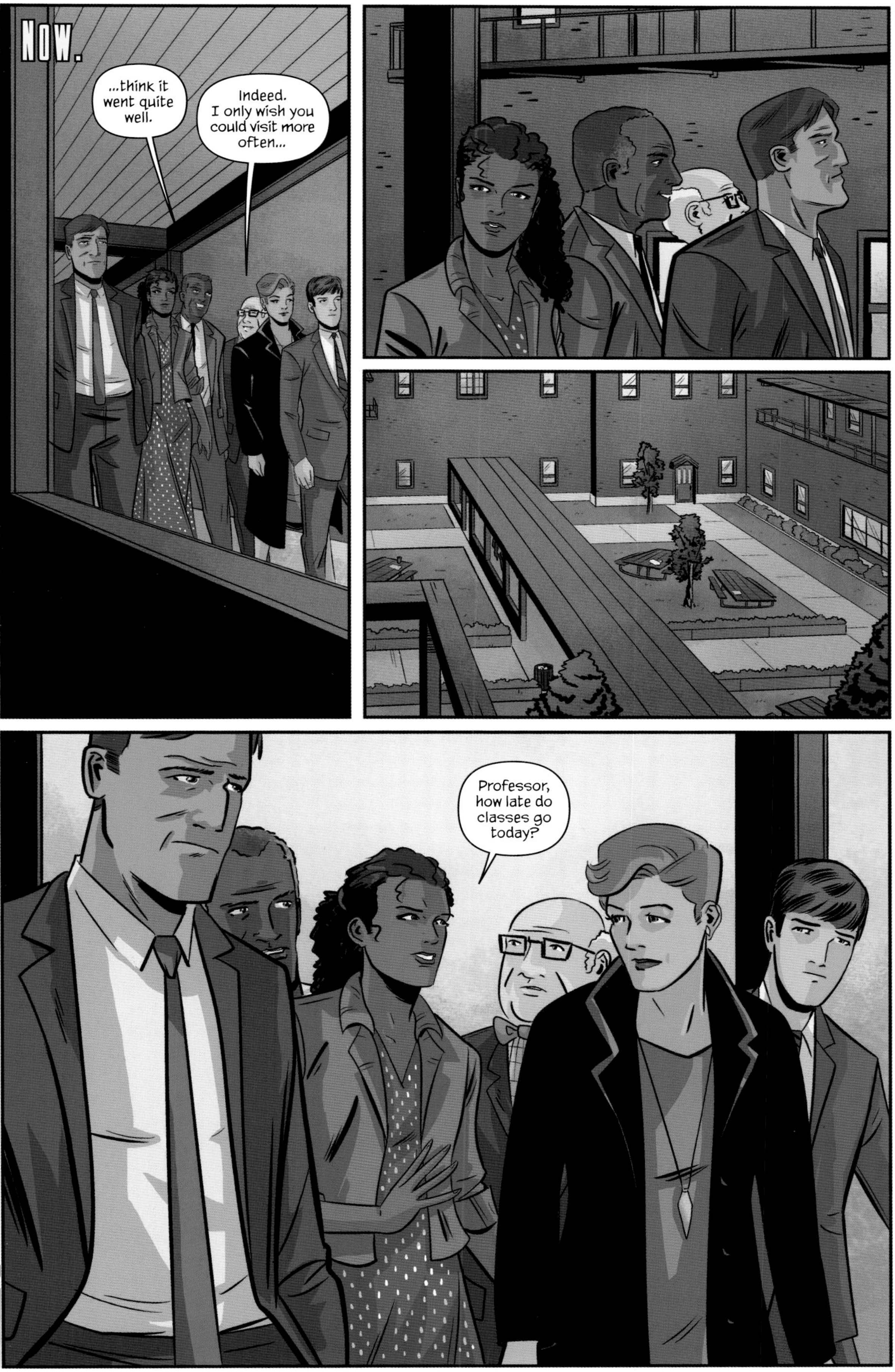
NOW.
...think it went quite well.
Indeed. I only wish you could visit more often...
Professor, how late do classes go today?

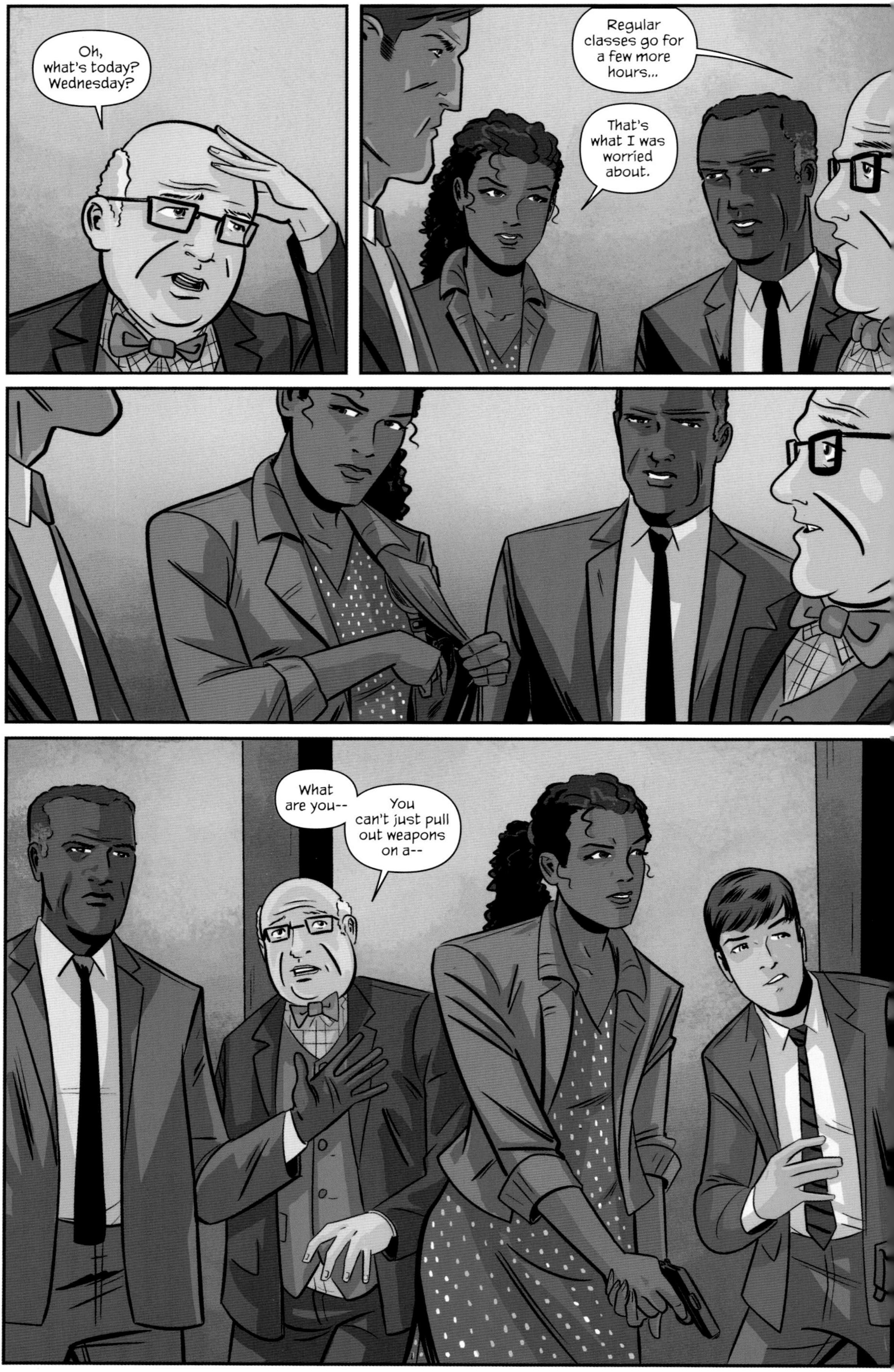
Oh, what's today? Wednesday?
Regular classes go for a few more hours...
That's what I was worried about.
What are you--
You can't just pull out weapons on a--

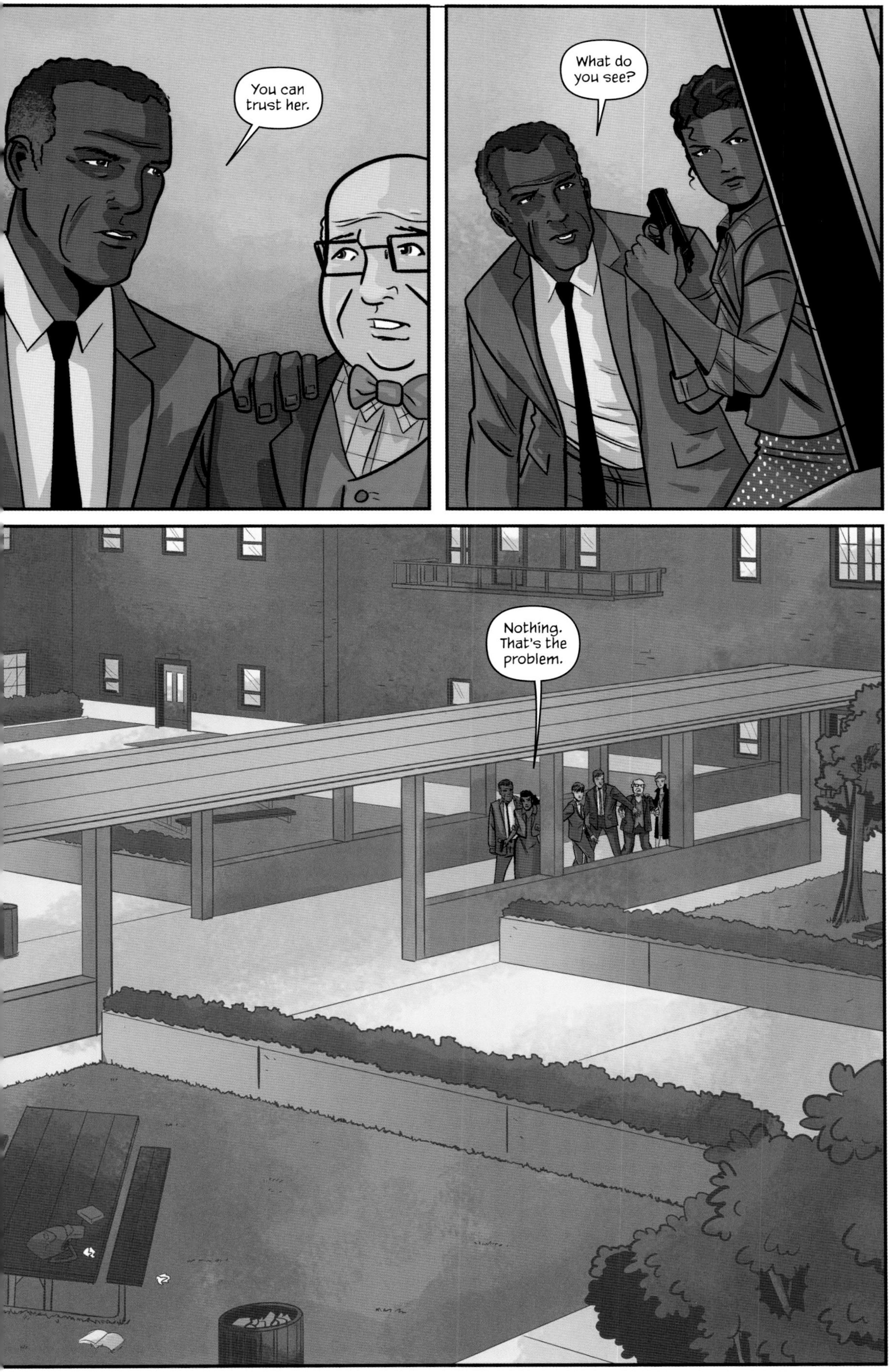
You can trust her.
What do you see?
Nothing. That's the problem.

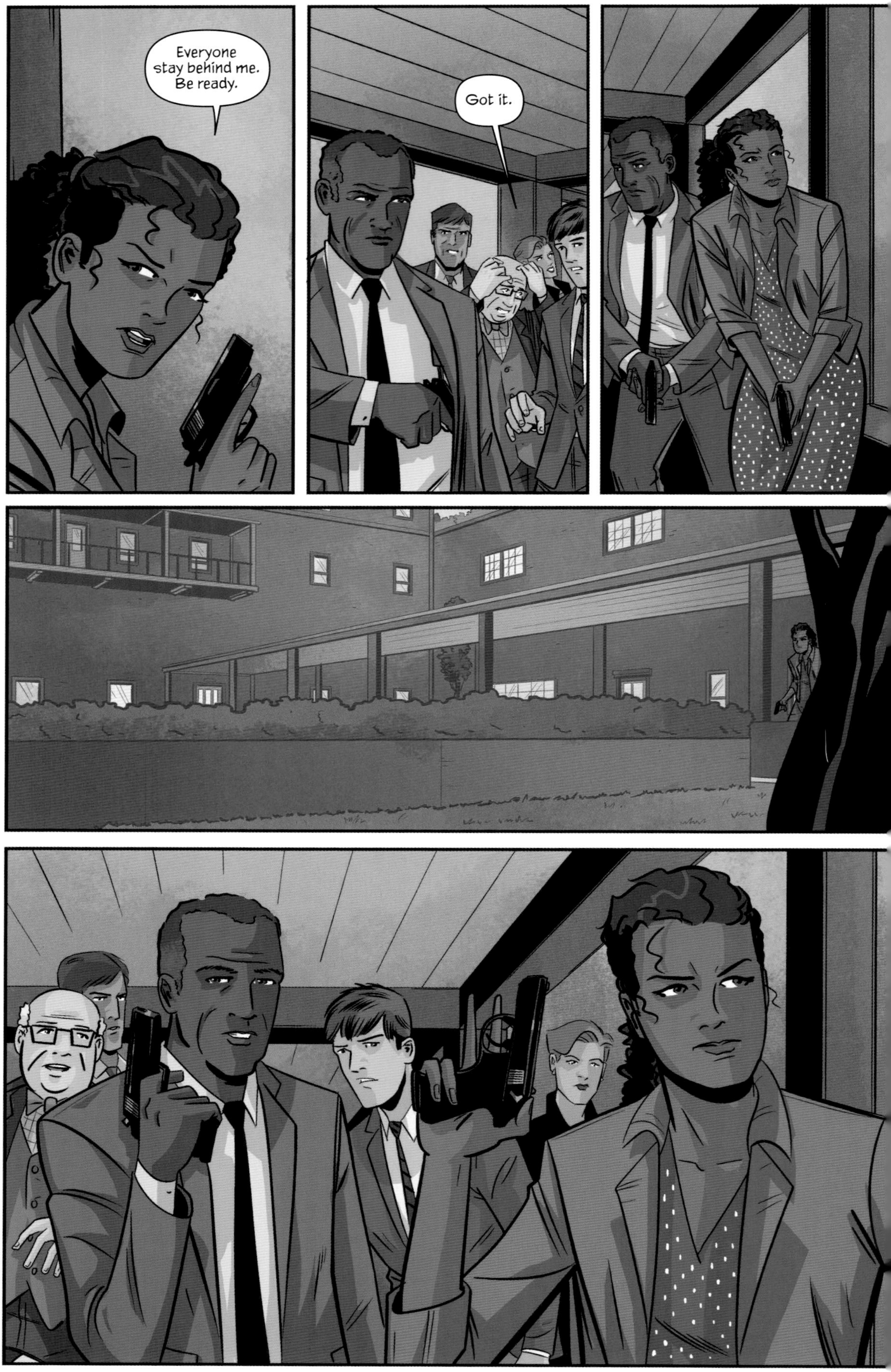

Everyone stay behind me. Be ready.
Got it.

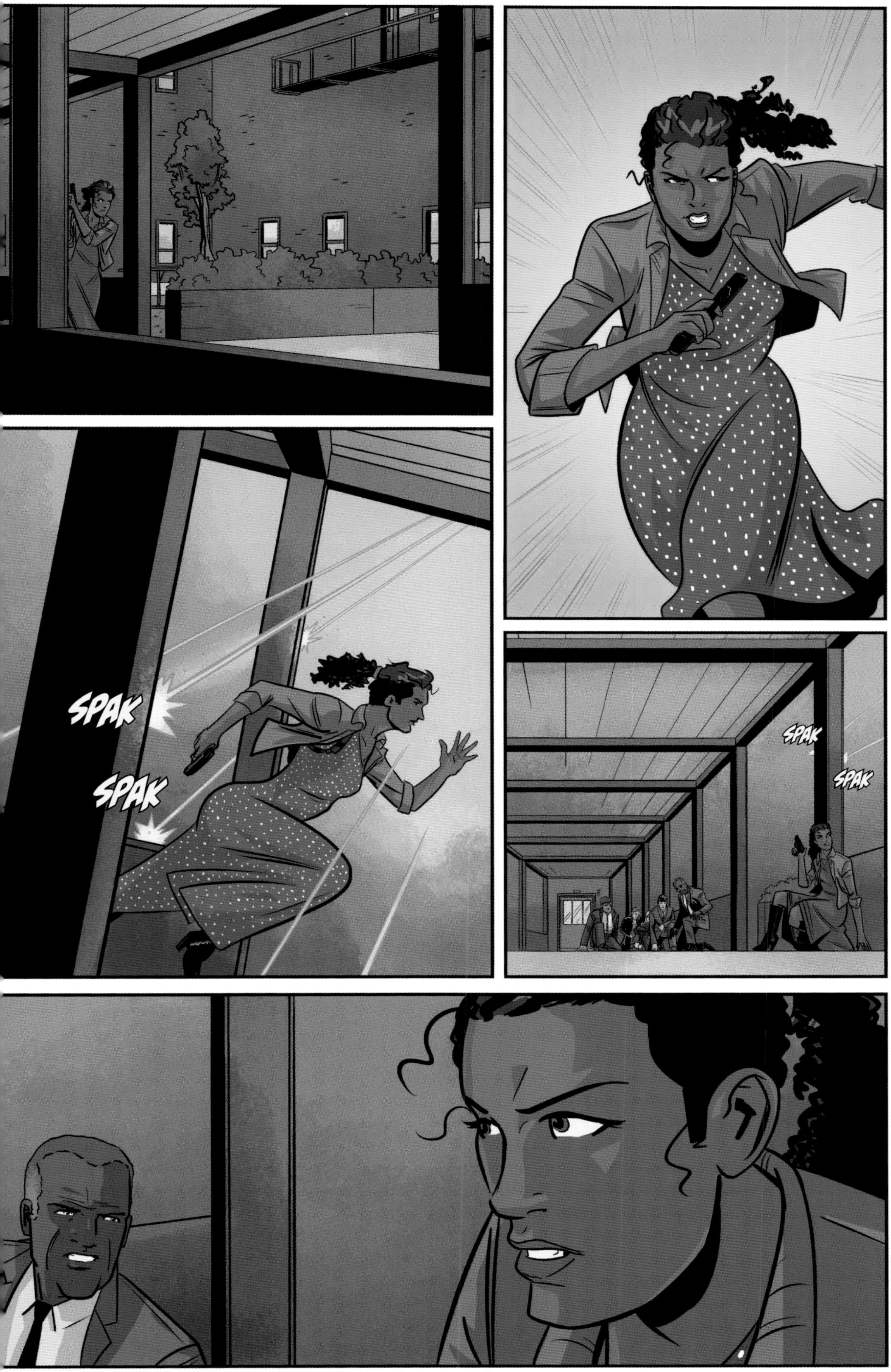
SPAK
SPAK
SPAK
SPAK

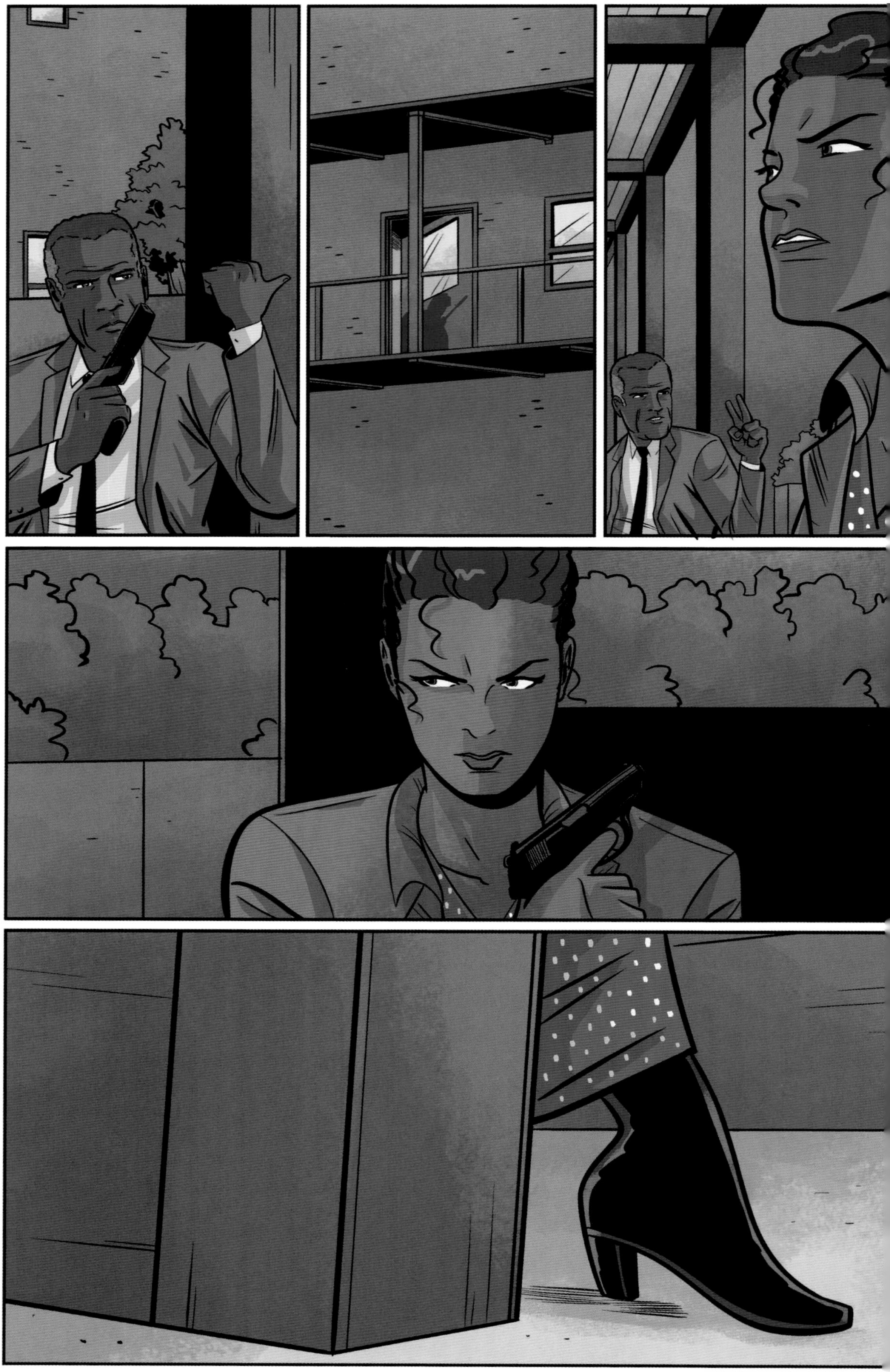

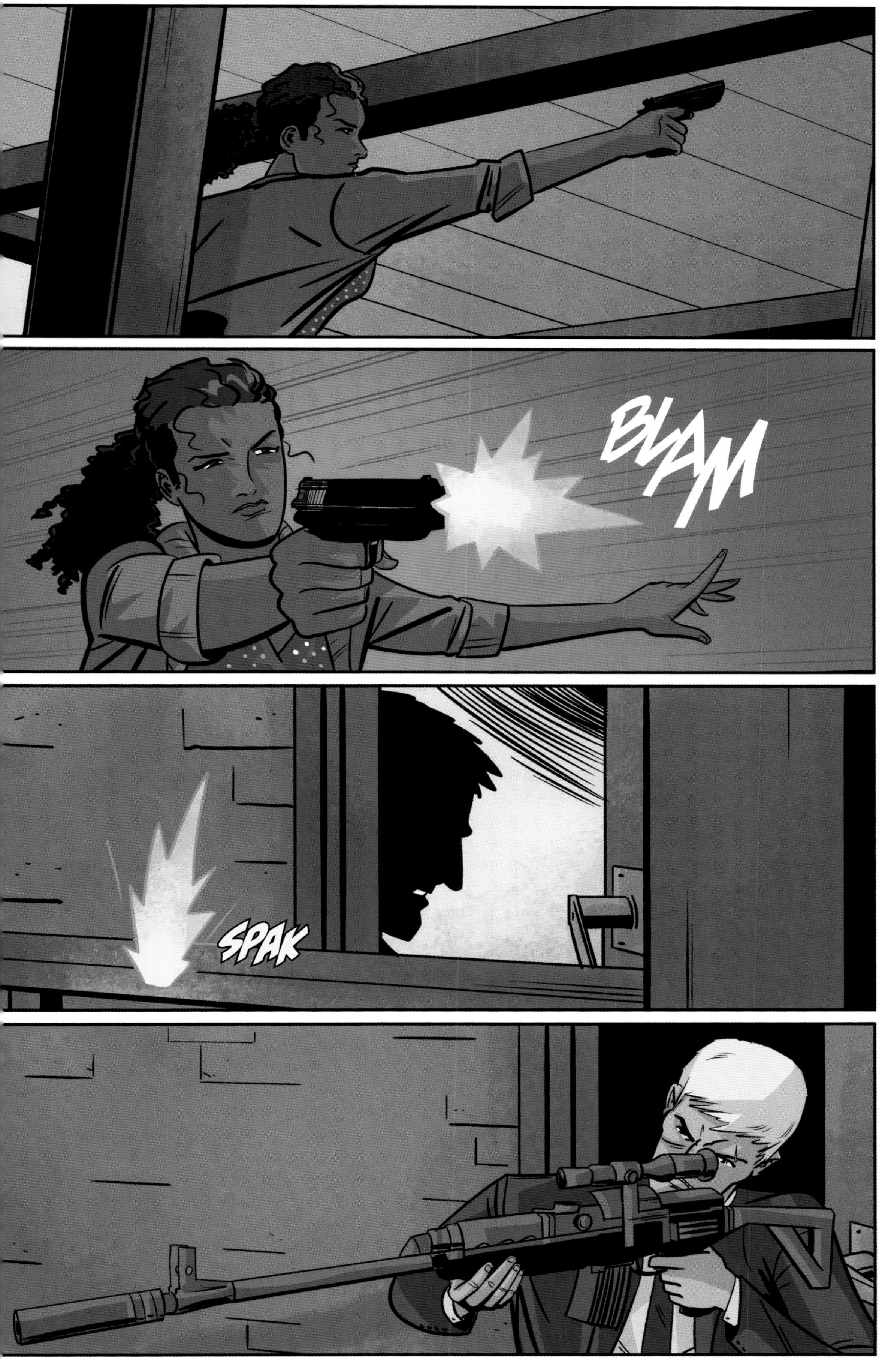
BLAM
SPAK

BLAM

Back the way we came. NOW.

But he's--

Move move move!

BLAM BLAM

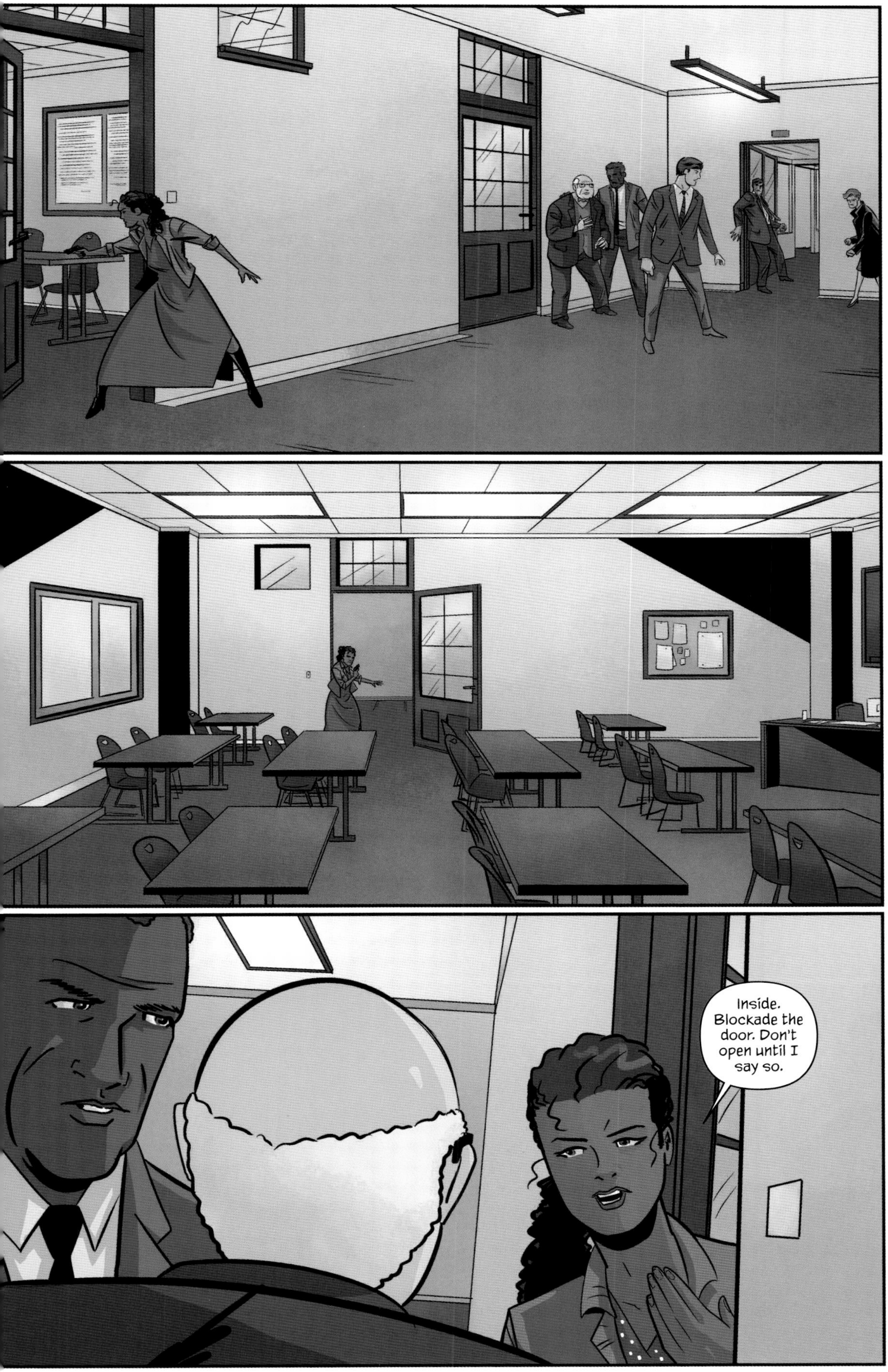
Inside. Blockade the door. Don't open until I say so.

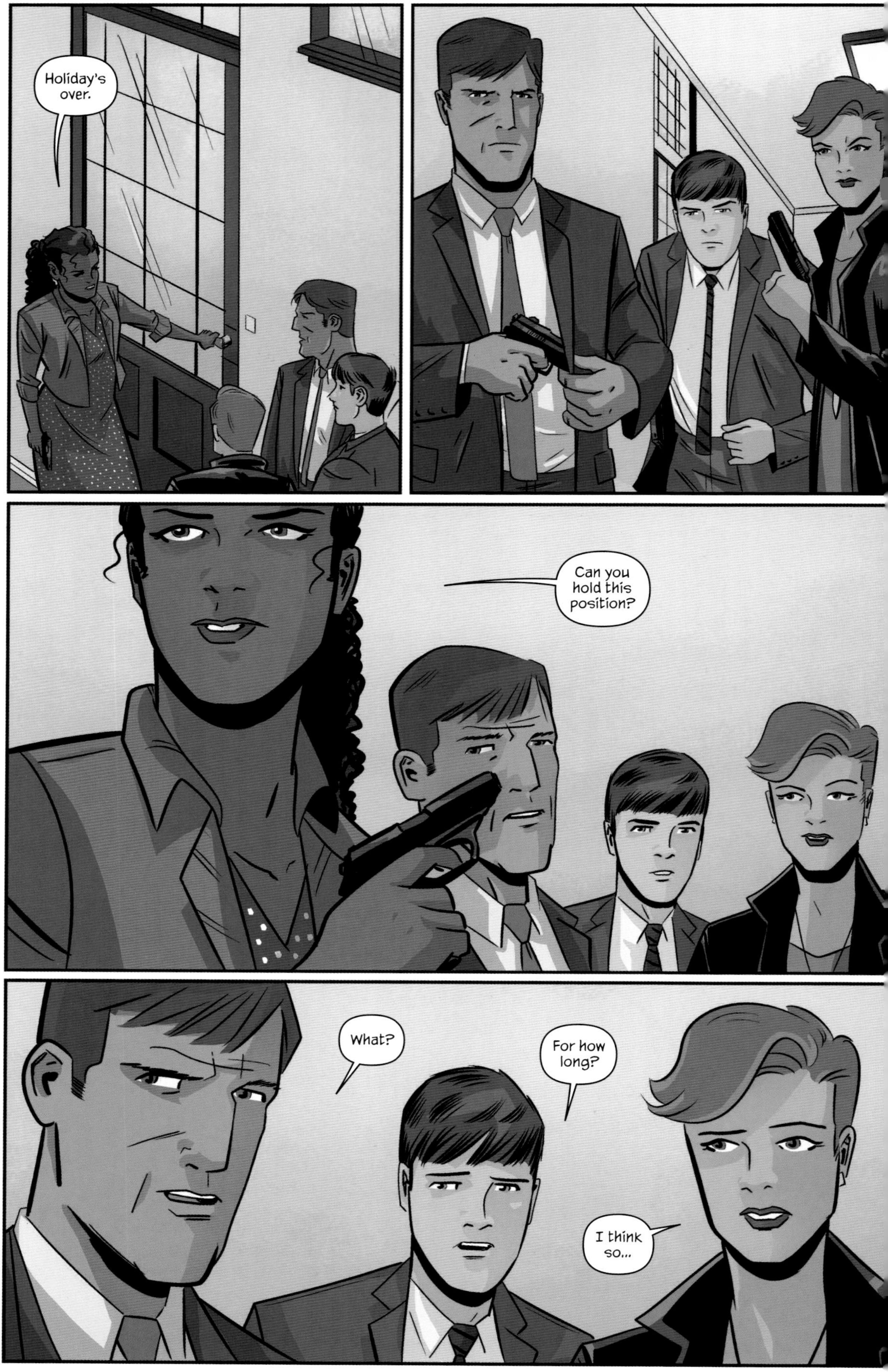
Holiday's over.
Can you hold this position?
What?
For how long?
I think so...

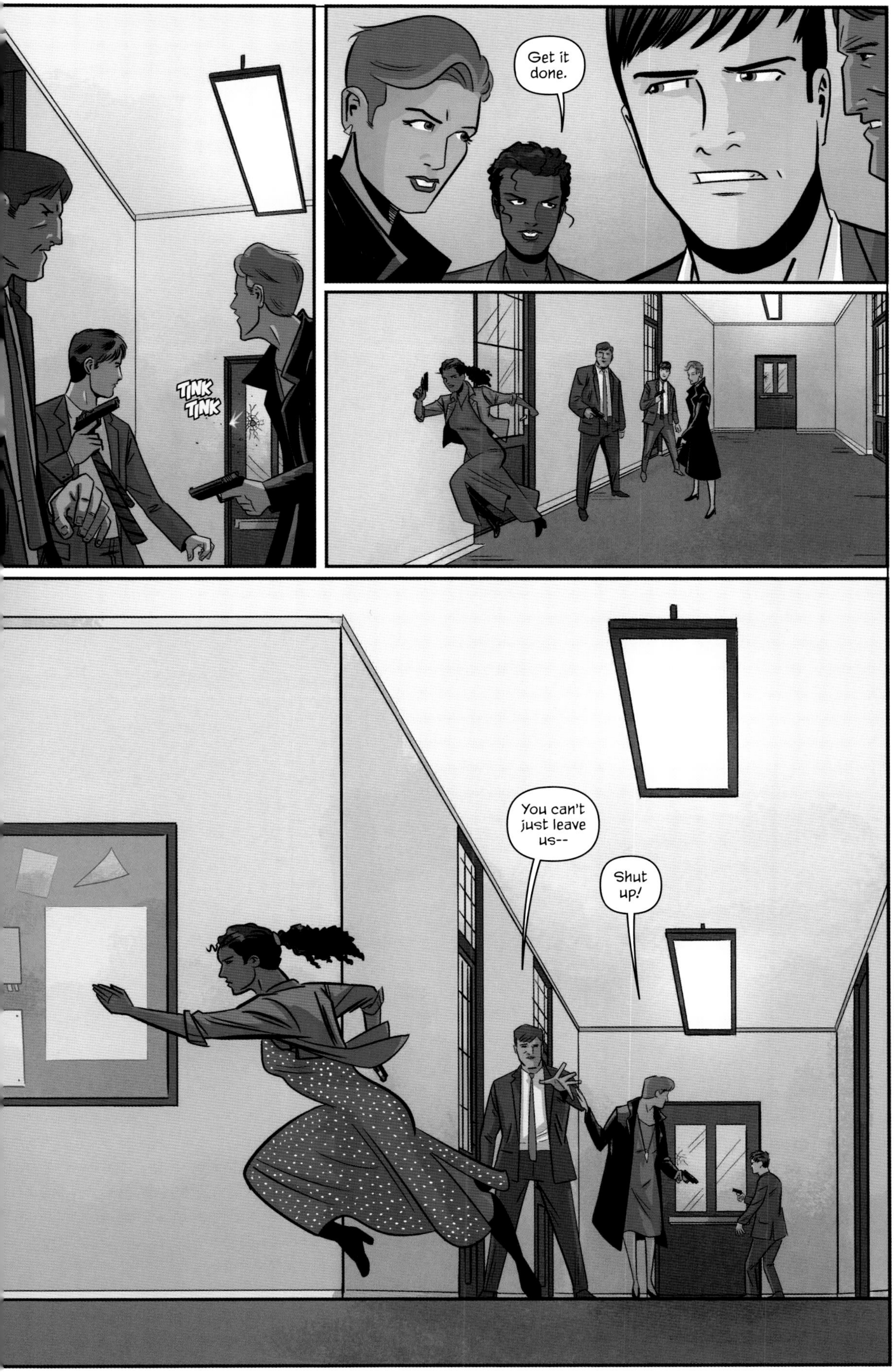
TINK
TINK
Get it done.
You can't just leave us--
Shut up!

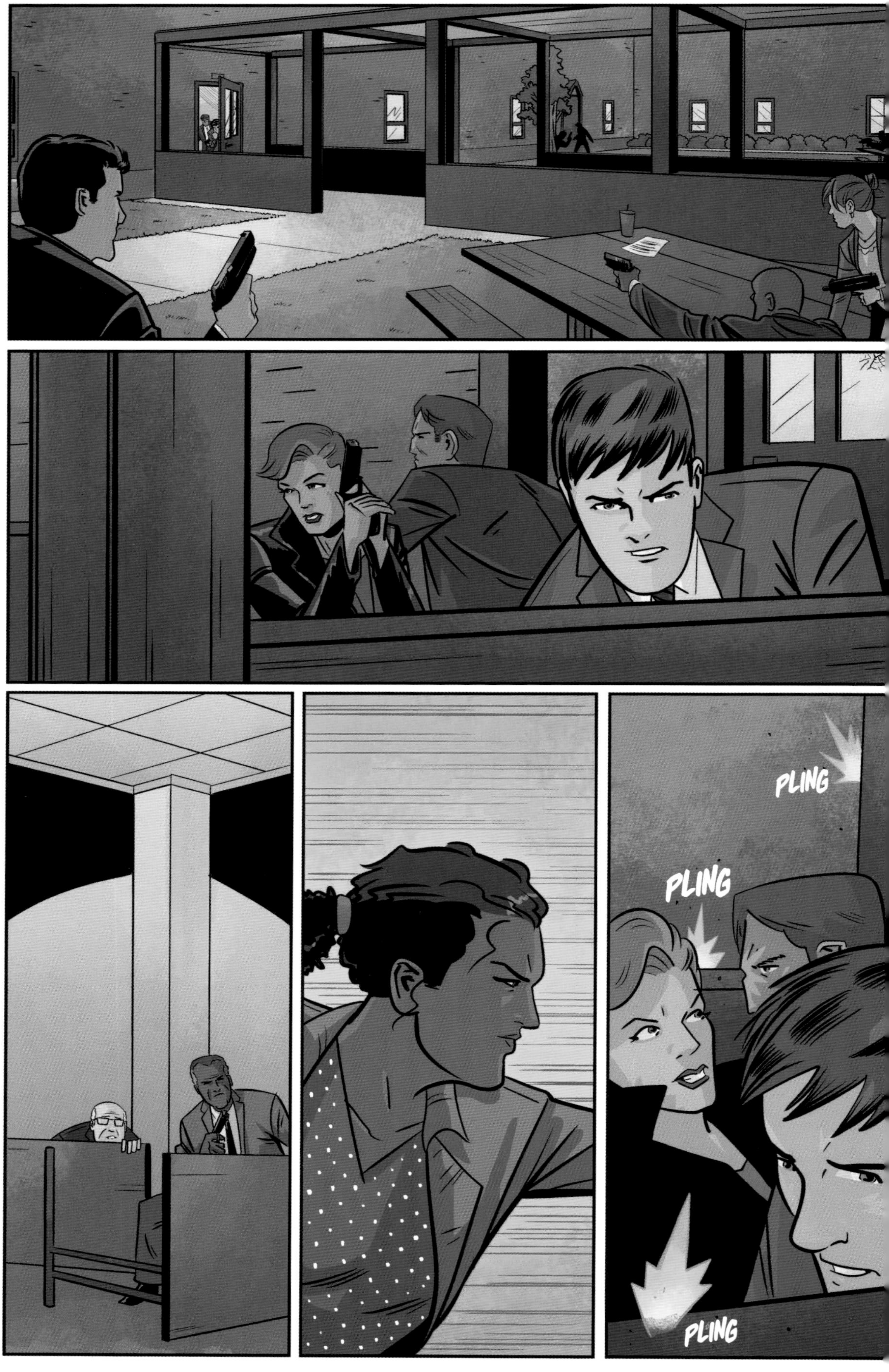
PLING
PLING
PLING

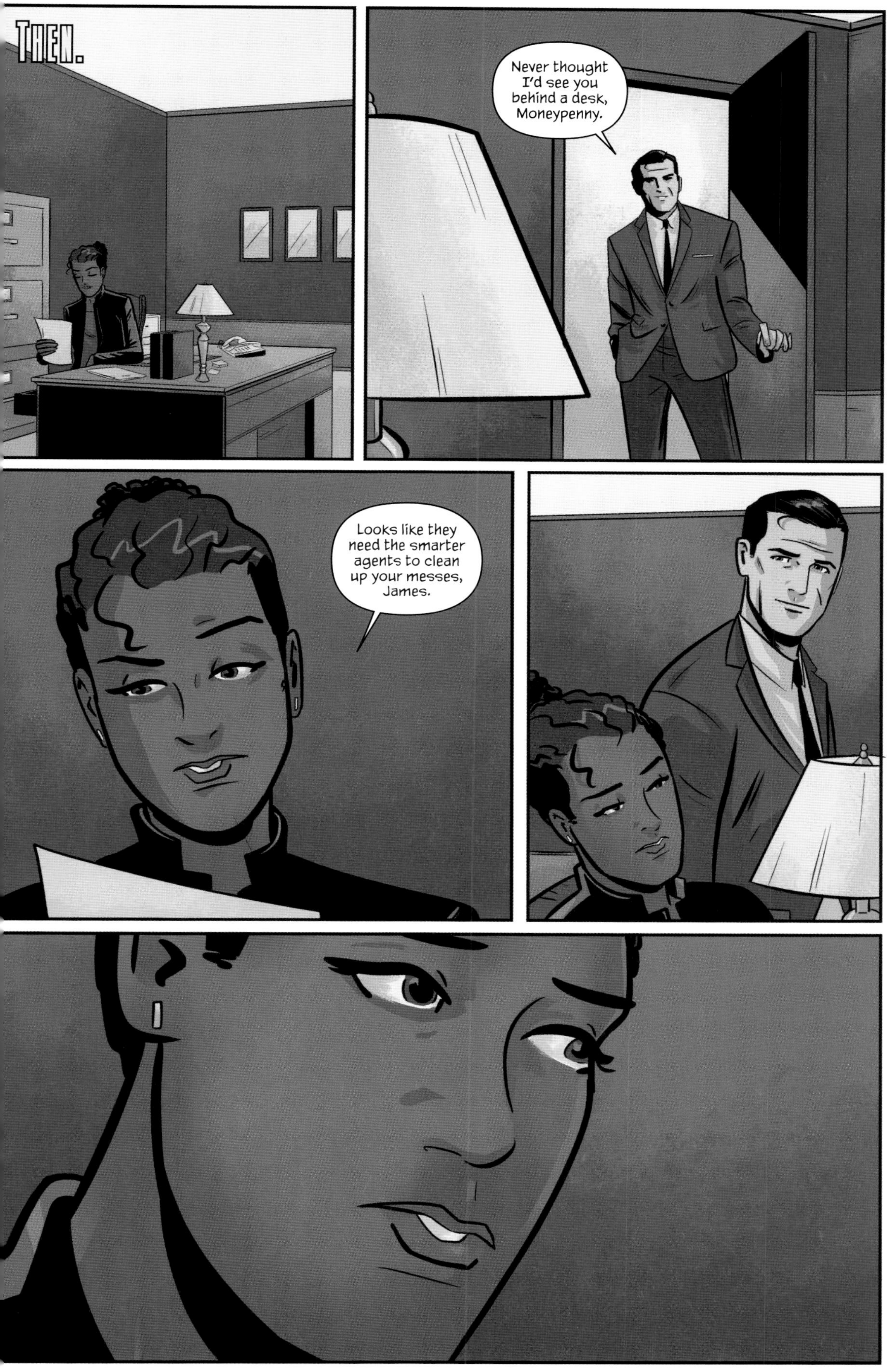
THEN.
Never thought I'd see you behind a desk, Moneypenny.
Looks like they need the smarter agents to clean up your messes, James.

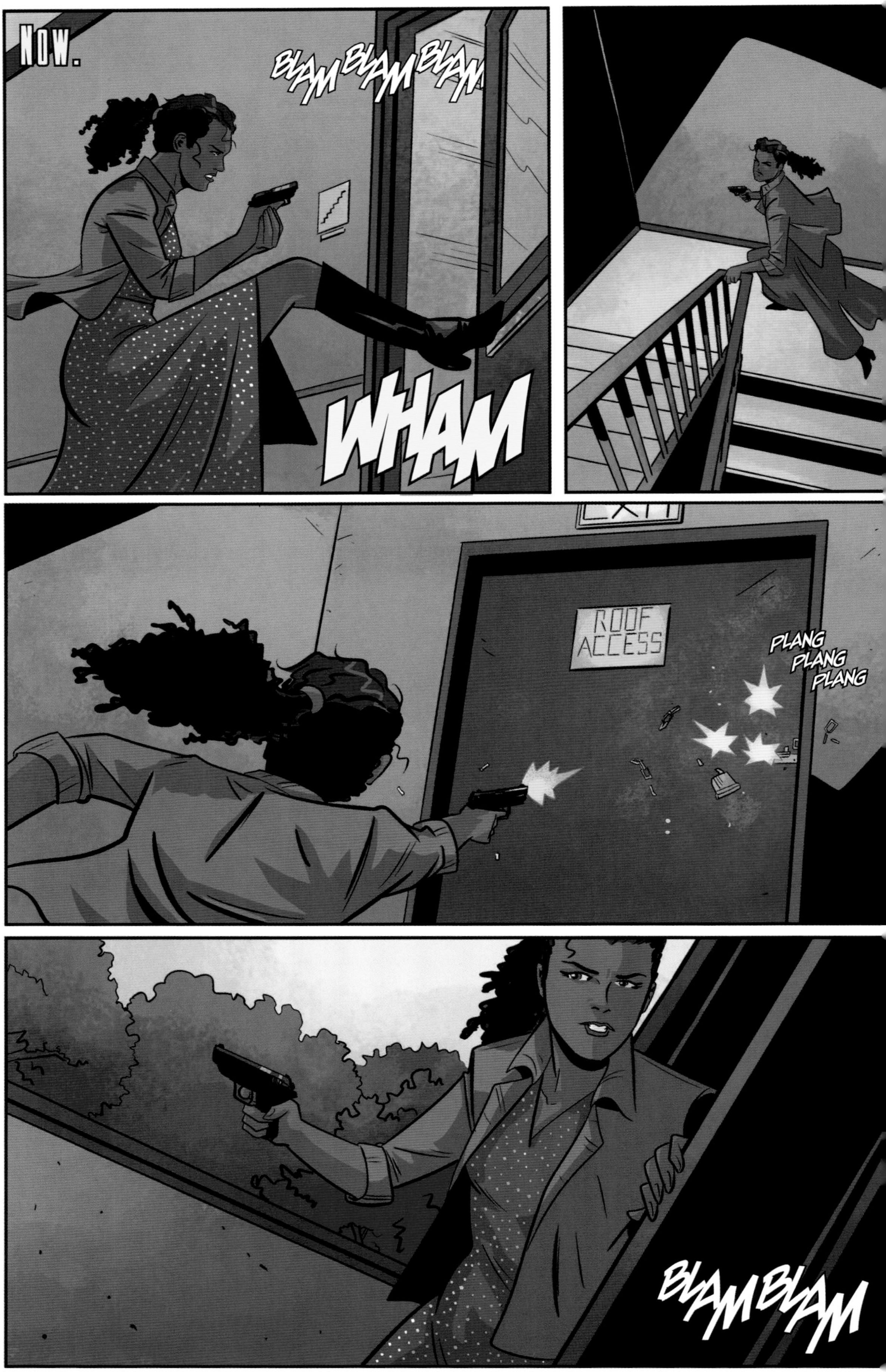
NOW.
BLAM BLAM BLAM
WHAM
EXIT
ROOF ACCESS
PLANG
PLANG
PLANG
BLAM BLAM

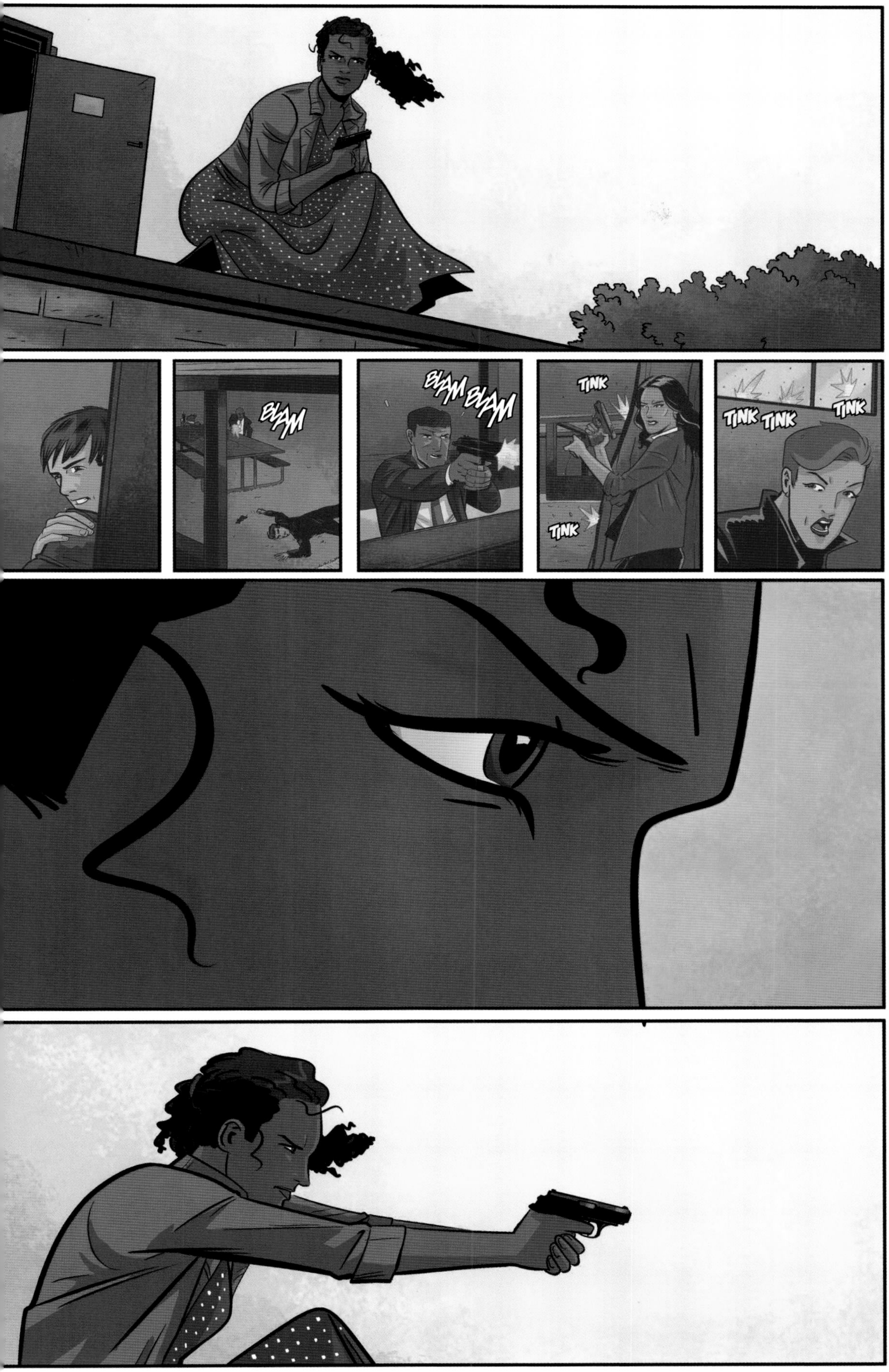
BLAM
BLAM BLAM
TINK
TINK
TINK TINK
TINK

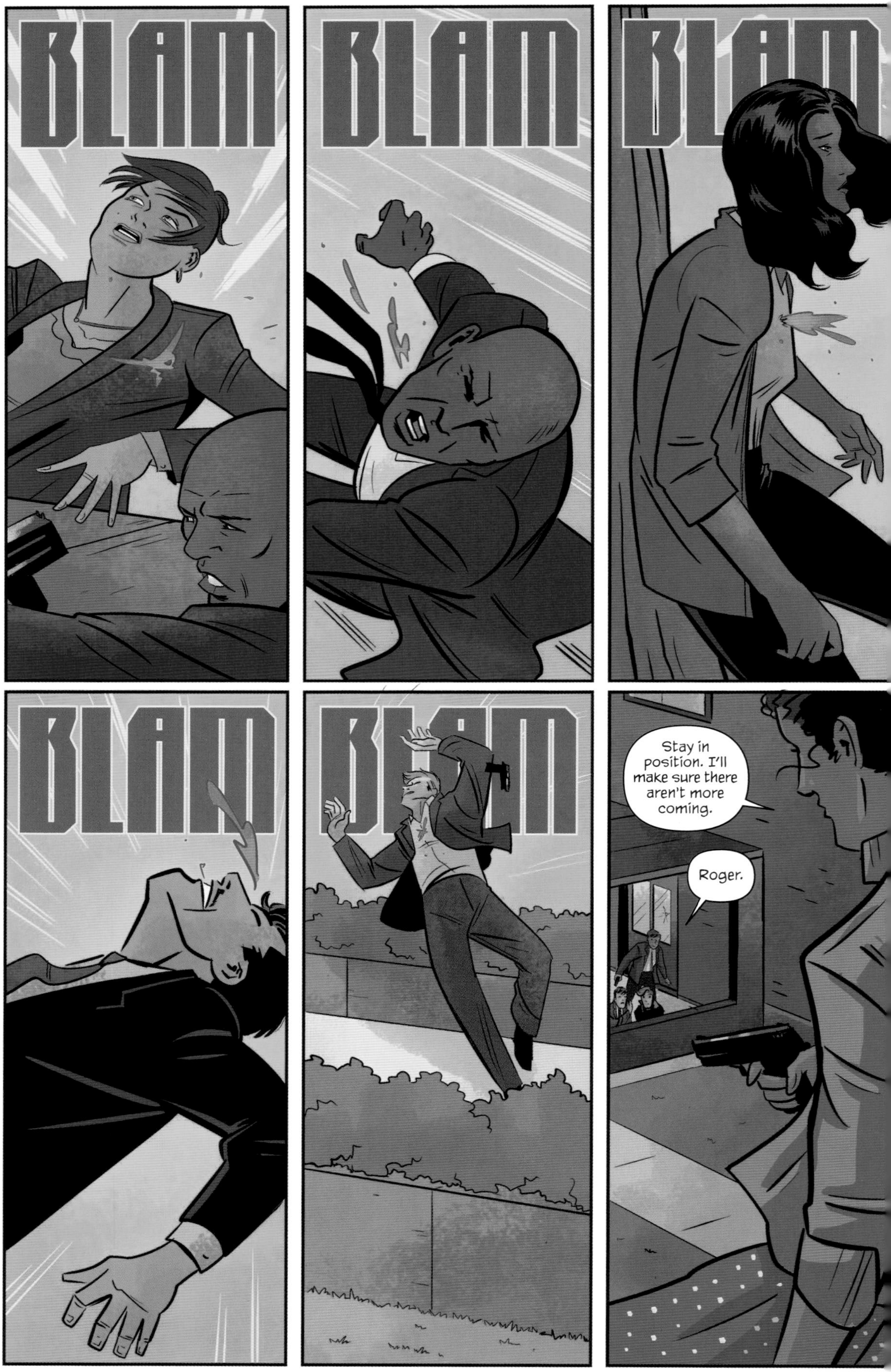
BLAM
BLAM
BLAM
BLAM
BLAM
Stay in position. I'll make sure there aren't more coming.
Roger.

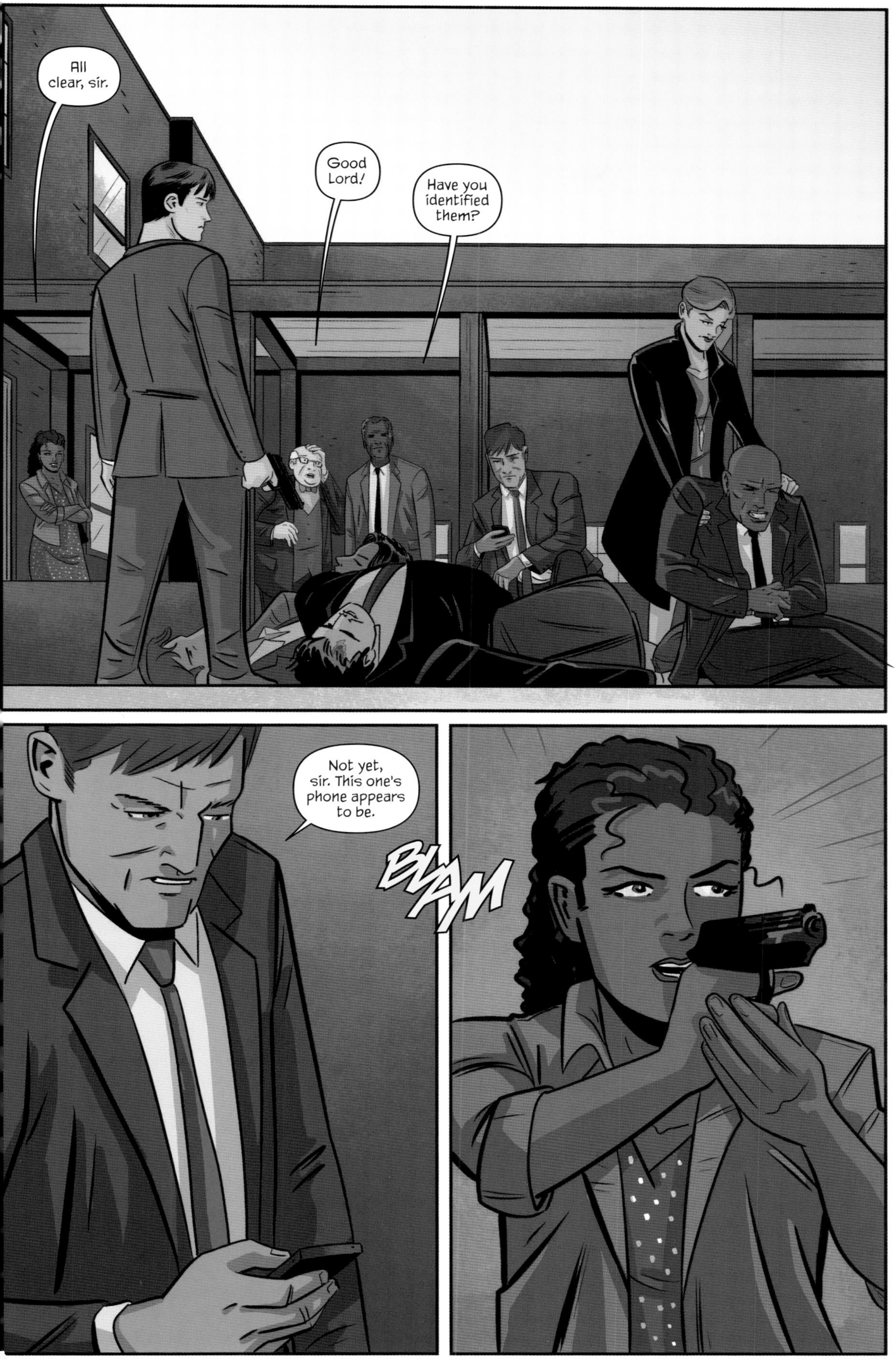
All clear, sir.
Good Lord!
Have you identified them?
Not yet, sir. This one's phone appears to be.
BLAM

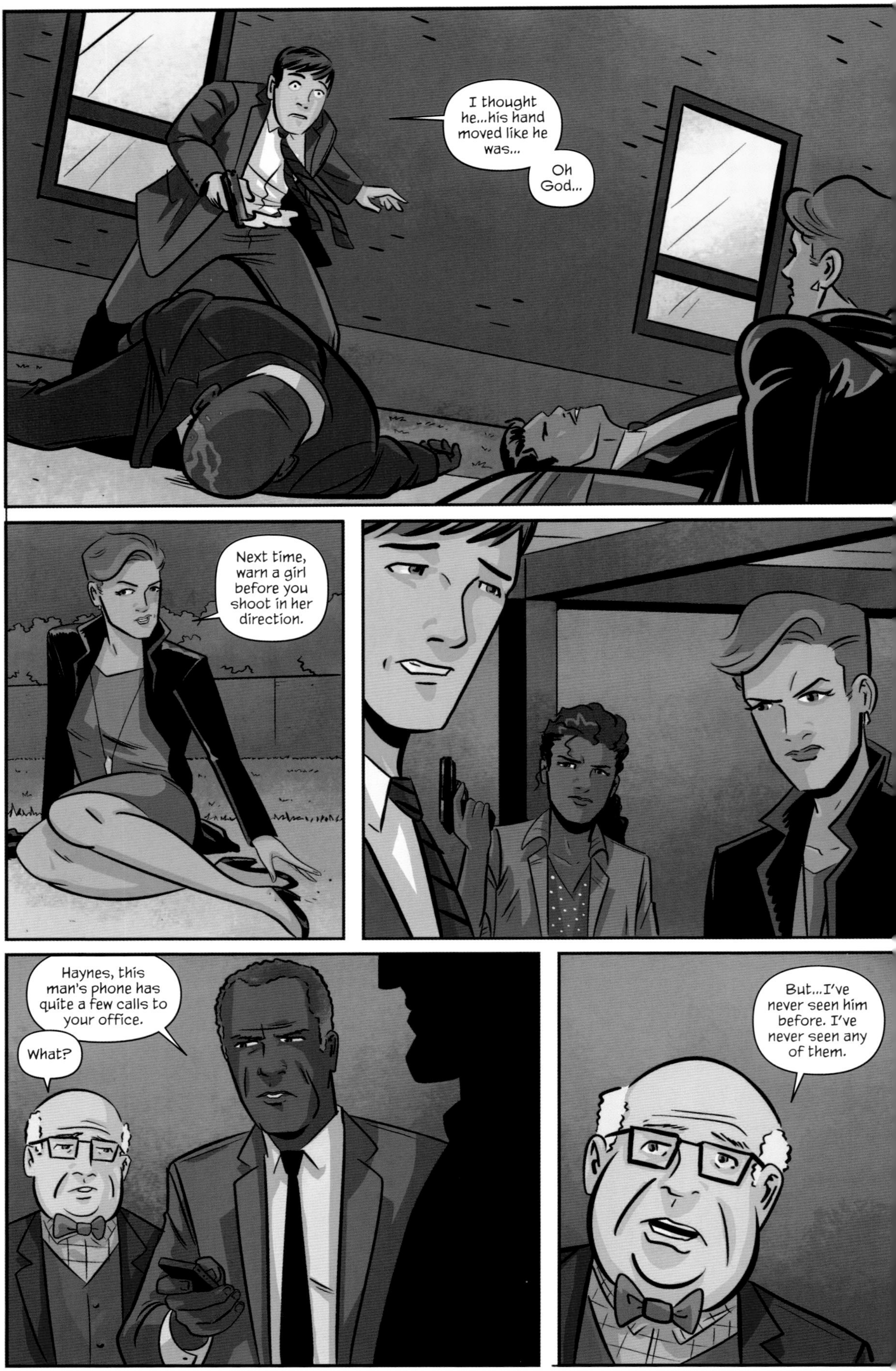
I thought he...his hand moved like he was...
Oh God...
Next time, warn a girl before you shoot in her direction.
Haynes, this man's phone has quite a few calls to your office.
What?
But...I've never seen him before. I've never seen any of them.

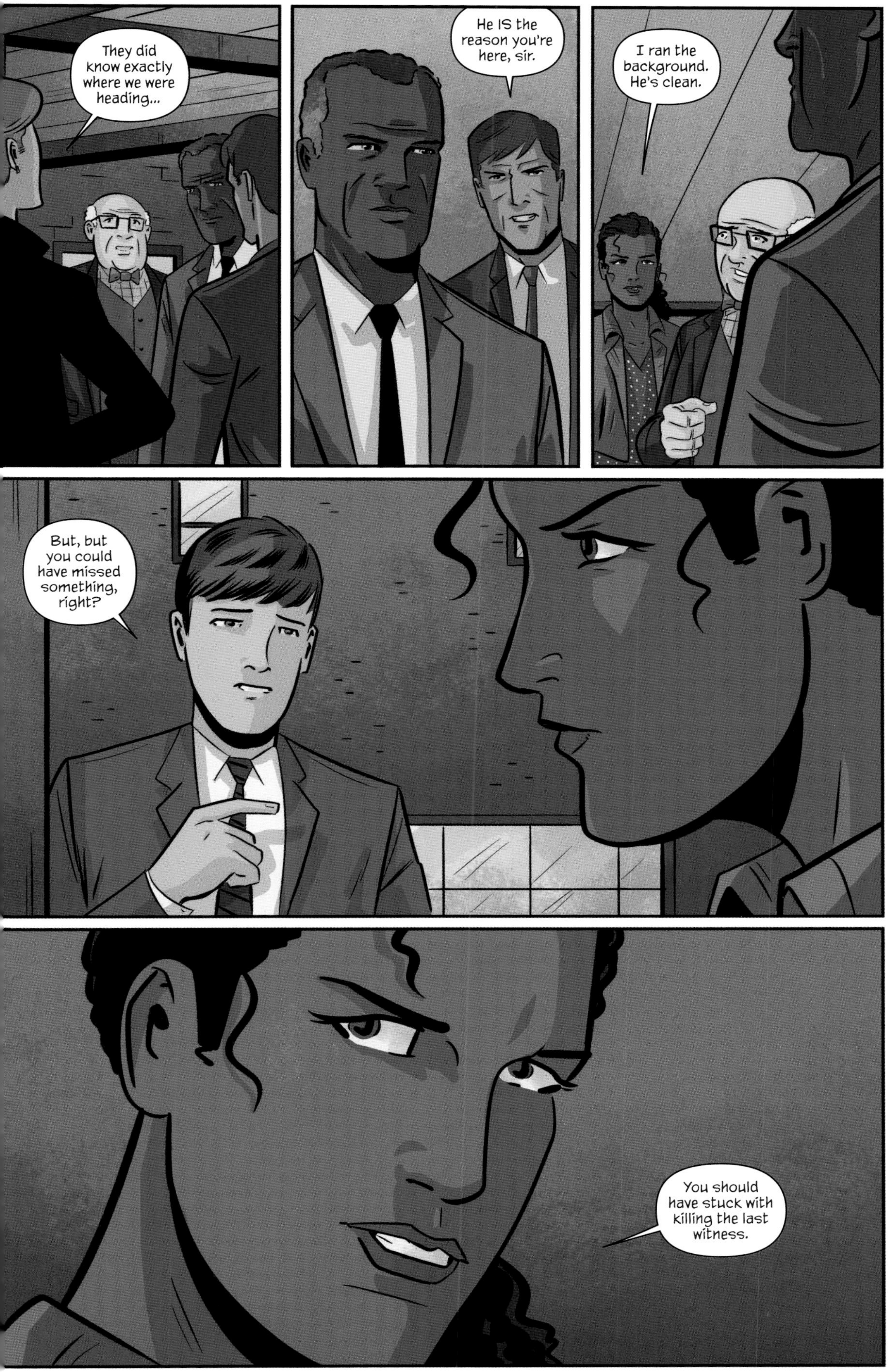
They did know exactly where we were heading...
He IS the reason you're here, sir.
I ran the background. He's clean.
But, but you could have missed something, right?
You should have stuck with killing the last witness.

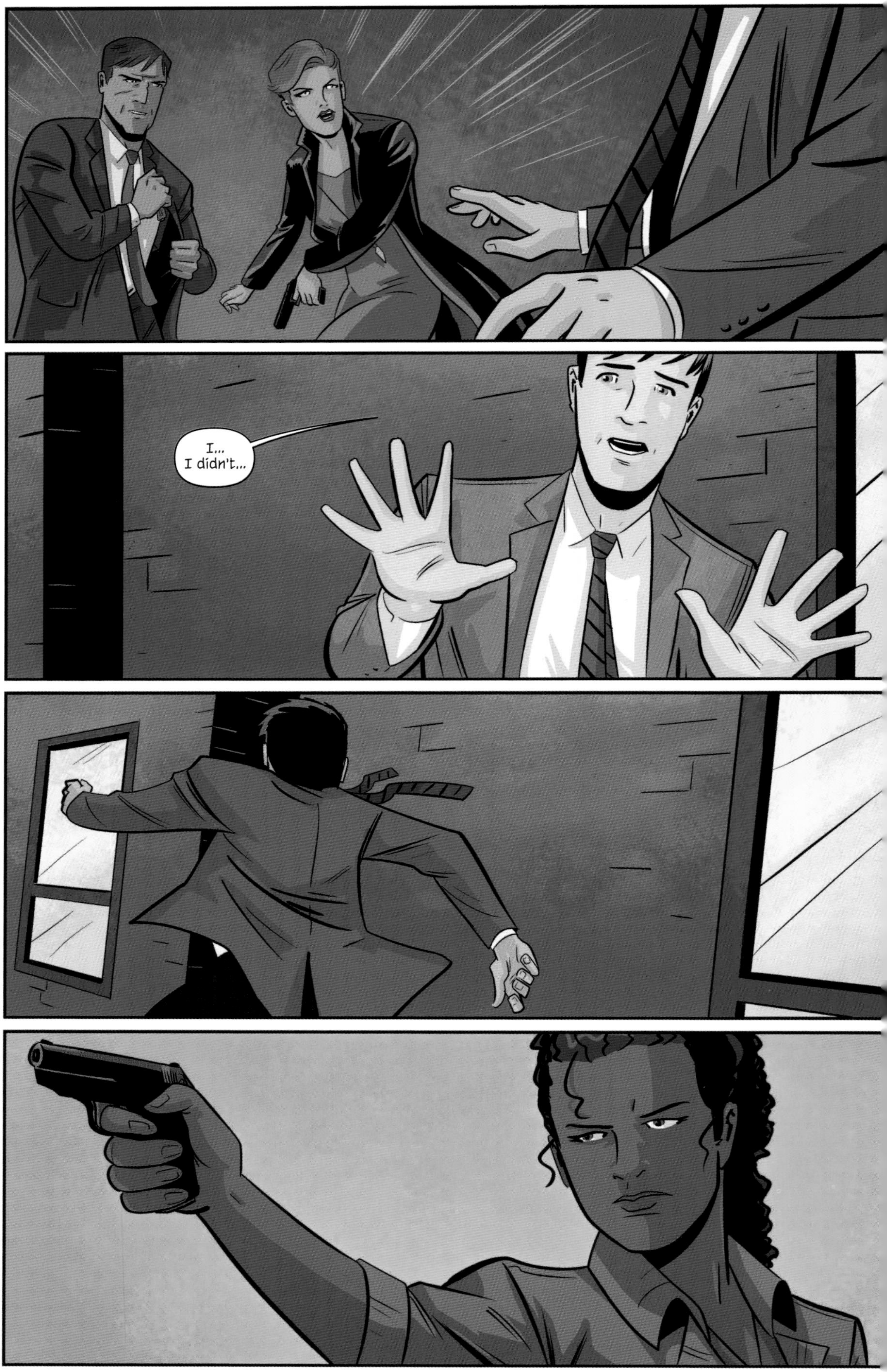
I... I didn't...

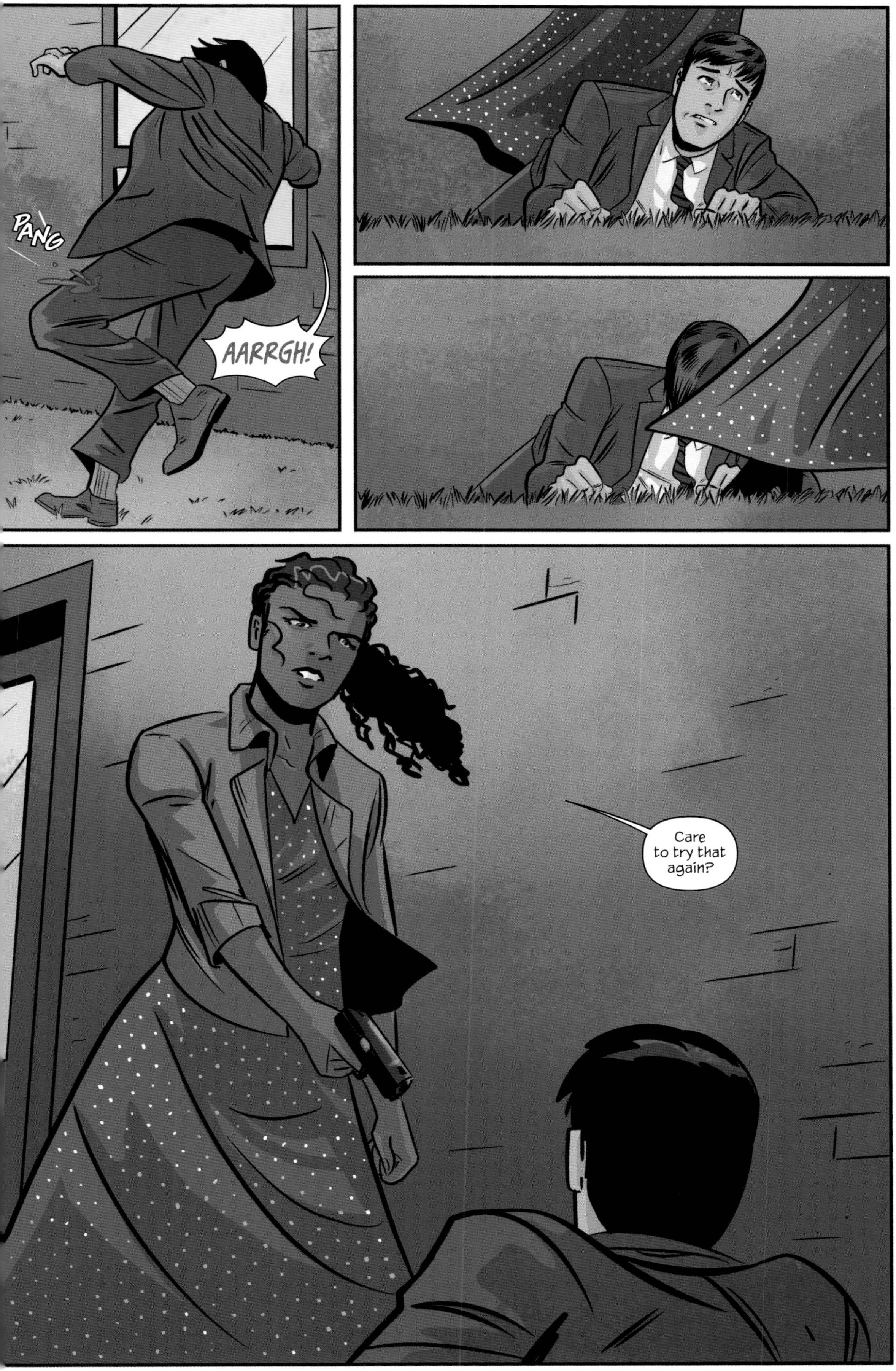
PANG
AARRGH!
Care to try that again?

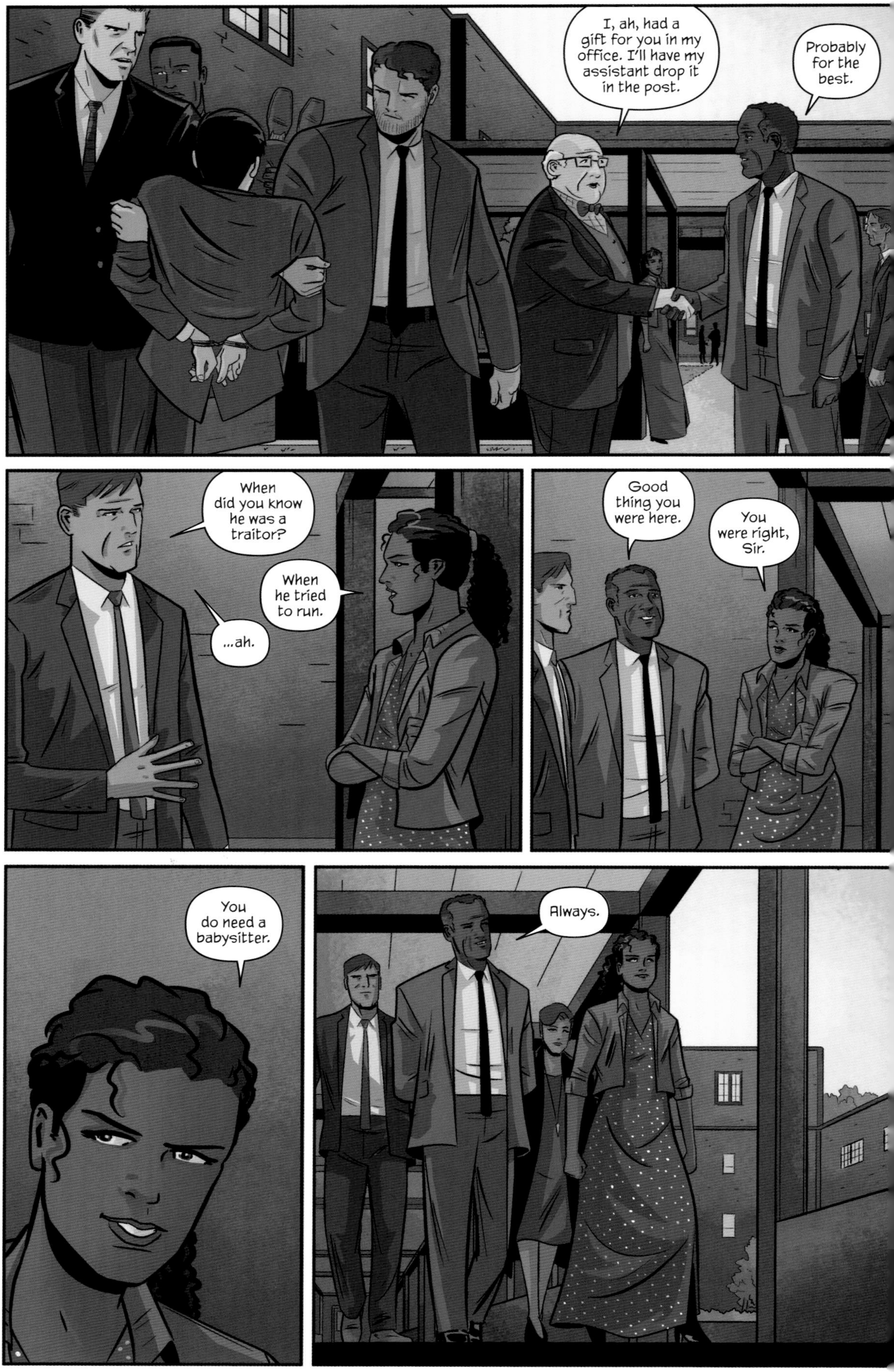
I, ah, had a gift for you in my office. I'll have my assistant drop it in the post.
Probably for the best.
When did you know he was a traitor?
When he tried to run.
...ah.
Good thing you were here.
You were right, Sir.
You do need a babysitter.
Always.

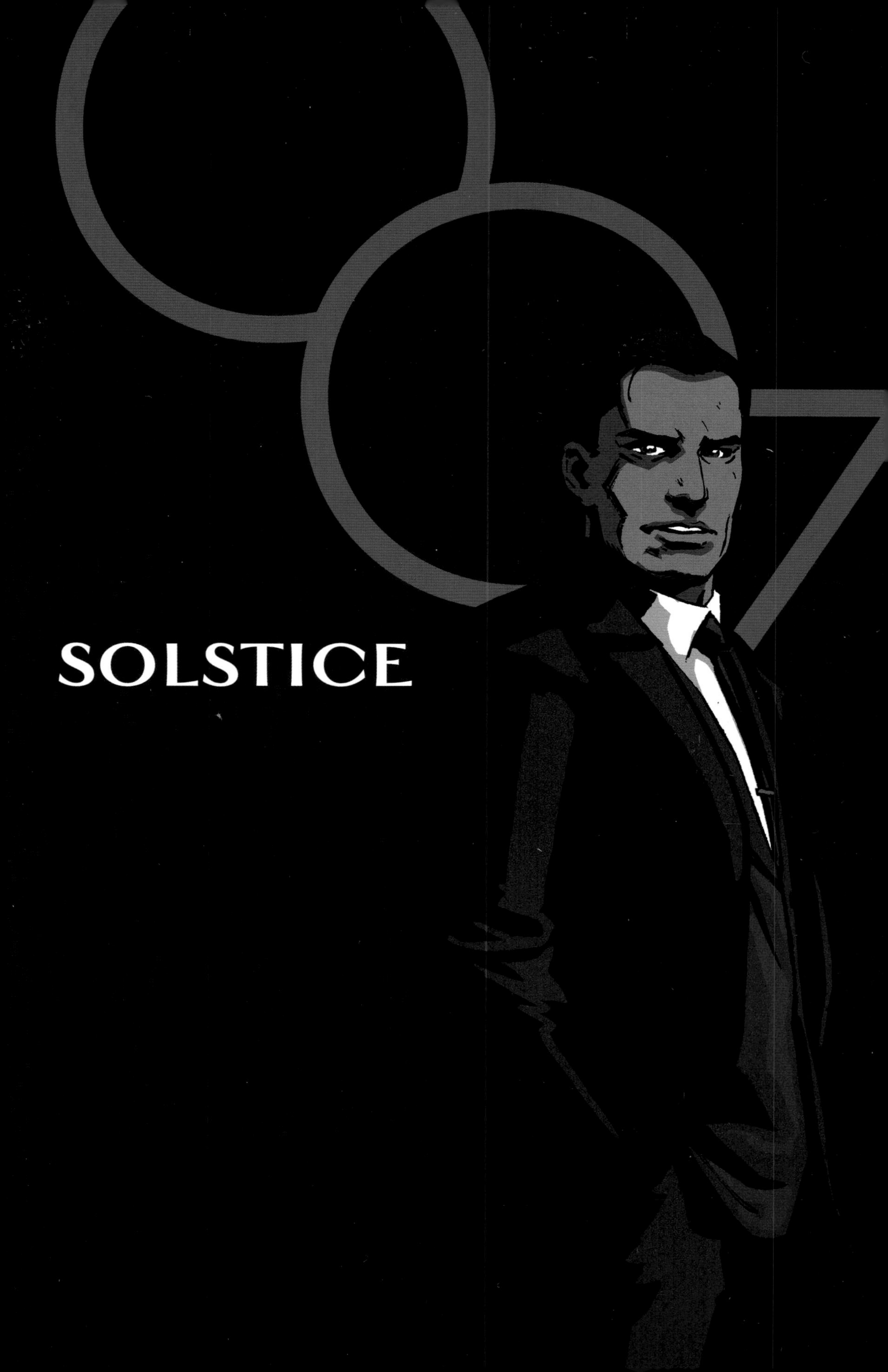
SOLSTICE

JAMES BOND: SOLSTICE
COVER BY IBRAHIM MOUSTAFA

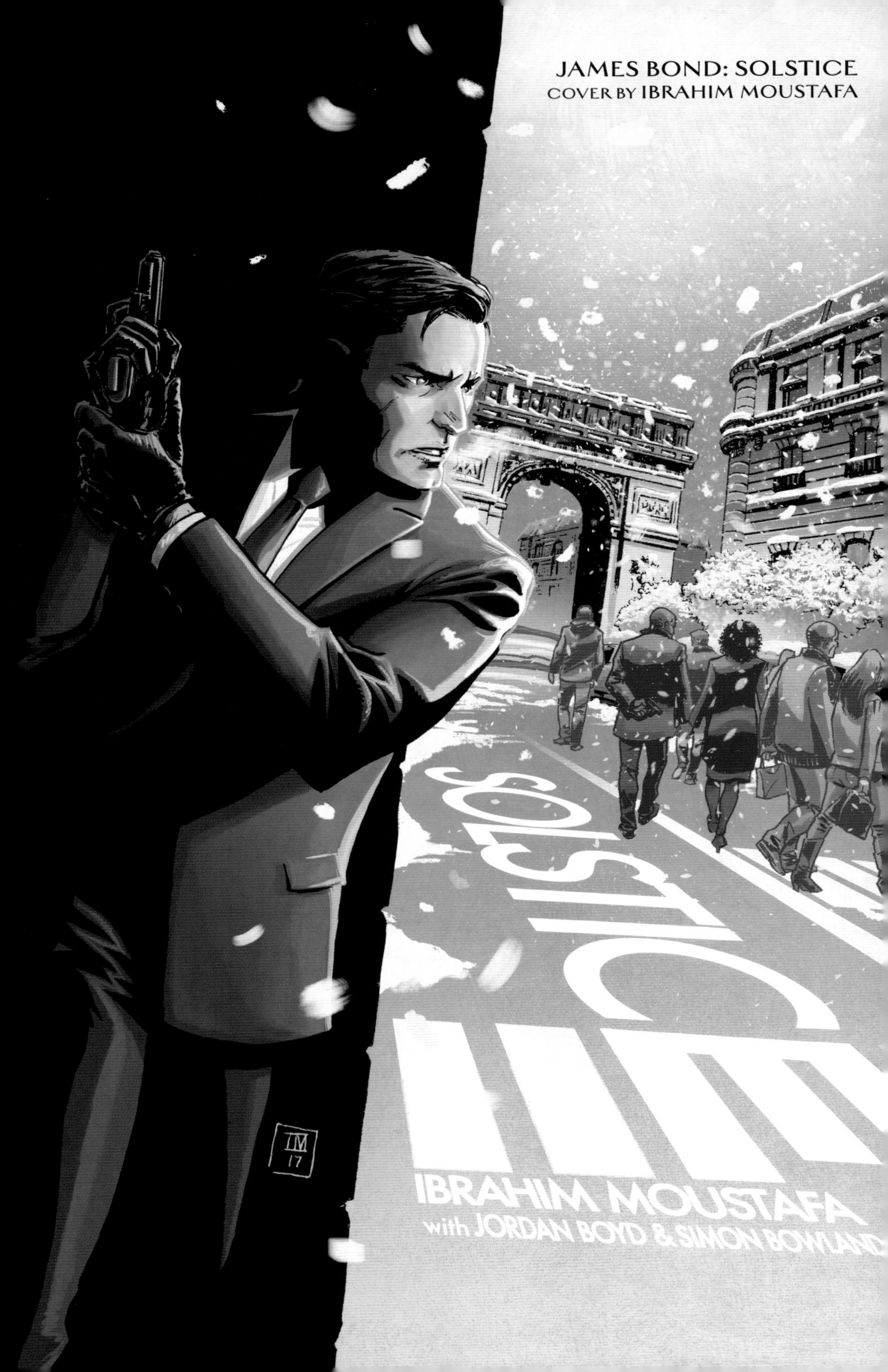
SOLSTICE
IBRAHIM MOUSTAFA
with JORDAN BOYD & SIMON BOWLAND
IM
17

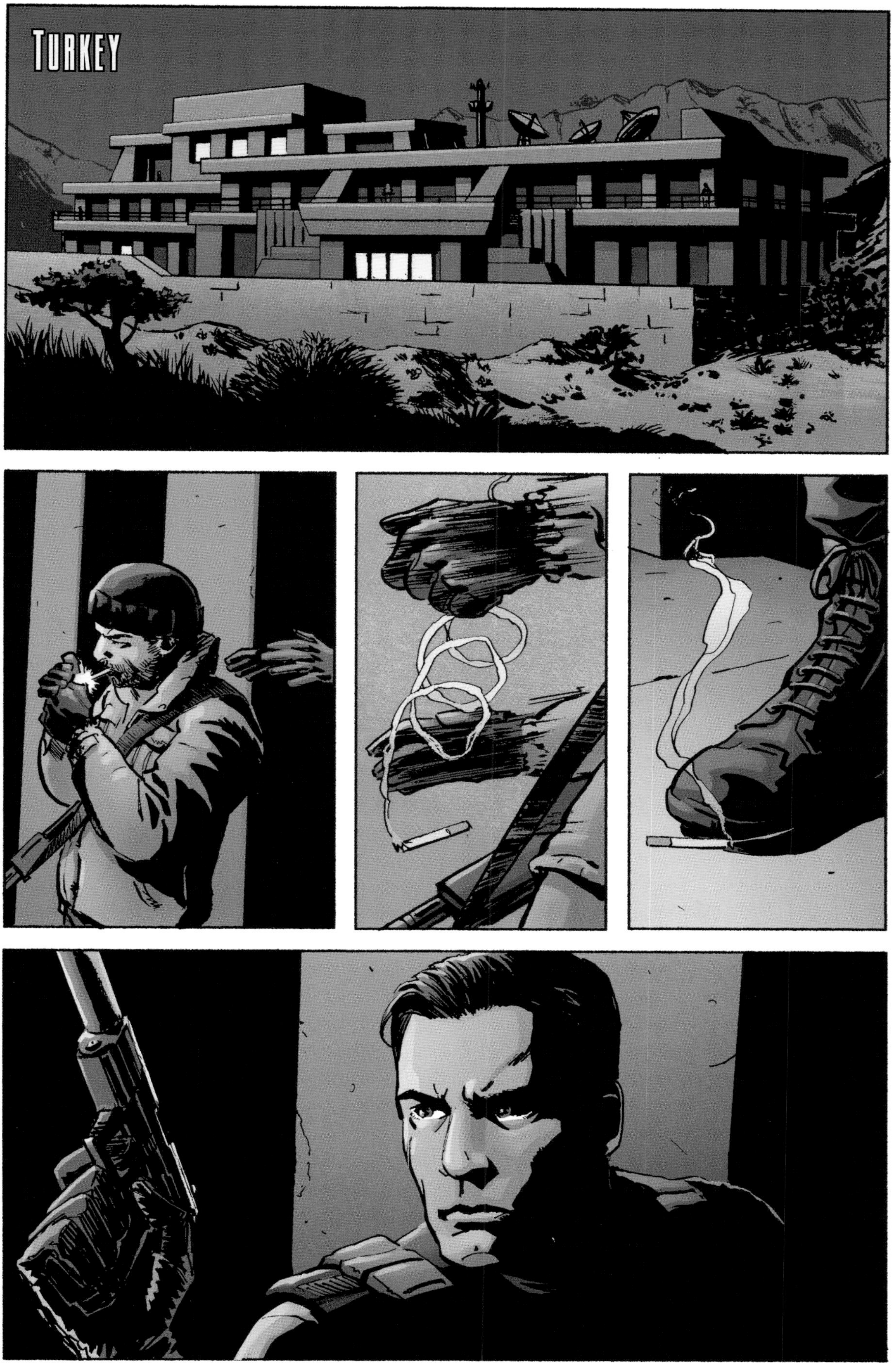
TURKEY

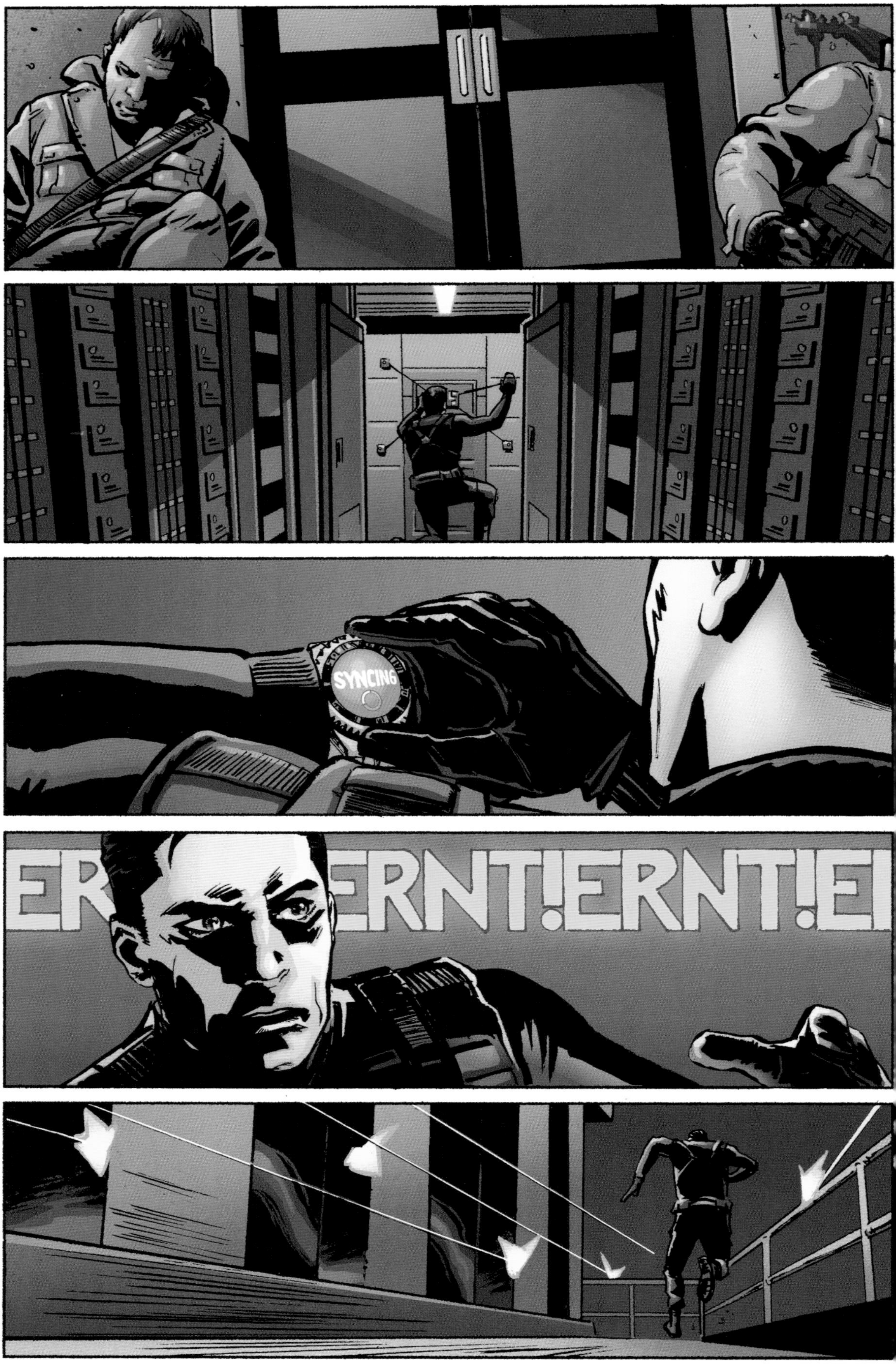
SYNCING
ERNT!ERNT!ERNT!EI

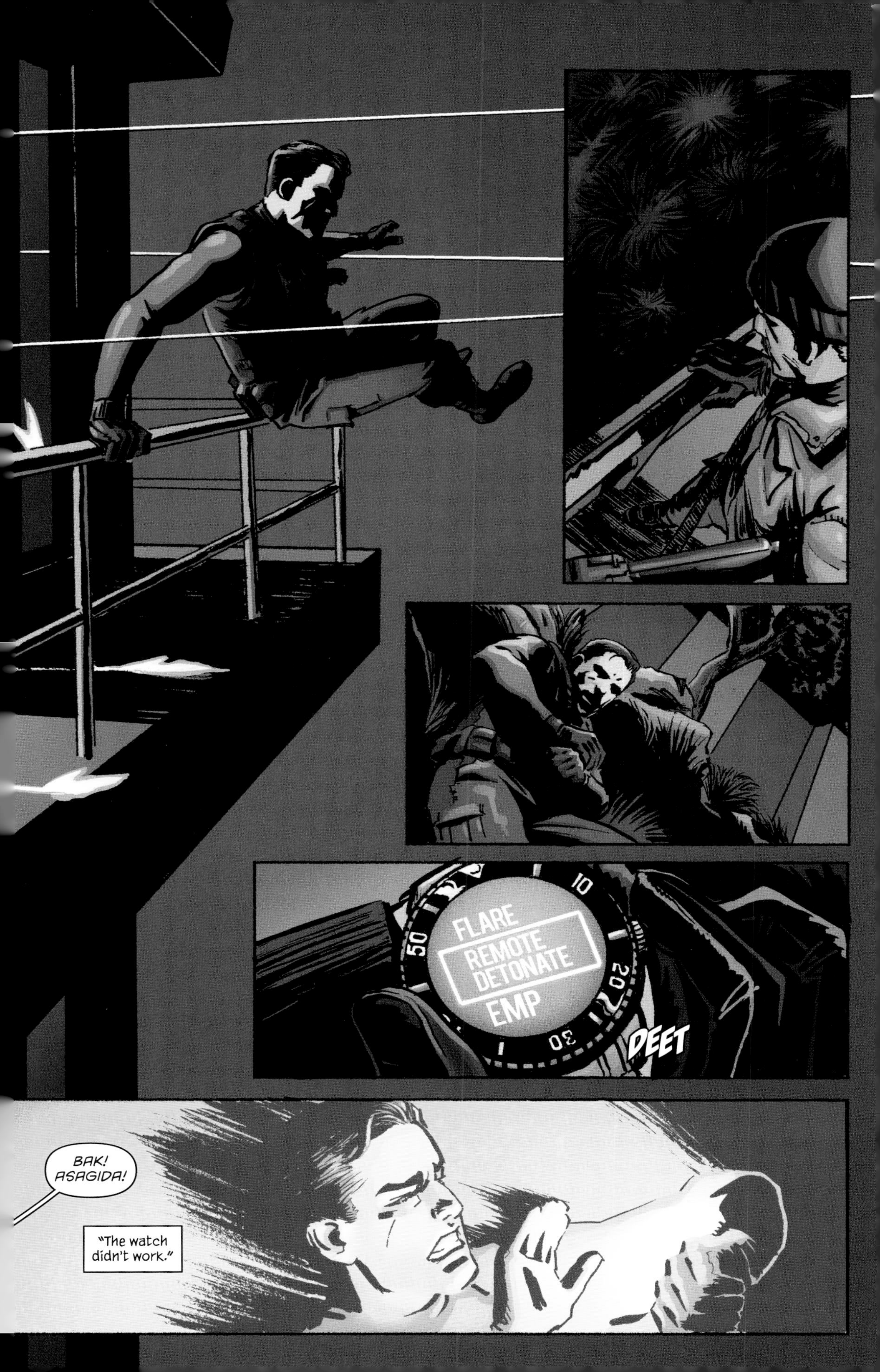
FLARE
REMOTE DETONATE
EMP
DEET
BAK! ASAGIDA!
"The watch didn't work."

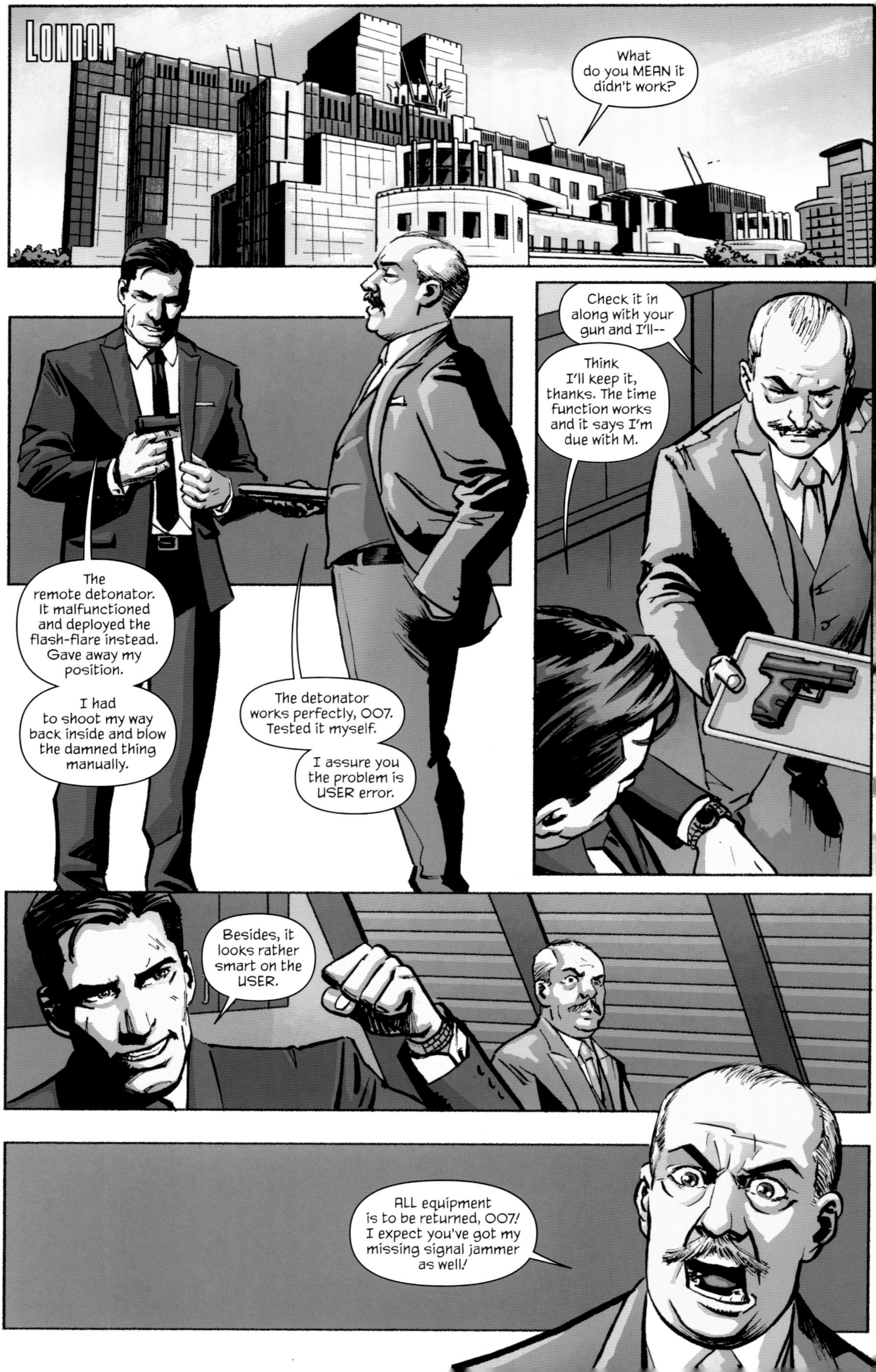
LONDON
What do you MEAN it didn't work?
The remote detonator. It malfunctioned and deployed the flash-flare instead. Gave away my position.
I had to shoot my way back inside and blow the damned thing manually.
The detonator works perfectly, 007. Tested it myself.
I assure you the problem is USER error.
Check it in along with your gun and I'll--
Think I'll keep it, thanks. The time function works and it says I'm due with M.
Besides, it looks rather smart on the USER.
ALL equipment is to be returned, 007! I expect you've got my missing signal jammer as well!

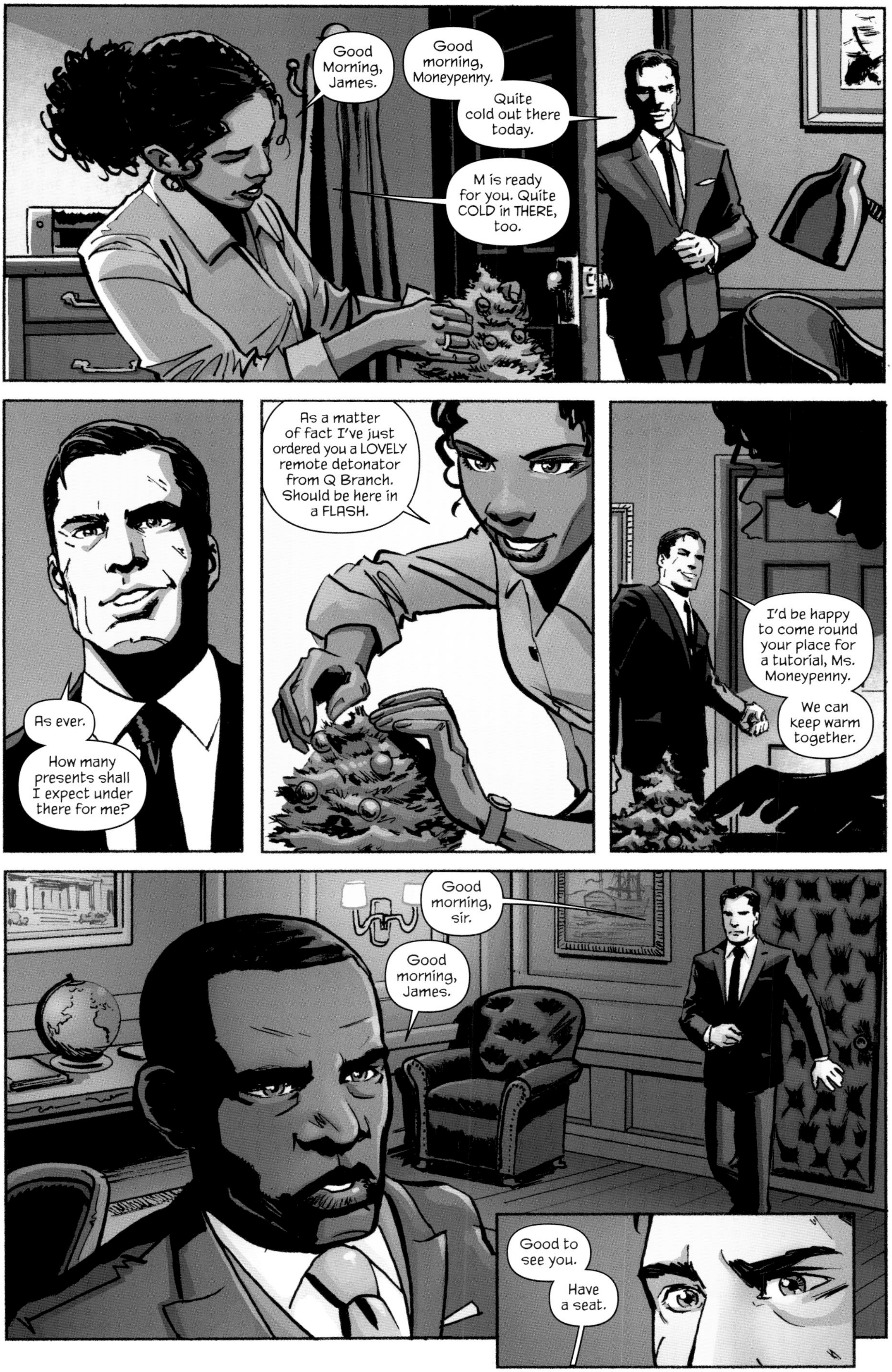
Good Morning, James.
Good morning, Moneypenny.
Quite cold out there today.
M is ready for you. Quite COLD in THERE, too.
As ever.
How many presents shall I expect under there for me?
As a matter of fact I've just ordered you a LOVELY remote detonator from Q Branch. Should be here in a FLASH.
I'd be happy to come round your place for a tutorial, Ms. Moneypenny.
We can keep warm together.
Good morning, sir.
Good morning, James.
Good to see you.
Have a seat.

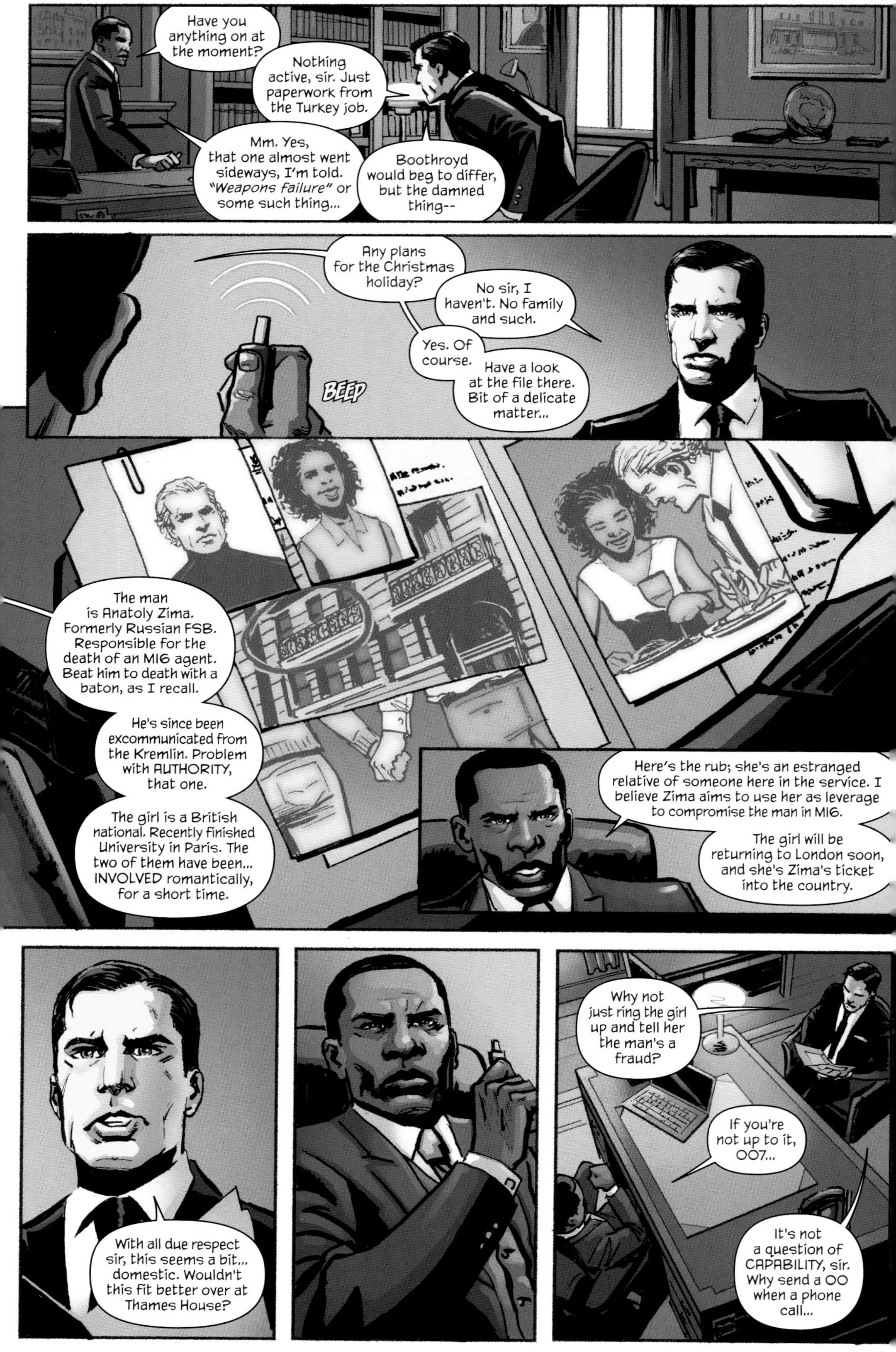

Have you anything on at the moment?
Nothing active, sir. Just paperwork from the Turkey job.
Mm. Yes, that one almost went sideways, I'm told. *"Weapons failure"* or some such thing...
Boothroyd would beg to differ, but the damned thing--
Any plans for the Christmas holiday?
No sir, I haven't. No family and such.
Yes. Of course.
Have a look at the file there. Bit of a delicate matter...
BEEP
The man is Anatoly Zima. Formerly Russian FSB. Responsible for the death of an MI6 agent. Beat him to death with a baton, as I recall.
He's since been excommunicated from the Kremlin. Problem with AUTHORITY, that one.
The girl is a British national. Recently finished University in Paris. The two of them have been... INVOLVED romantically, for a short time.
Here's the rub; she's an estranged relative of someone here in the service. I believe Zima aims to use her as leverage to compromise the man in MI6.
The girl will be returning to London soon, and she's Zima's ticket into the country.
With all due respect sir, this seems a bit... domestic. Wouldn't this fit better over at Thames House?
Why not just ring the girl up and tell her the man's a fraud?
If you're not up to it, 007...
It's not a question of CAPABILITY, sir. Why send a 00 when a phone call...

What's to be done?

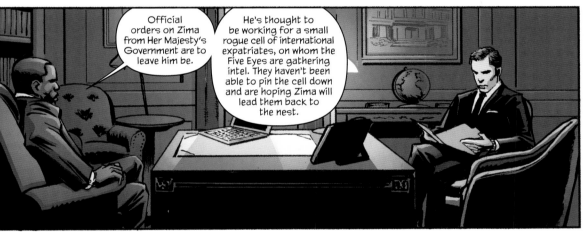

Official orders on Zima from Her Majesty's Government are to leave him be.

He's thought to be working for a small rogue cell of international expatriates, on whom the Five Eyes are gathering intel. They haven't been able to pin the cell down and are hoping Zima will lead them back to the nest.

Unofficially...

He is to be removed from the equation.

They've dinner reservations for this evening and a show after. Locations in the file.

It goes without saying, but discretion is vital.

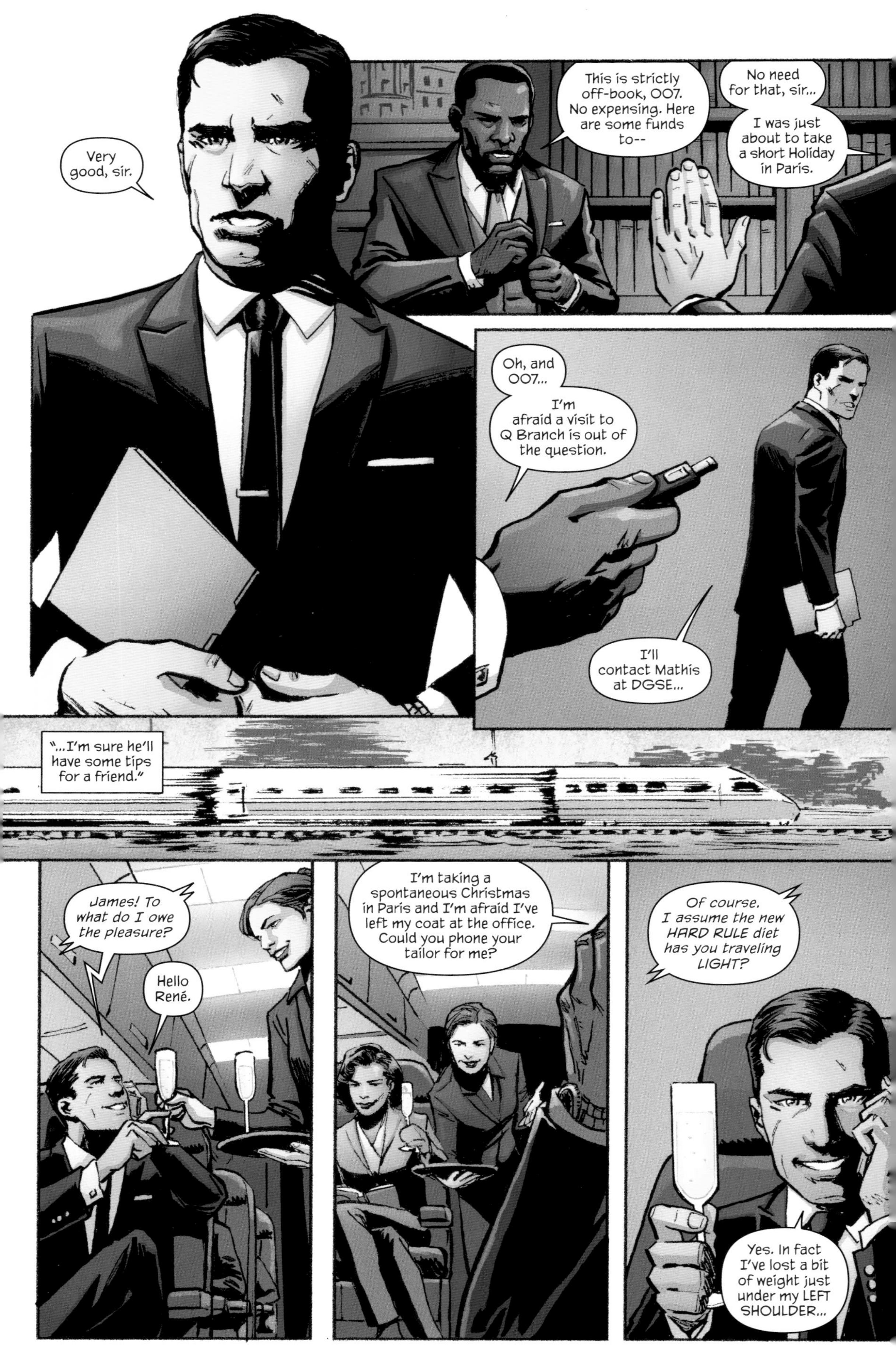
Very good, sir.
This is strictly off-book, 007. No expensing. Here are some funds to--
No need for that, sir...
I was just about to take a short Holiday in Paris.
Oh, and 007...
I'm afraid a visit to Q Branch is out of the question.
I'll contact Mathis at DGSE...
"...I'm sure he'll have some tips for a friend."
James! To what do I owe the pleasure?
Hello René.
I'm taking a spontaneous Christmas in Paris and I'm afraid I've left my coat at the office. Could you phone your tailor for me?
Of course. I assume the new HARD RULE diet has you traveling LIGHT?
Yes. In fact I've lost a bit of weight just under my LEFT SHOULDER...

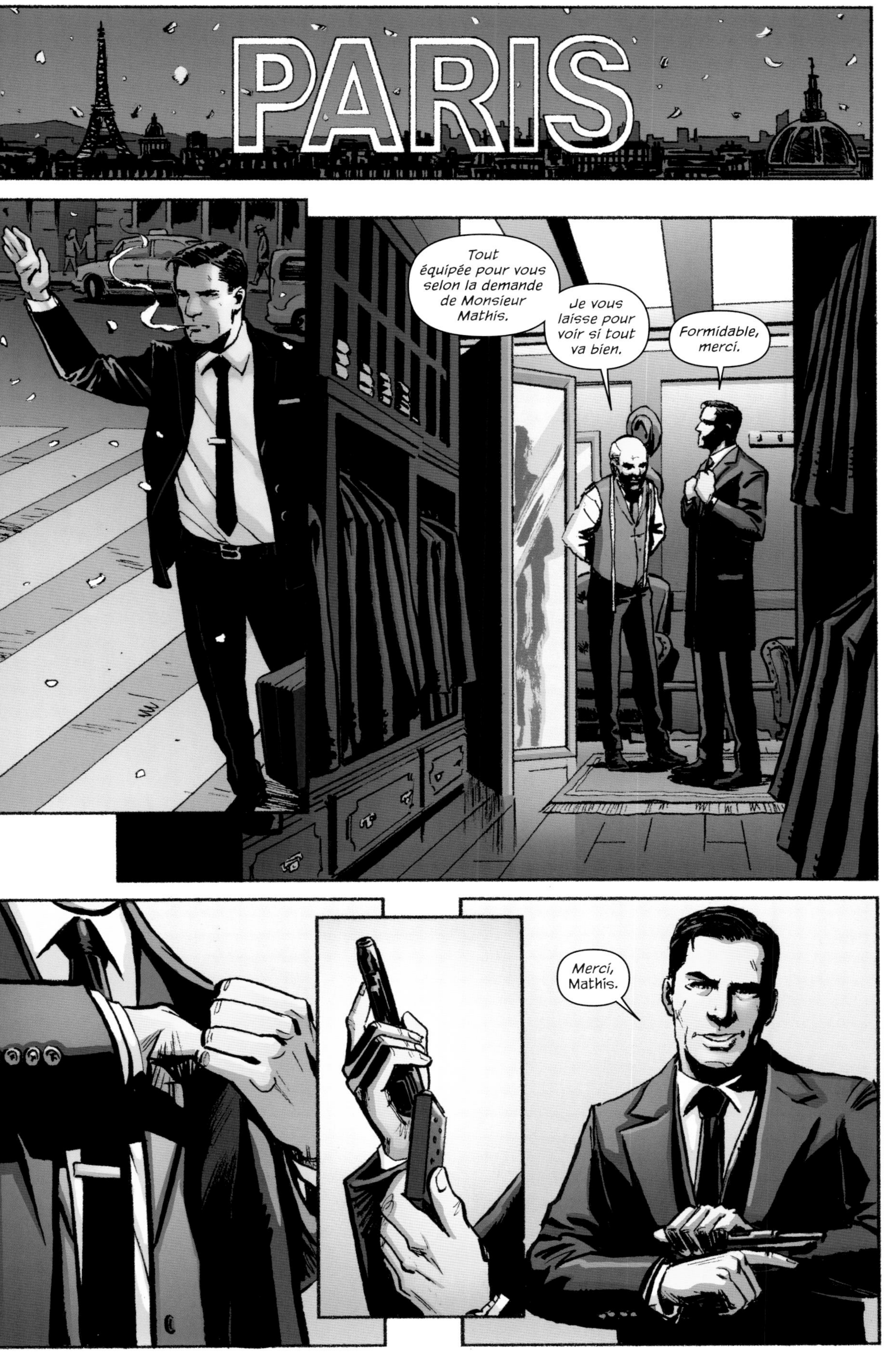
PARIS
Tout équipée pour vous selon la demande de Monsieur Mathis.
Je vous laisse pour voir si tout va bien.
Formidable, merci.
Merci, Mathis.

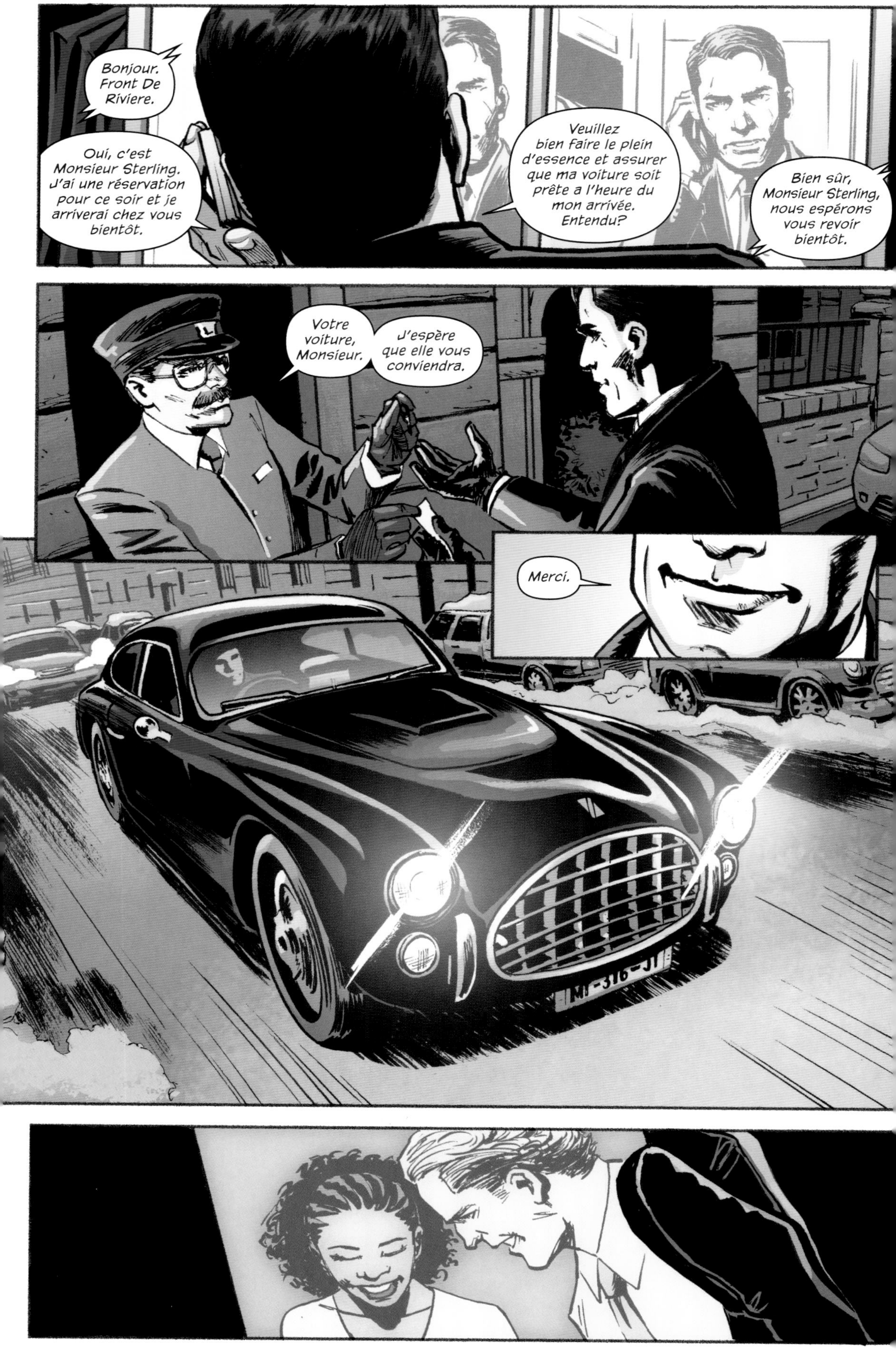
Bonjour. Front De Riviere.
Oui, c'est Monsieur Sterling. J'ai une réservation pour ce soir et je arriverai chez vous bientôt.
Veuillez bien faire le plein d'essence et assurer que ma voiture soit prête a l'heure du mon arrivée. Entendu?
Bien sûr, Monsieur Sterling, nous espérons vous revoir bientôt.
Votre voiture, Monsieur.
J'espère que elle vous conviendra.
Merci.
MJ-316-JT

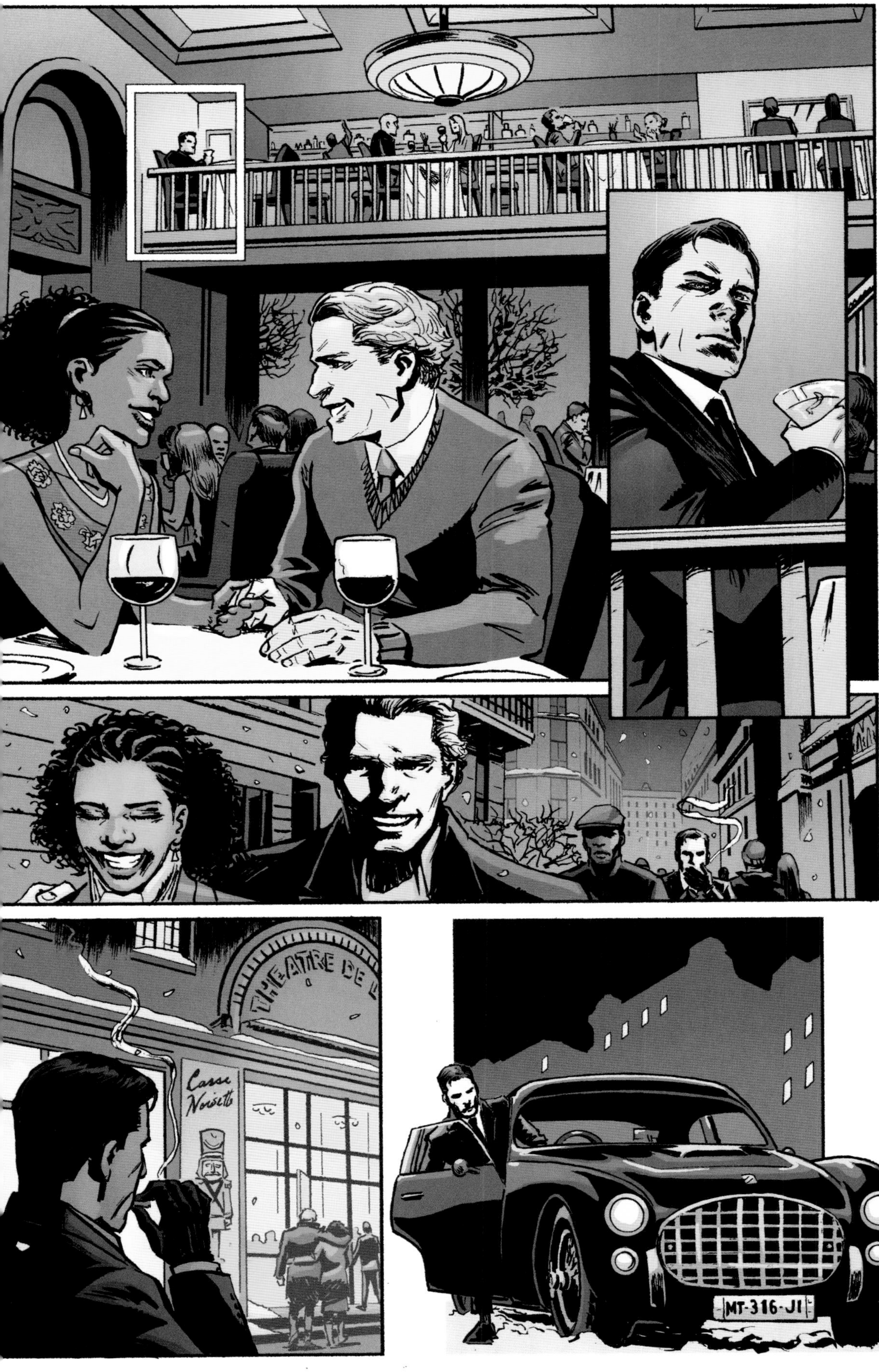
THEATRE DE L
Casse Noisette
MT-316-JI

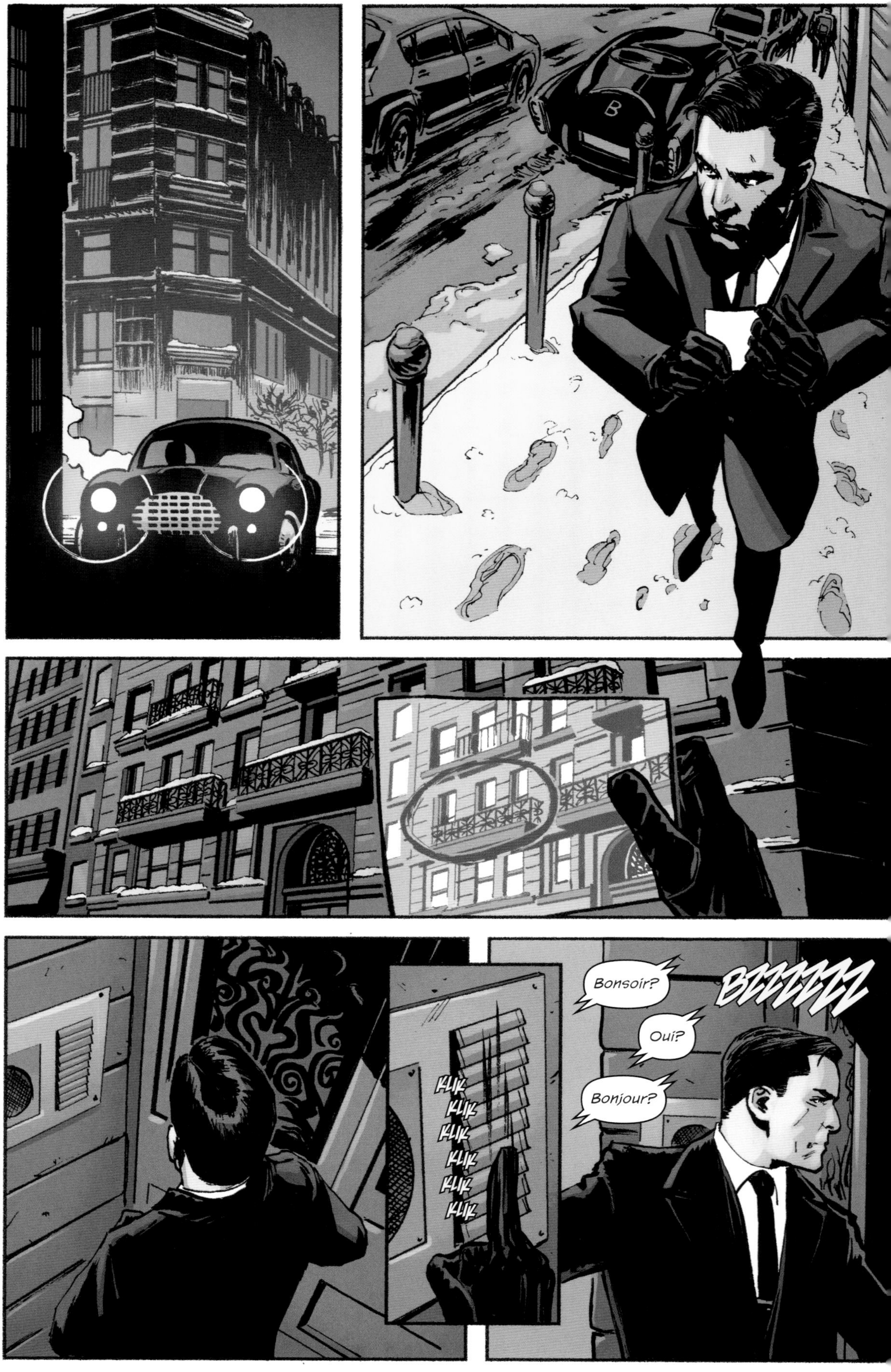
Bonsoir?
BZZZZZZ
Oui?
Bonjour?
KLIK
KLIK
KLIK
KLIK
KLIK
KLIK

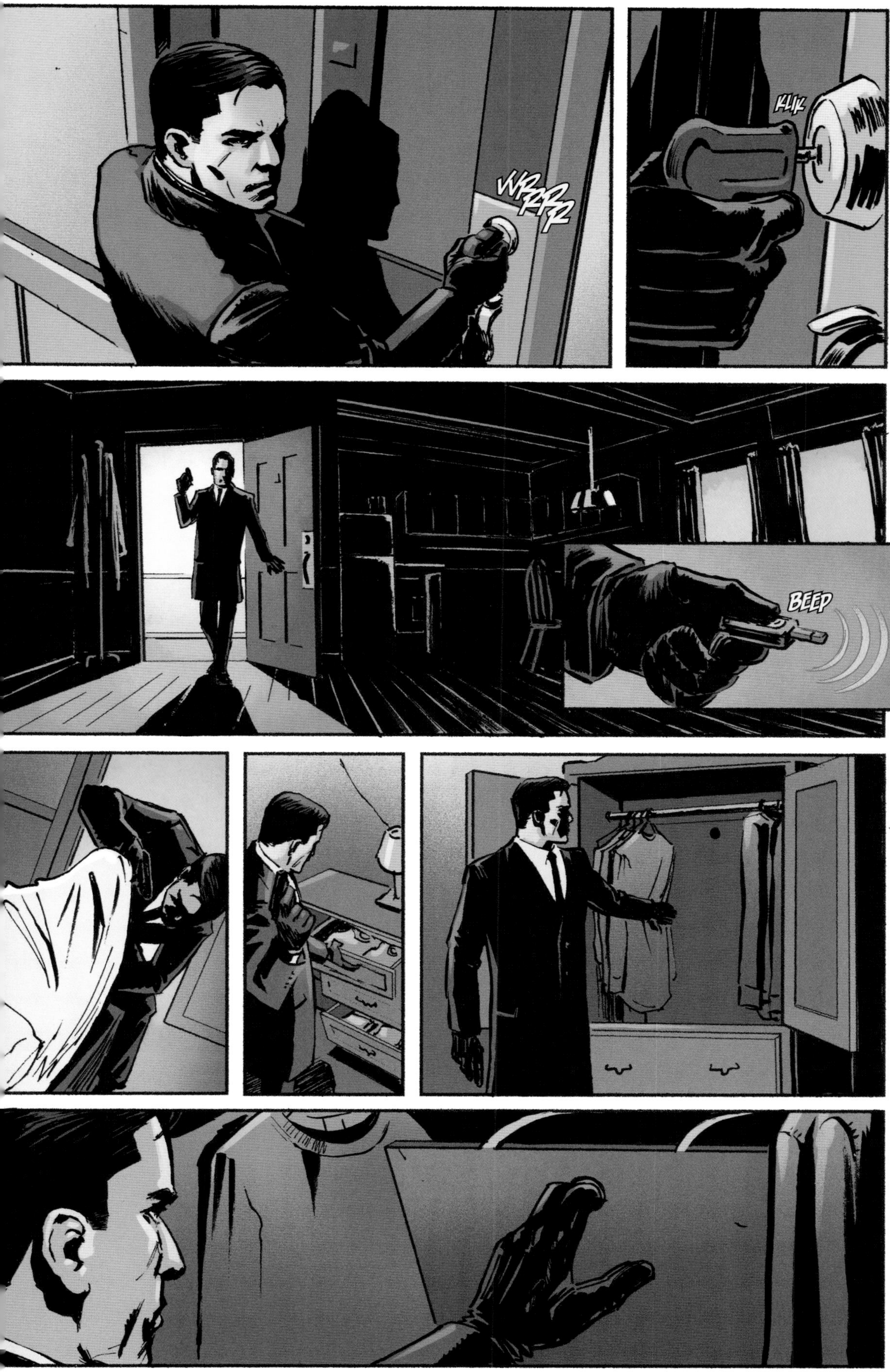
VRRRR
KLIK
BEEP

Got you.

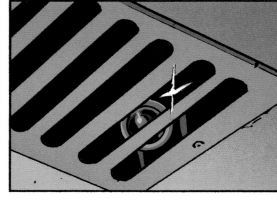

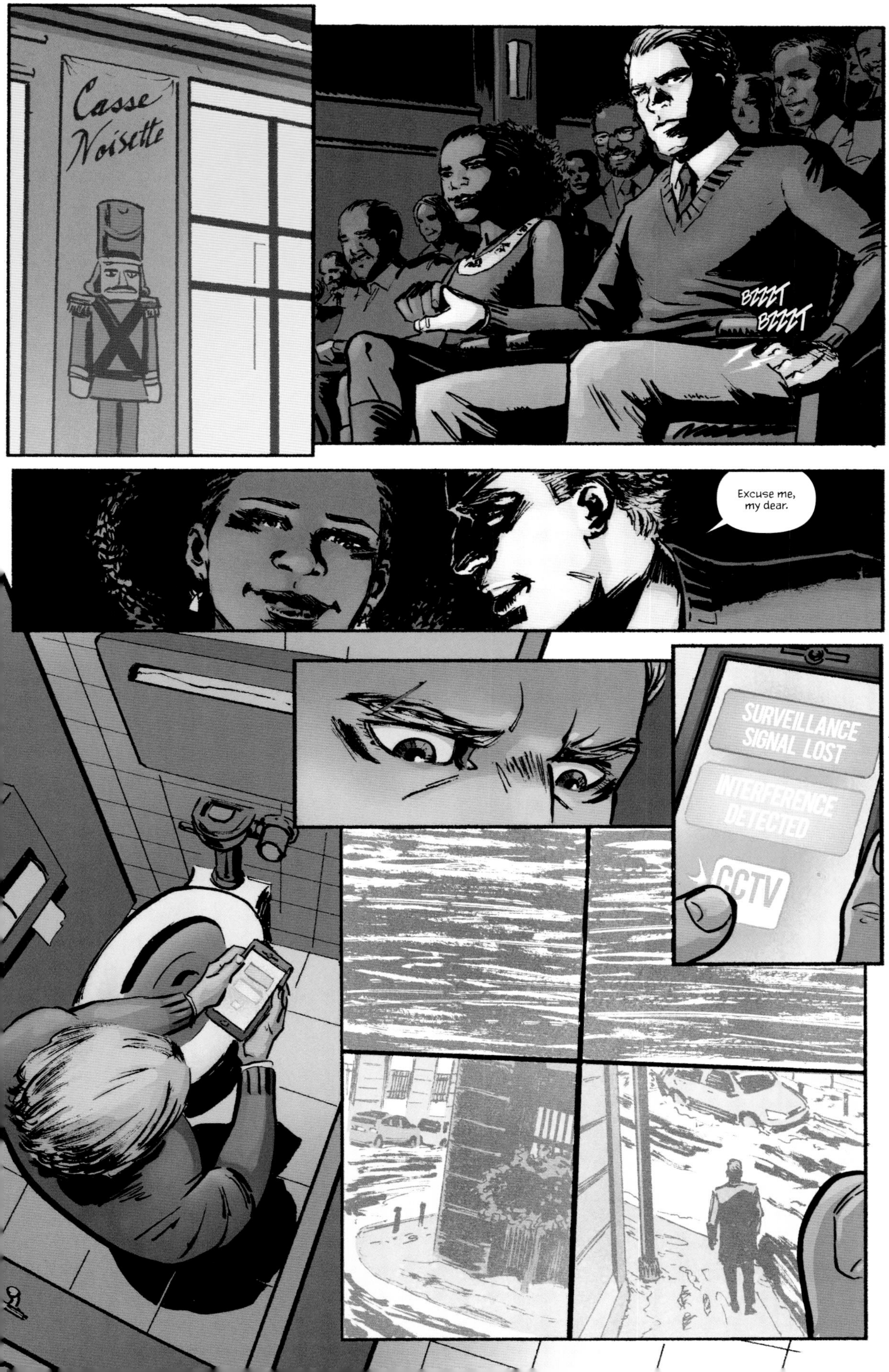
Casse Noisette
BZZZT BZZZT
Excuse me, my dear.
SURVEILLANCE SIGNAL LOST
INTERFERENCE DETECTED
CCTV

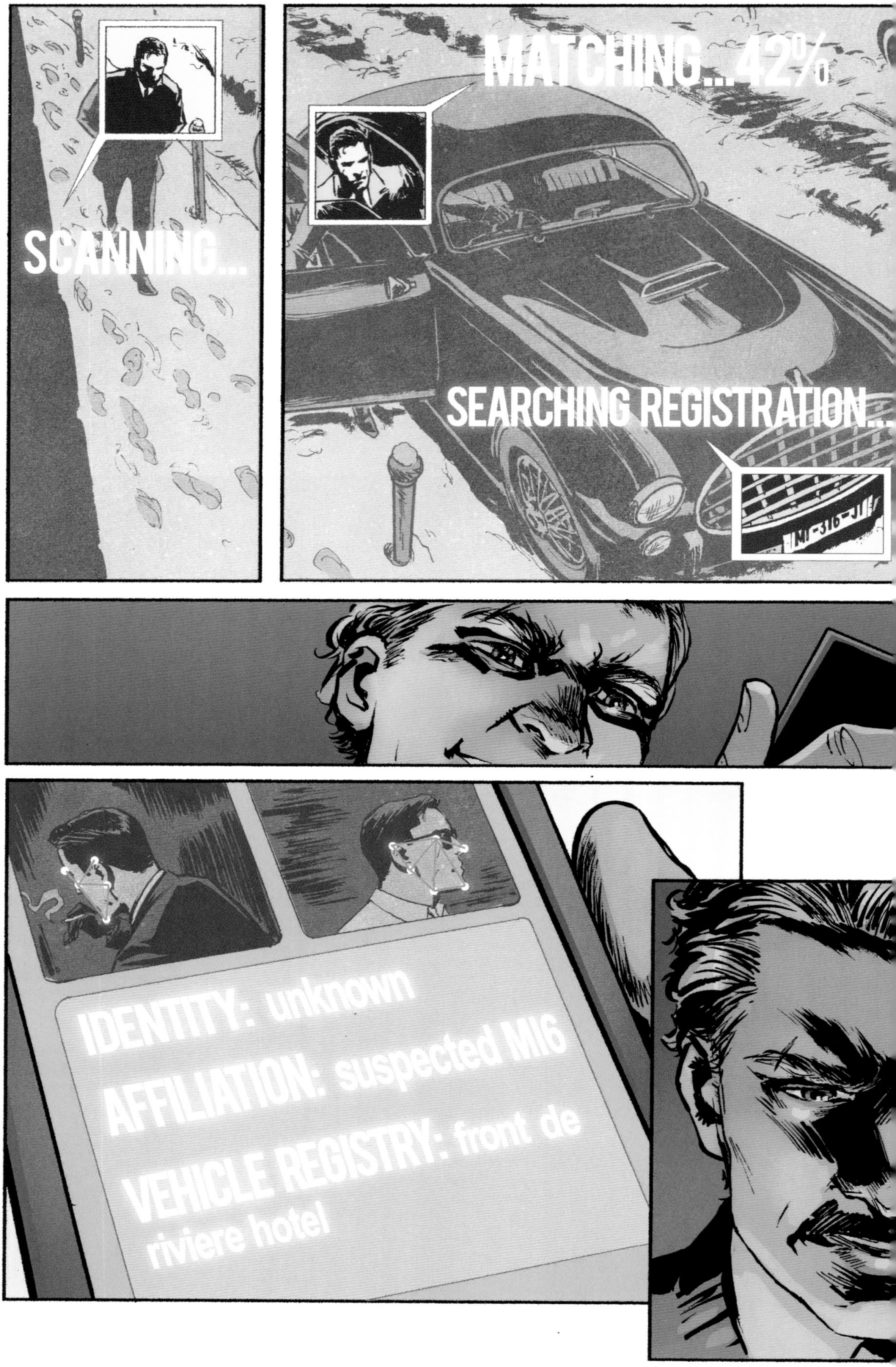
SCANNING...
MATCHING...42%
SEARCHING REGISTRATION...
IDENTITY: unknown
AFFILIATION: suspected MI6
VEHICLE REGISTRY: front de riviere hotel

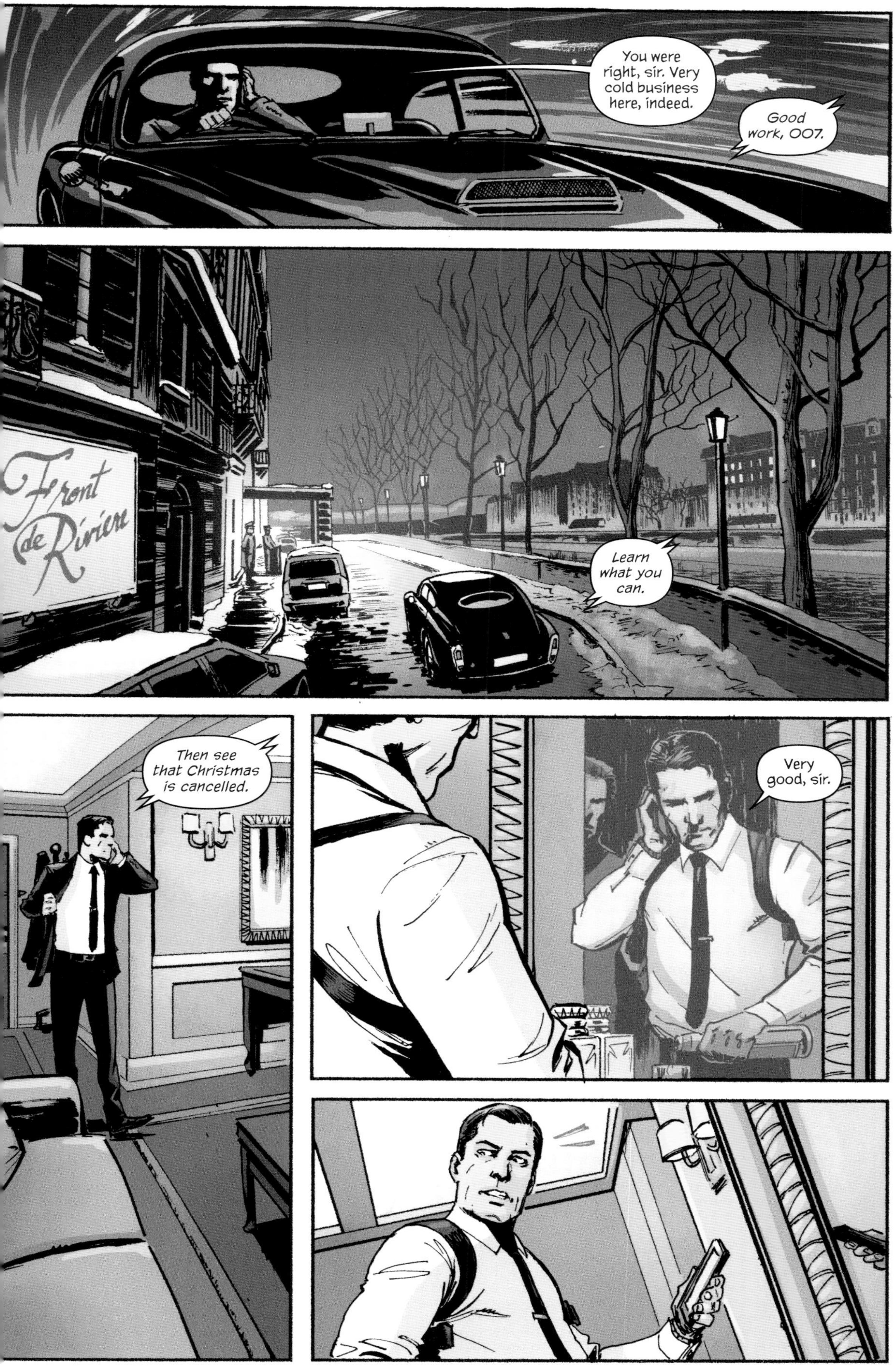
You were right, sir. Very cold business here, indeed.
Good work, 007.
Front de Rivière
Learn what you can.
Then see that Christmas is cancelled.
Very good, sir.

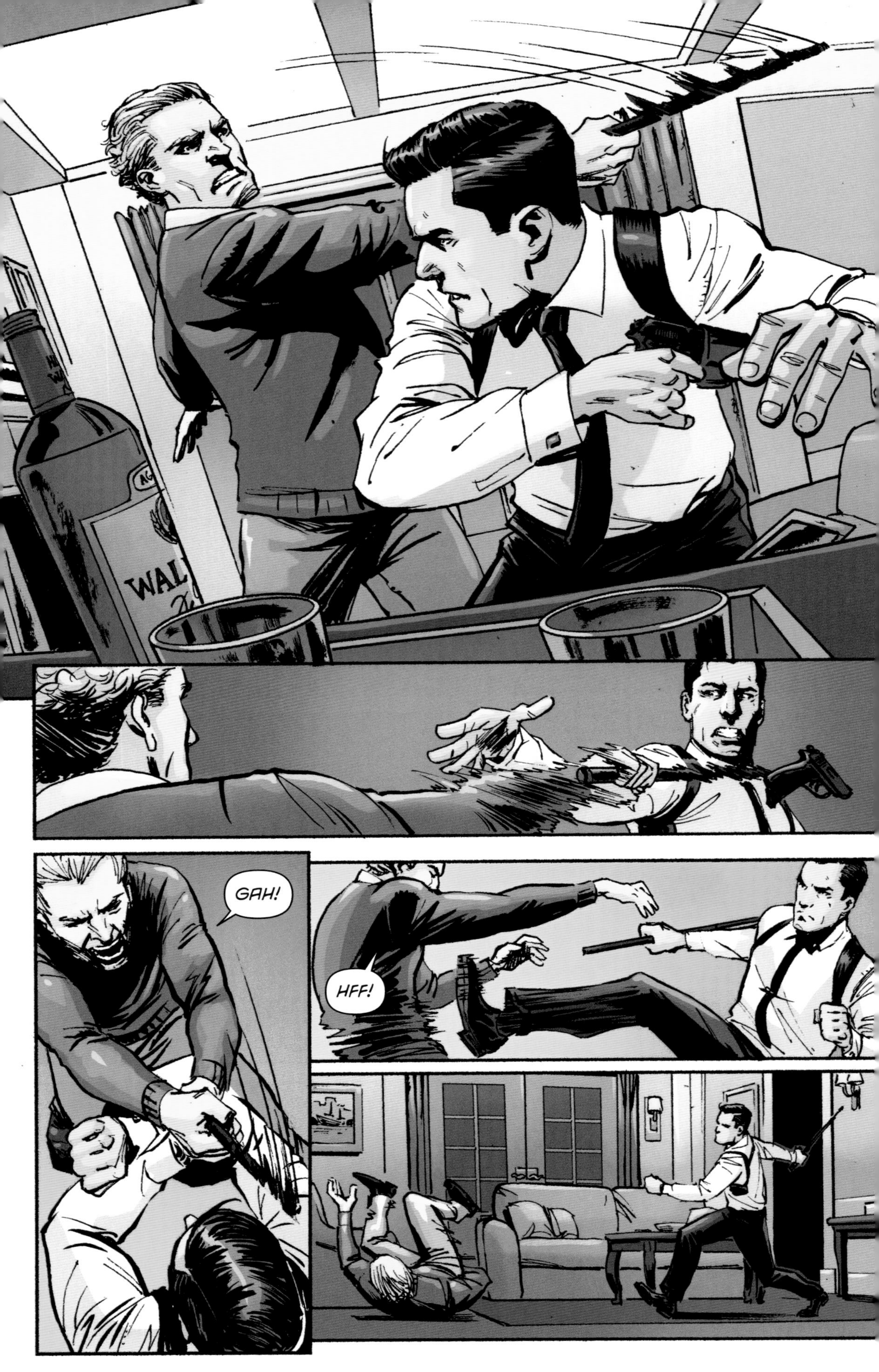
GAH!
HFF!

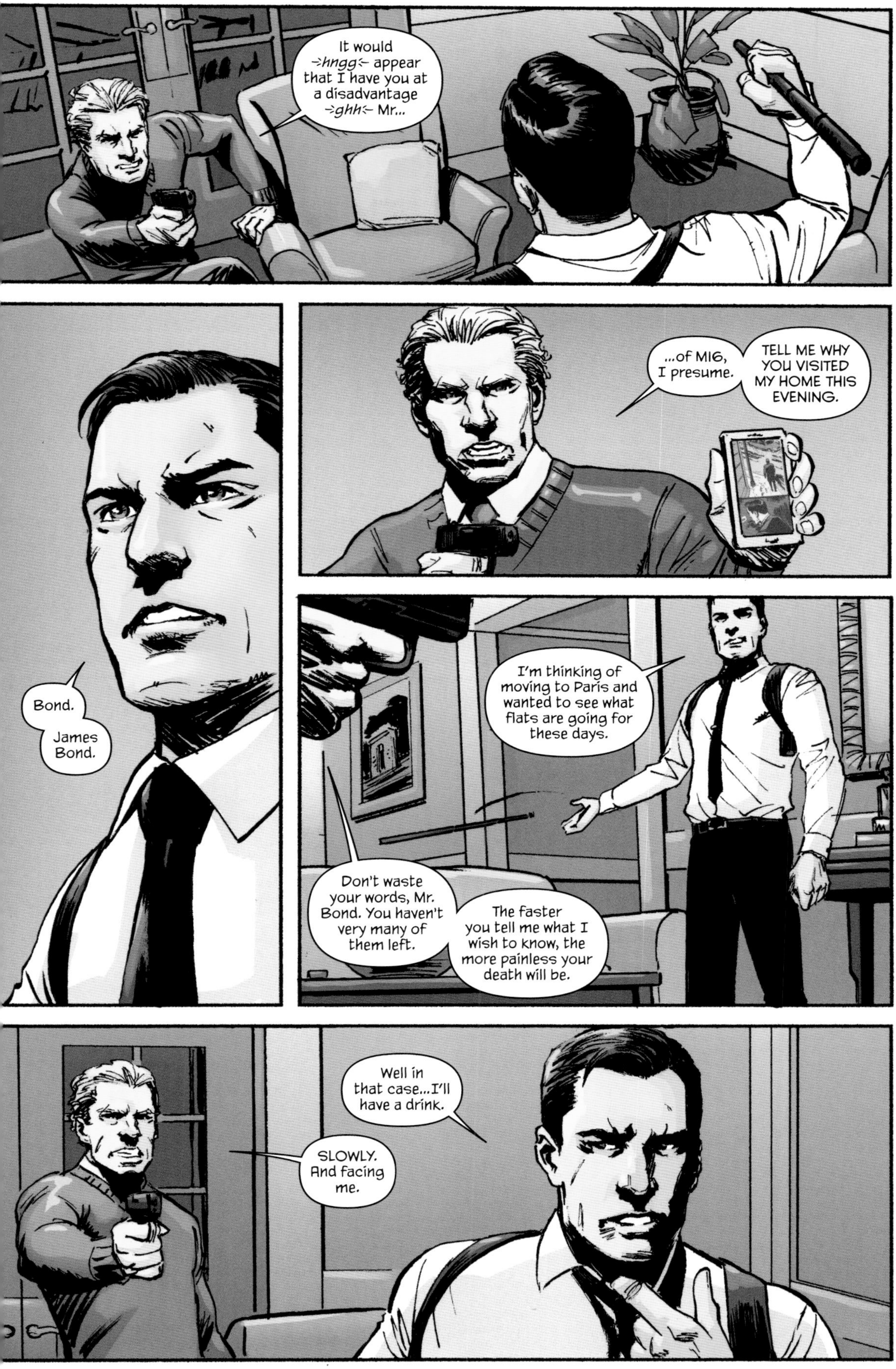
It would ->hngg<- appear that I have you at a disadvantage ->ghh<- Mr...
Bond.
James Bond.
...of MI6, I presume.
TELL ME WHY YOU VISITED MY HOME THIS EVENING.
I'm thinking of moving to Paris and wanted to see what flats are going for these days.
Don't waste your words, Mr. Bond. You haven't very many of them left.
The faster you tell me what I wish to know, the more painless your death will be.
Well in that case...I'll have a drink.
SLOWLY. And facing me.

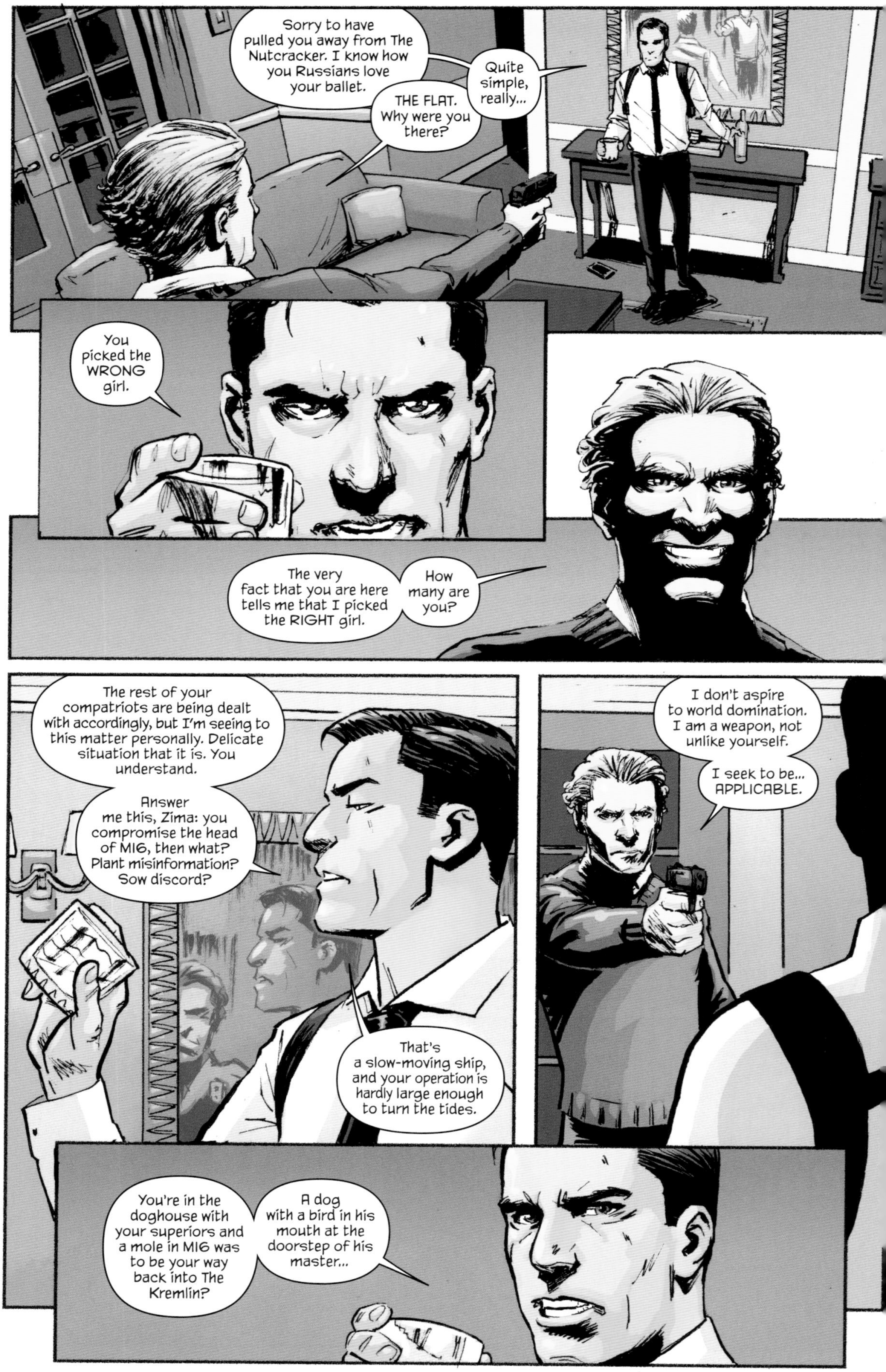
Sorry to have pulled you away from The Nutcracker. I know how you Russians love your ballet.
Quite simple, really...
THE FLAT. Why were you there?
You picked the WRONG girl.
The very fact that you are here tells me that I picked the RIGHT girl.
How many are you?
The rest of your compatriots are being dealt with accordingly, but I'm seeing to this matter personally. Delicate situation that it is. You understand.
Answer me this, Zima: you compromise the head of MI6, then what? Plant misinformation? Sow discord?
That's a slow-moving ship, and your operation is hardly large enough to turn the tides.
I don't aspire to world domination. I am a weapon, not unlike yourself.
I seek to be... APPLICABLE.
You're in the doghouse with your superiors and a mole in MI6 was to be your way back into The Kremlin?
A dog with a bird in his mouth at the doorstep of his master...

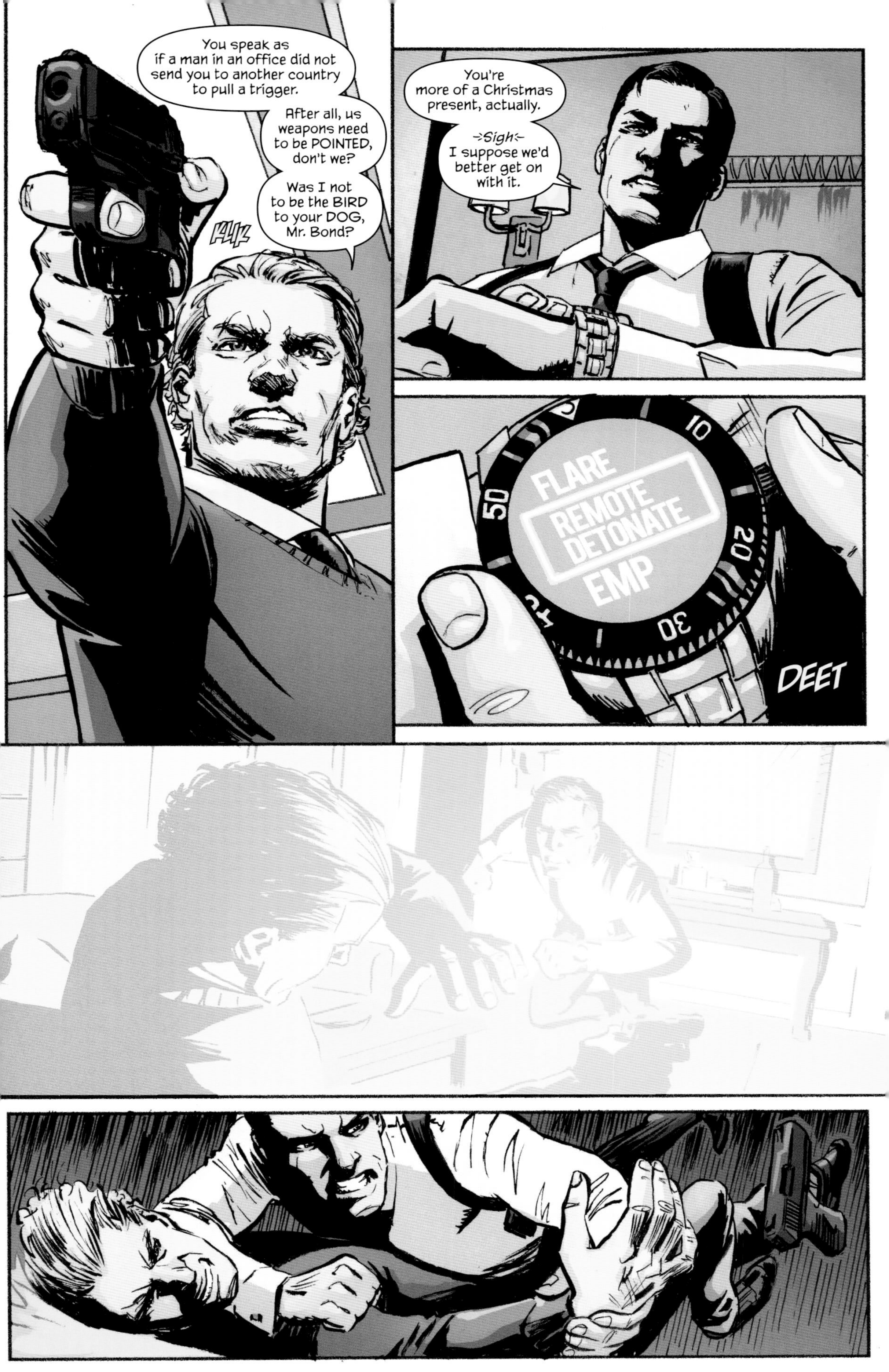
You speak as if a man in an office did not send you to another country to pull a trigger.
After all, us weapons need to be POINTED, don't we?
Was I not to be the BIRD to your DOG, Mr. Bond?
KLIK
You're more of a Christmas present, actually.
Sigh
I suppose we'd better get on with it.
FLARE
REMOTE DETONATE
EMP
10
20
30
50
DEET

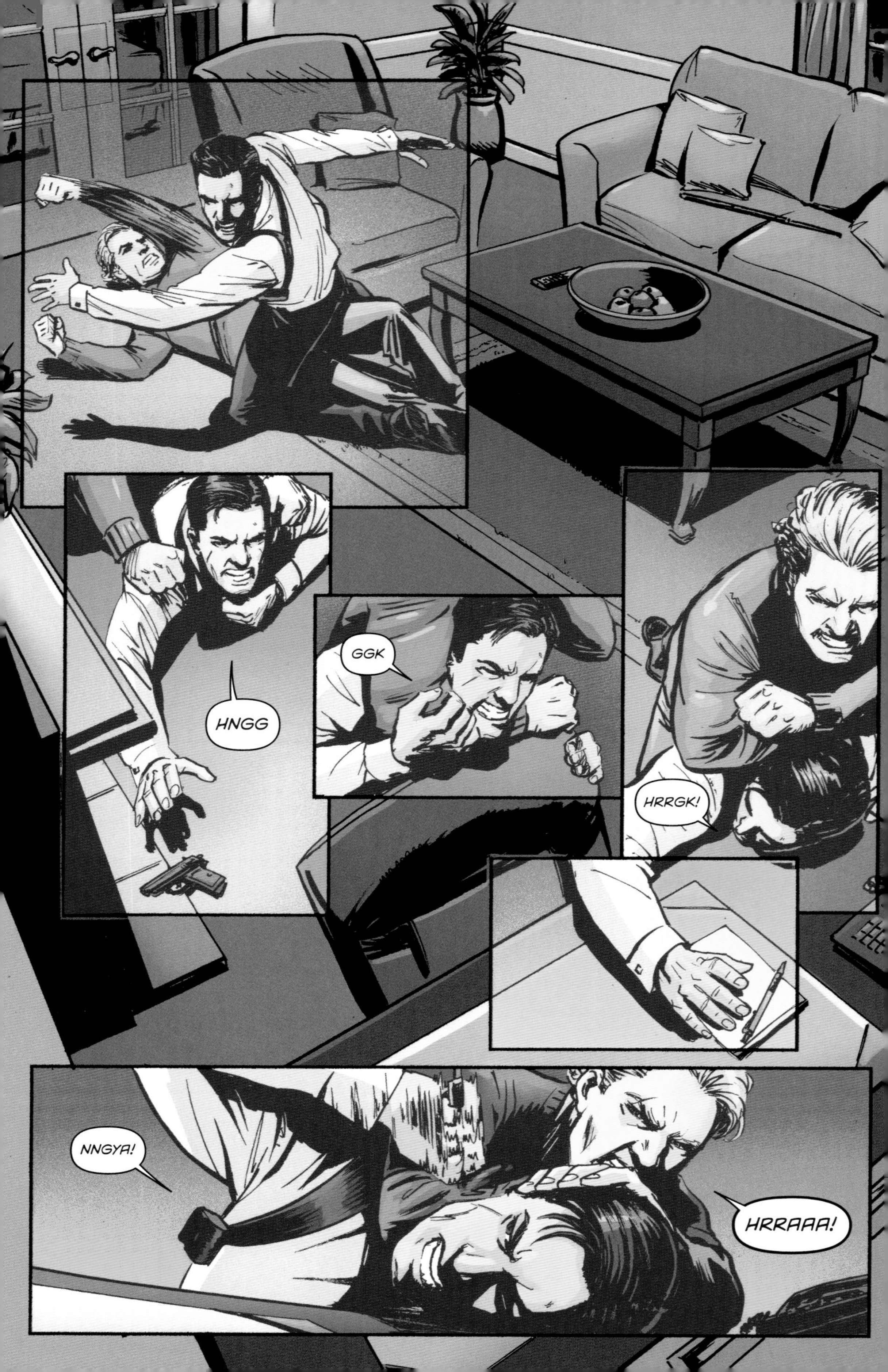
HNGG
GGK
HRRGK!
NNGYA!
HRRAAA!

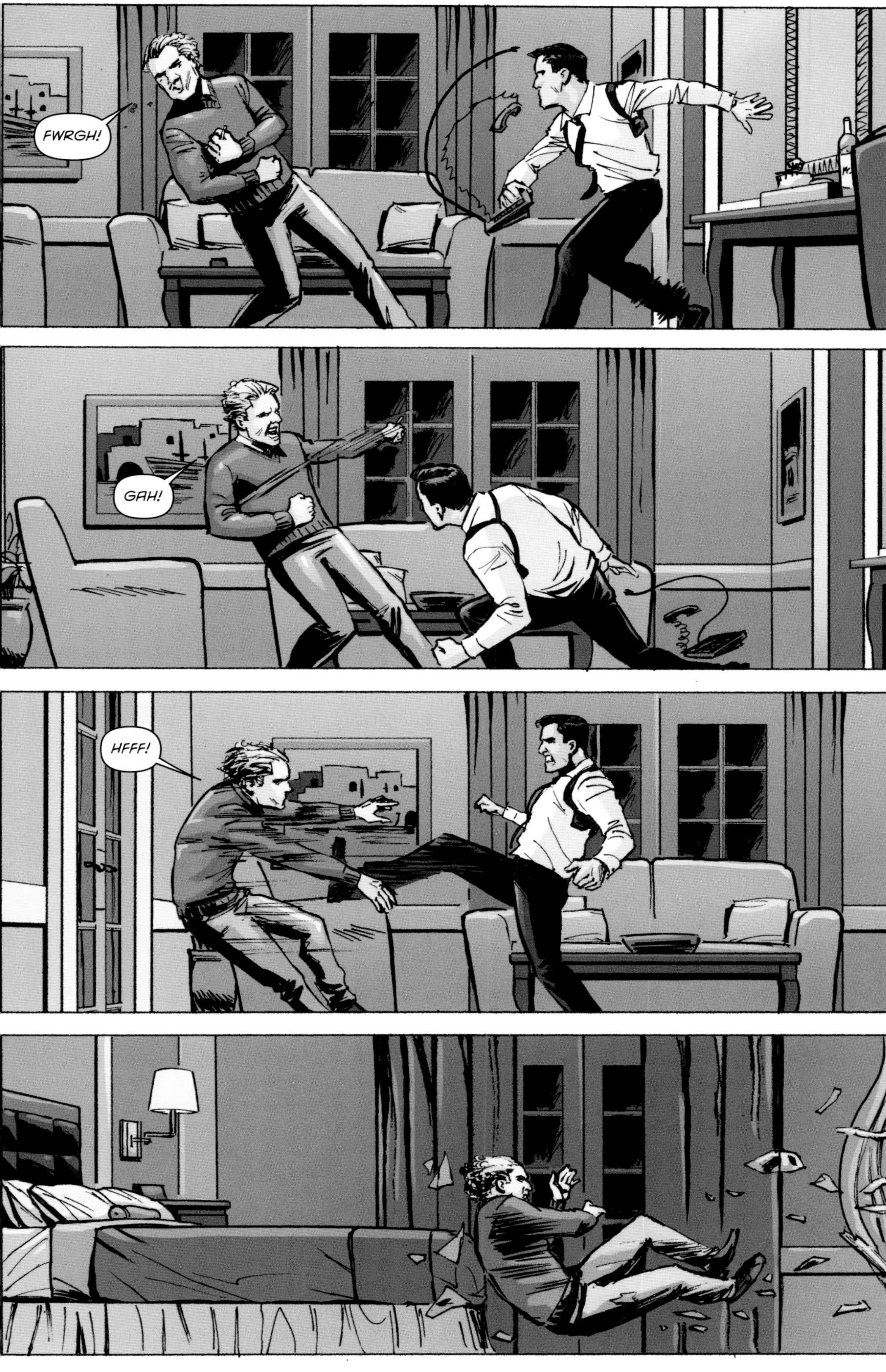
FWRGH!
GAH!
HFFF!

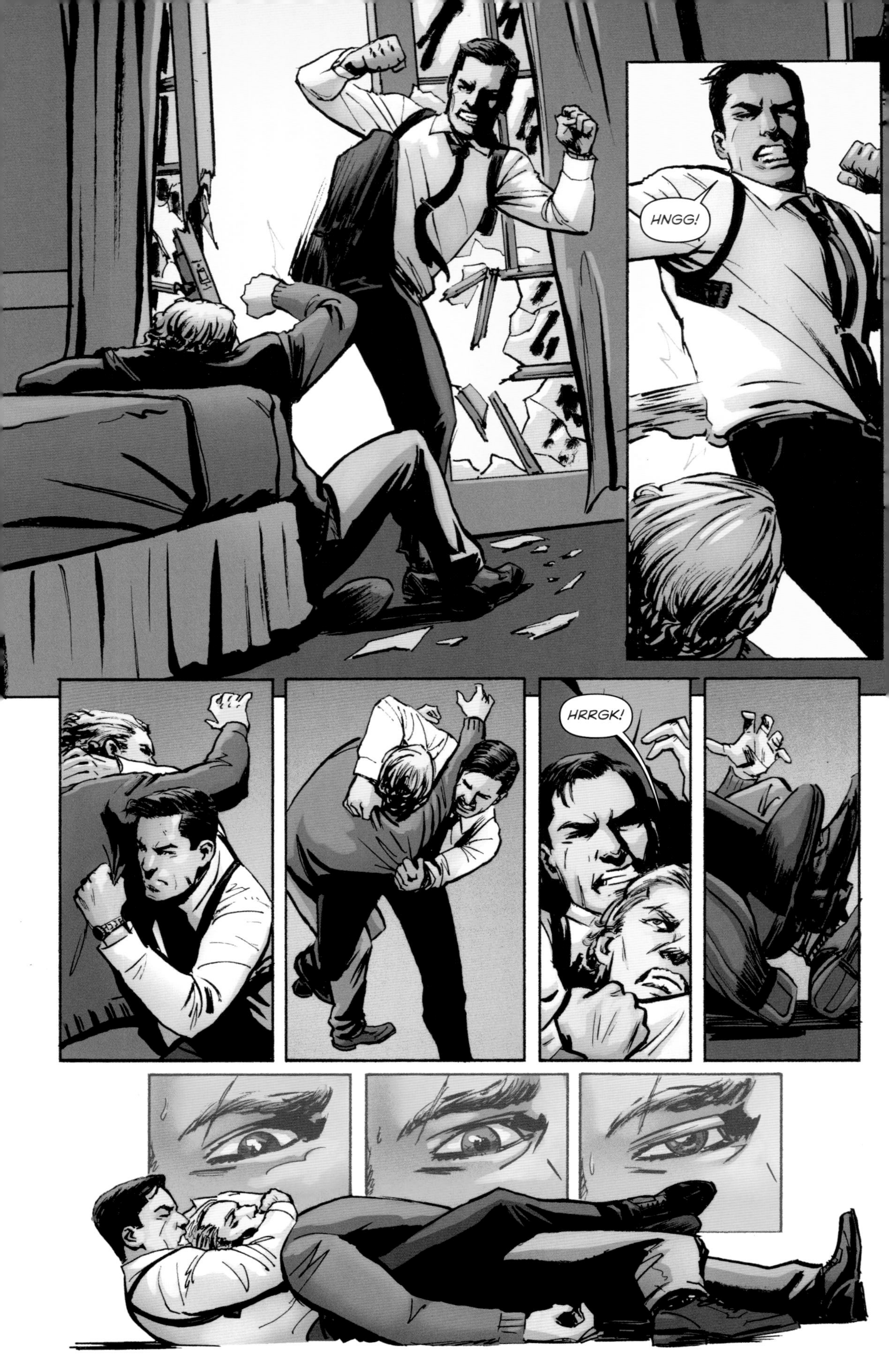
HNGG!
HRRGK!

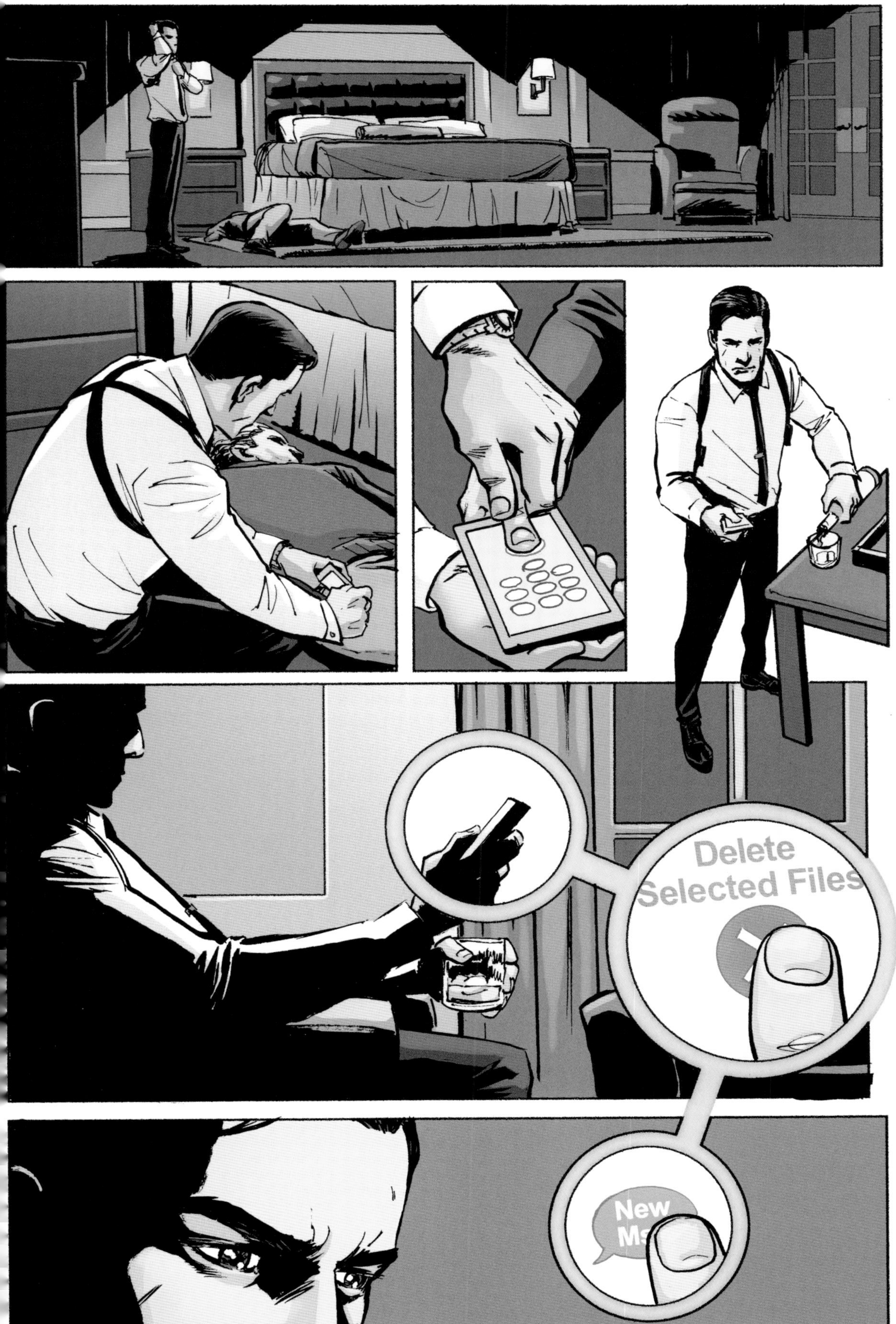
Delete
Selected Files
New

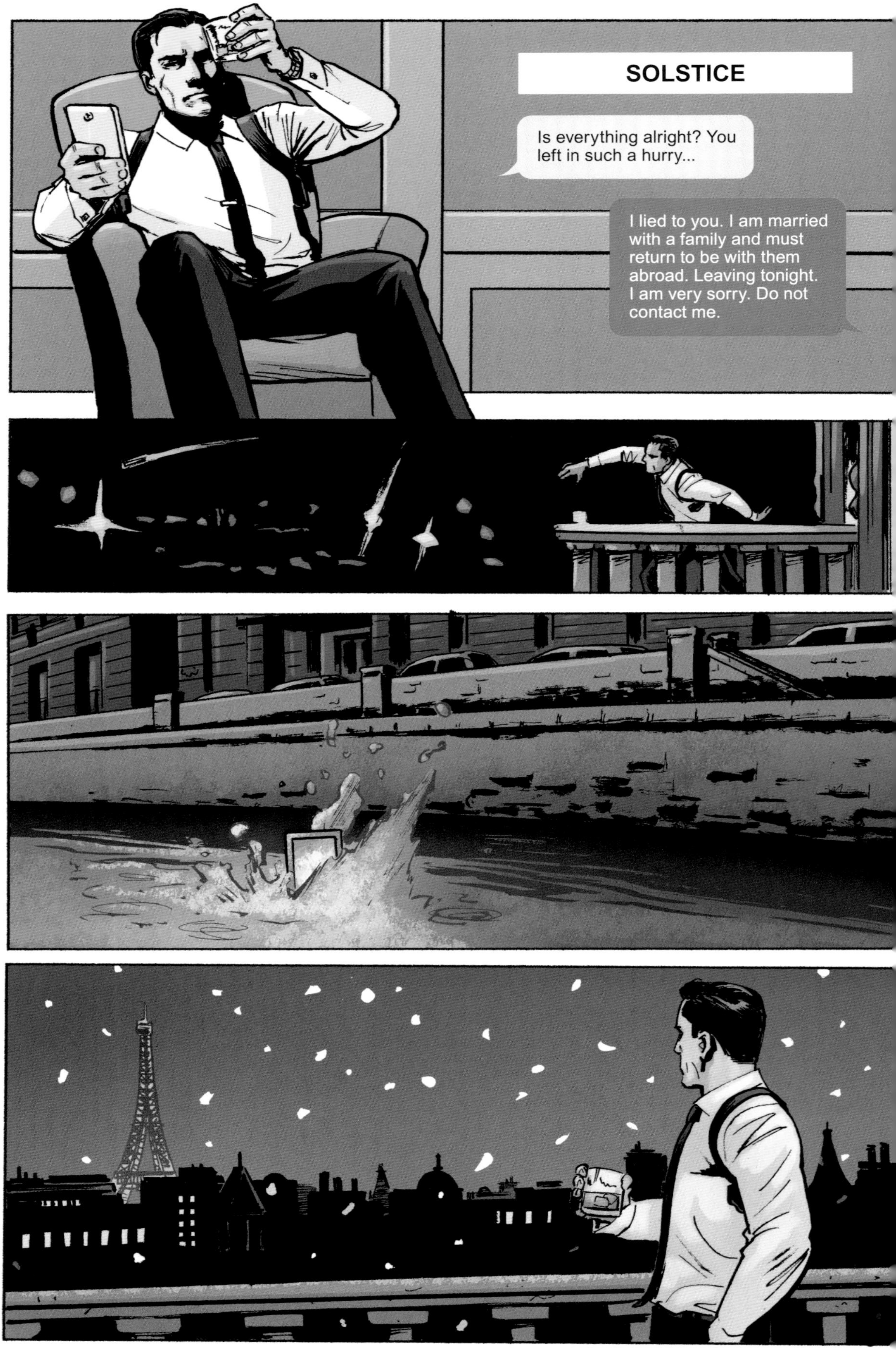
SOLSTICE
Is everything alright? You left in such a hurry...
I lied to you. I am married with a family and must return to be with them abroad. Leaving tonight. I am very sorry. Do not contact me.

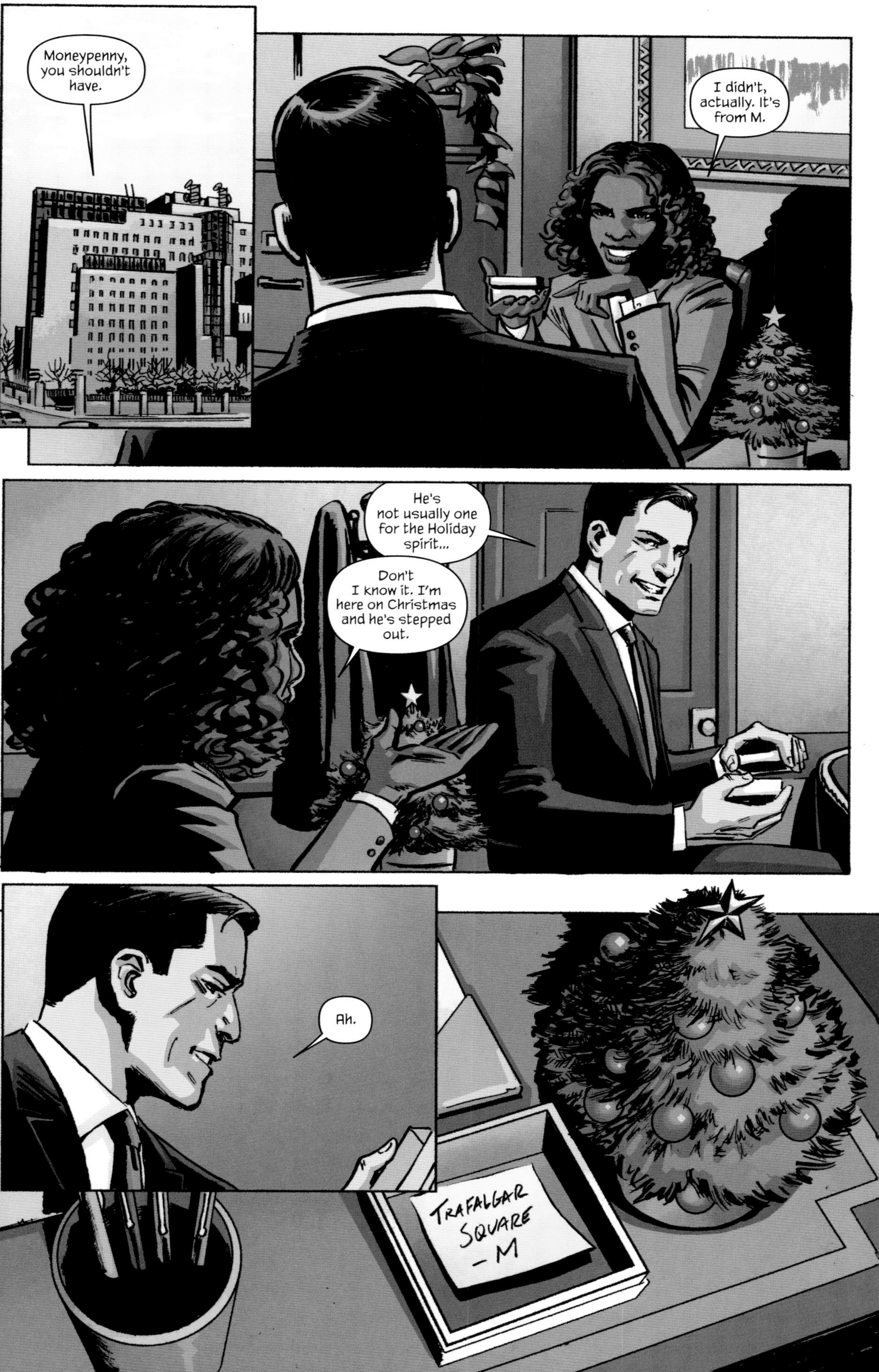
Moneypenny, you shouldn't have.
I didn't, actually. It's from M.
He's not usually one for the Holiday spirit...
Don't I know it. I'm here on Christmas and he's stepped out.
Ah.
TRAFALGAR SQUARE
– M

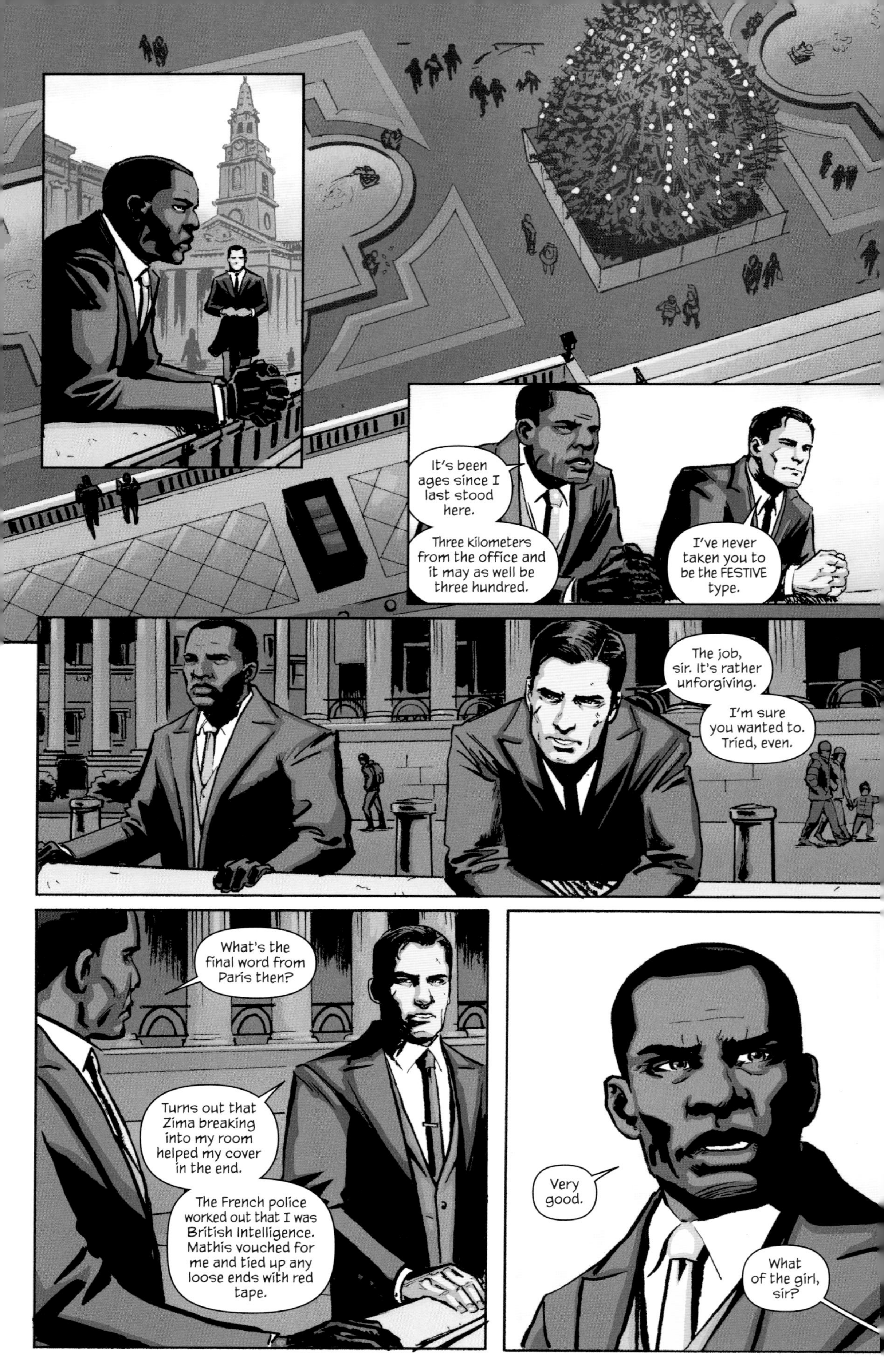
It's been ages since I last stood here.
Three kilometers from the office and it may as well be three hundred.
I've never taken you to be the FESTIVE type.
The job, sir. It's rather unforgiving.
I'm sure you wanted to. Tried, even.
What's the final word from Paris then?
Turns out that Zima breaking into my room helped my cover in the end.
The French police worked out that I was British Intelligence. Mathis vouched for me and tied up any loose ends with red tape.
Very good.
What of the girl, sir?

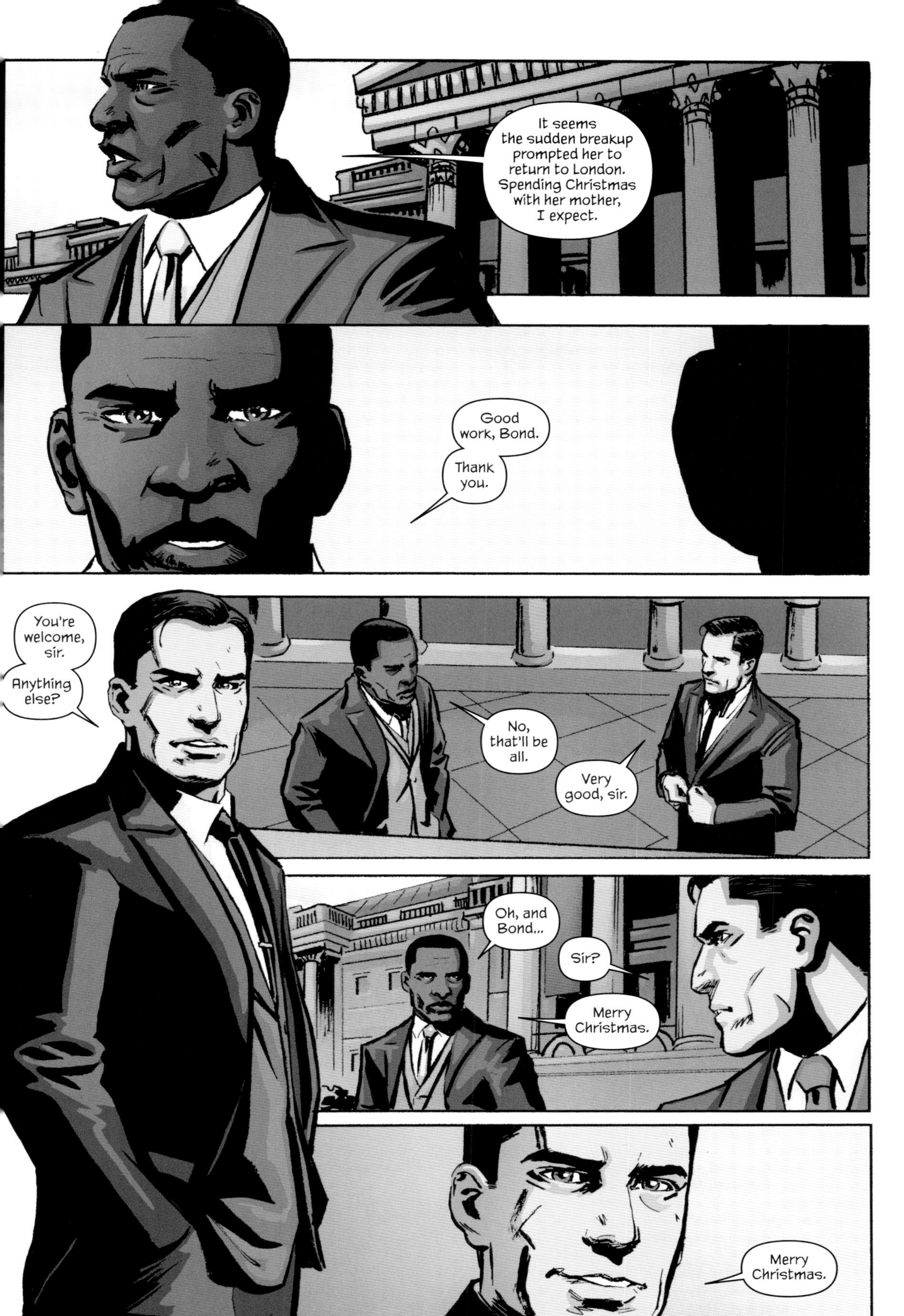
It seems the sudden breakup prompted her to return to London. Spending Christmas with her mother, I expect.
Good work, Bond.
Thank you.
You're welcome, sir.
Anything else?
No, that'll be all.
Very good, sir.
Oh, and Bond...
Sir?
Merry Christmas.
Merry Christmas.

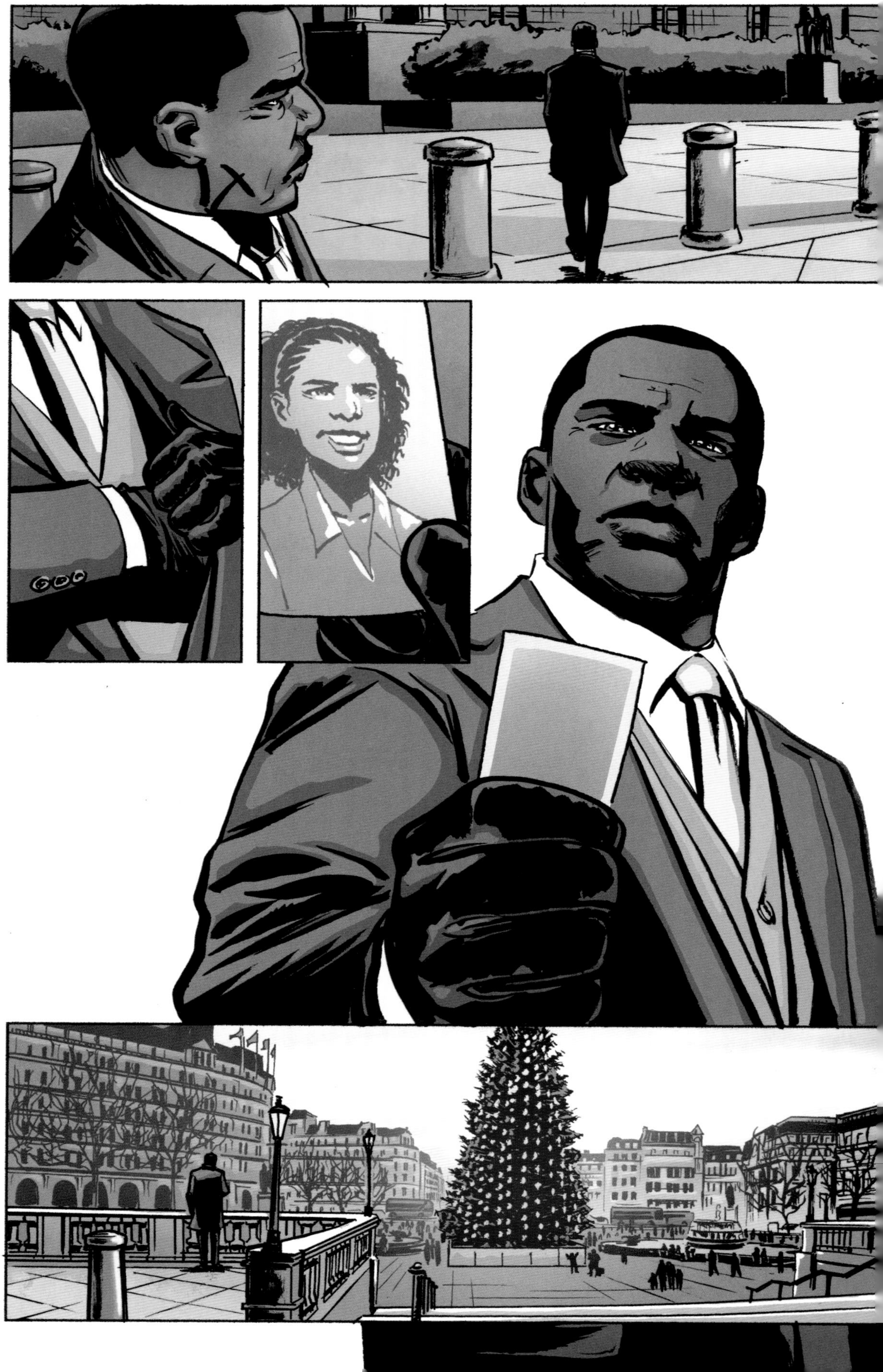

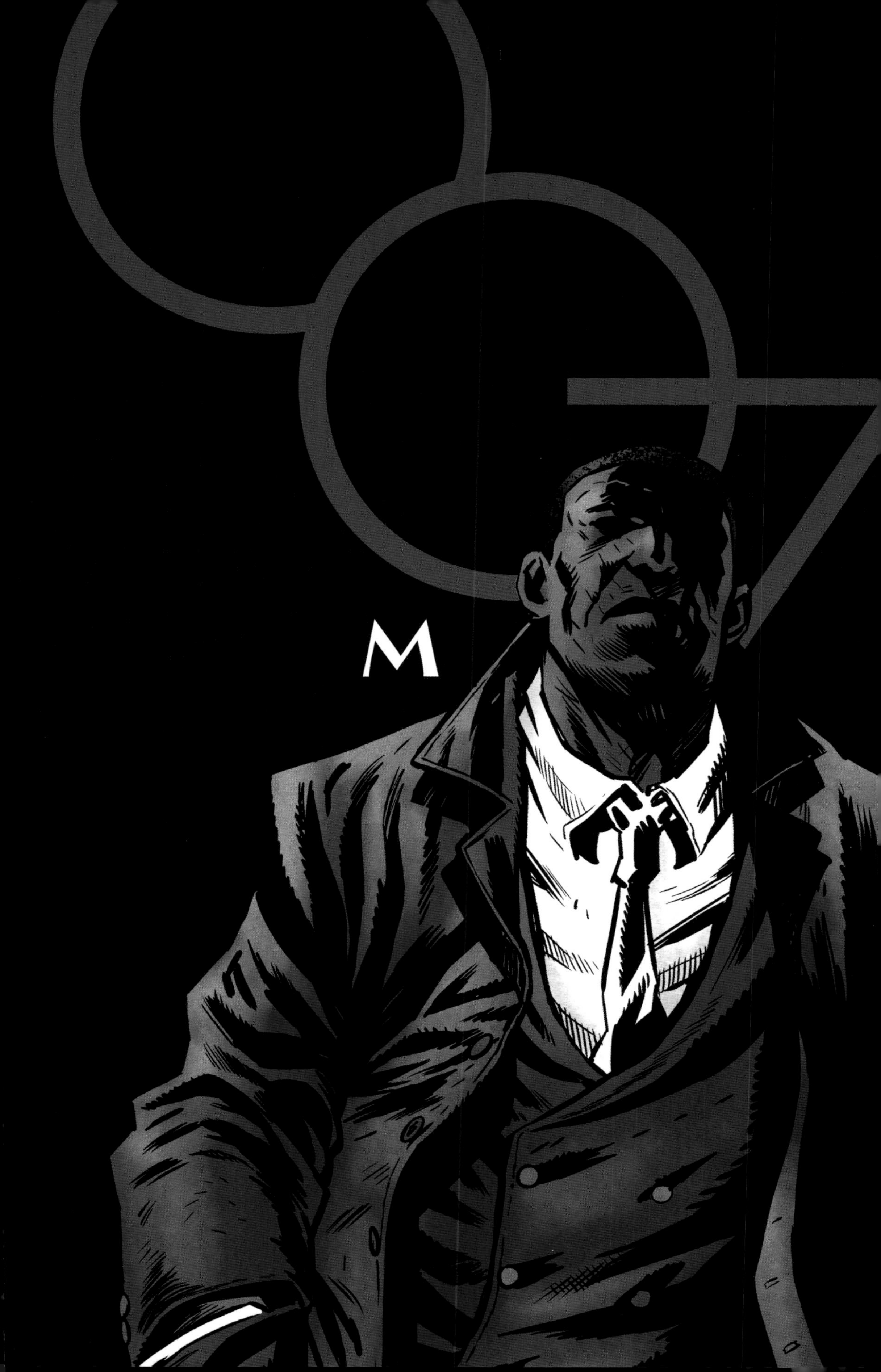
M

JAMES BOND: M
COVER BY DECLAN SHALVEY
COLORS BY JORDIE BELLAIRE

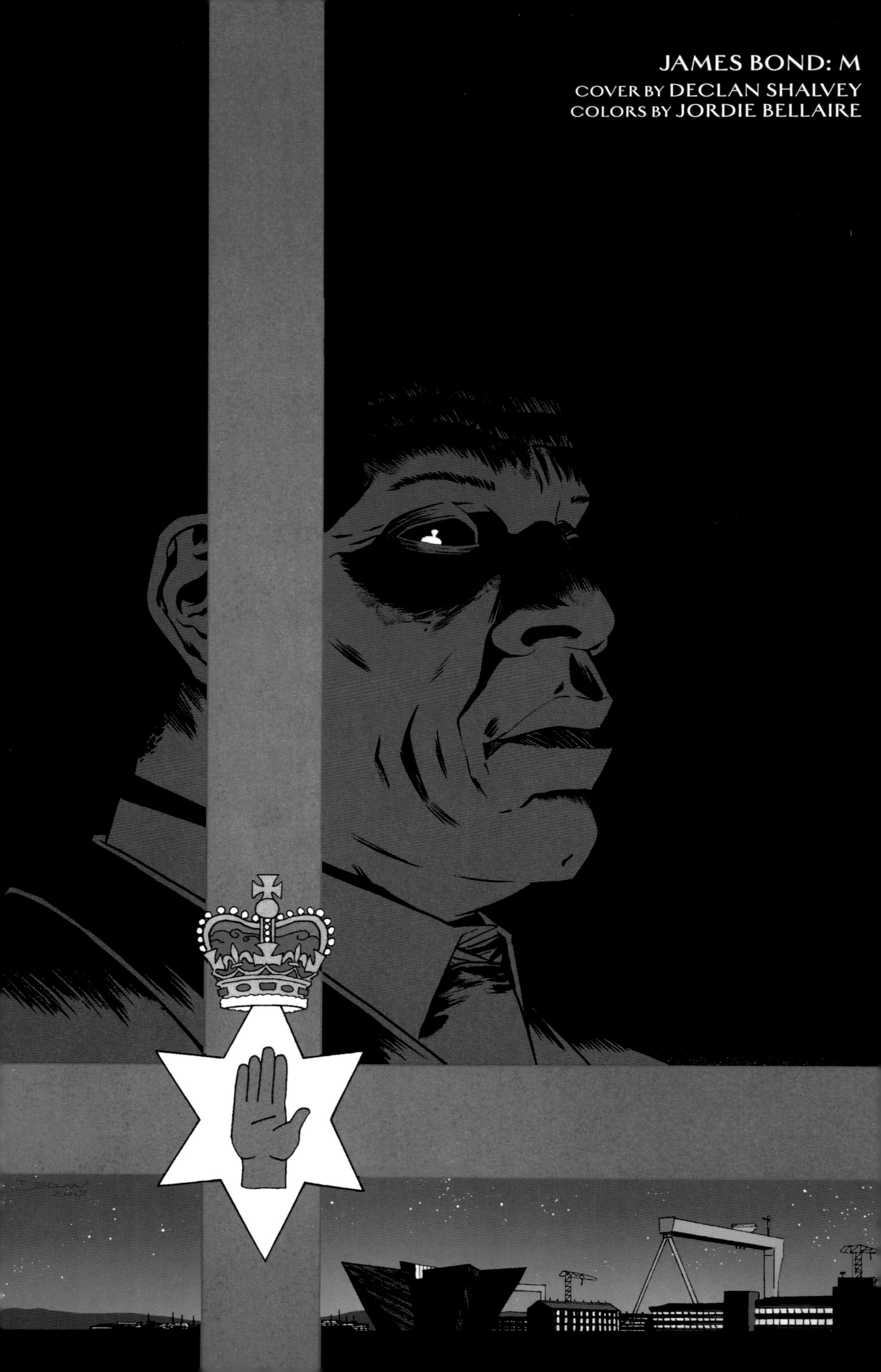

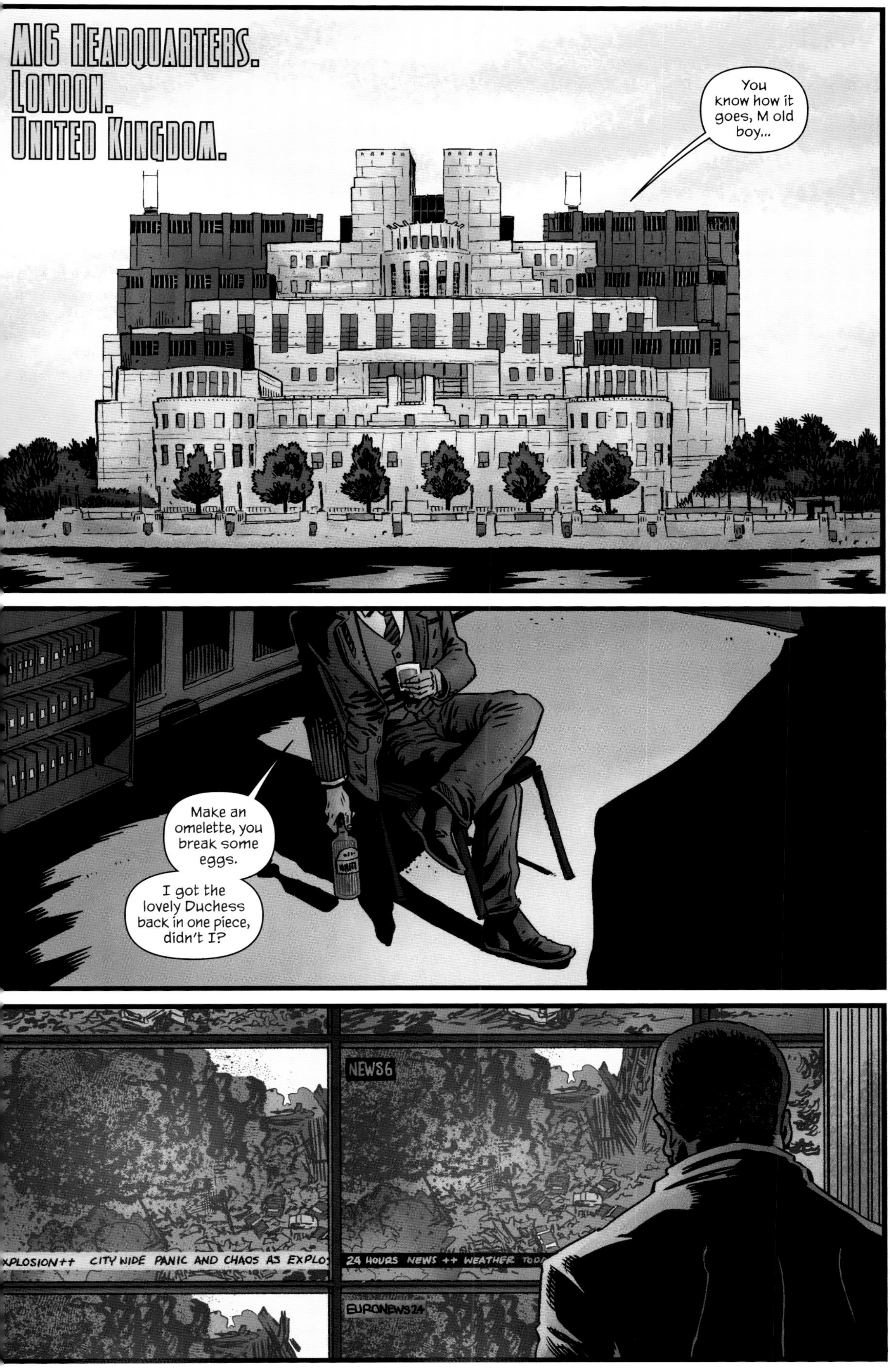
MI6 Headquarters.
London.
United Kingdom.
You know how it goes, M old boy...
Make an omelette, you break some eggs.
I got the lovely Duchess back in one piece, didn't I?
NEWS6
XPLOSION++ CITY WIDE PANIC AND CHAOS AS EXPLO
24 HOURS NEWS ++ WEATHER TODA
EURONEWS24

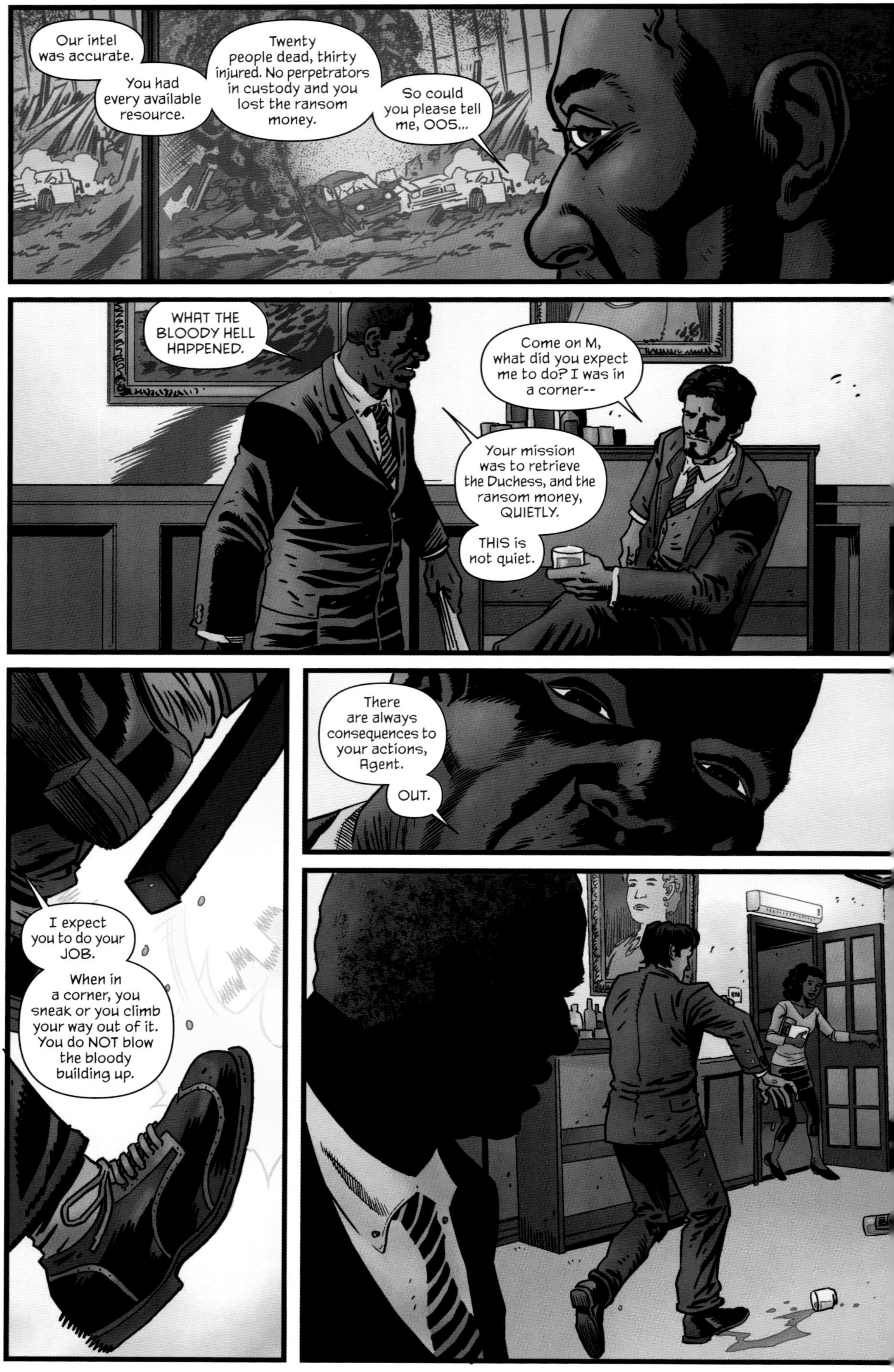
Our intel was accurate.
You had every available resource.
Twenty people dead, thirty injured. No perpetrators in custody and you lost the ransom money.
So could you please tell me, 005...
WHAT THE BLOODY HELL HAPPENED.
Come on M, what did you expect me to do? I was in a corner--
Your mission was to retrieve the Duchess, and the ransom money, QUIETLY.
THIS is not quiet.
I expect you to do your JOB.
When in a corner, you sneak or you climb your way out of it. You do NOT blow the bloody building up.
There are always consequences to your actions, Agent.
OUT.

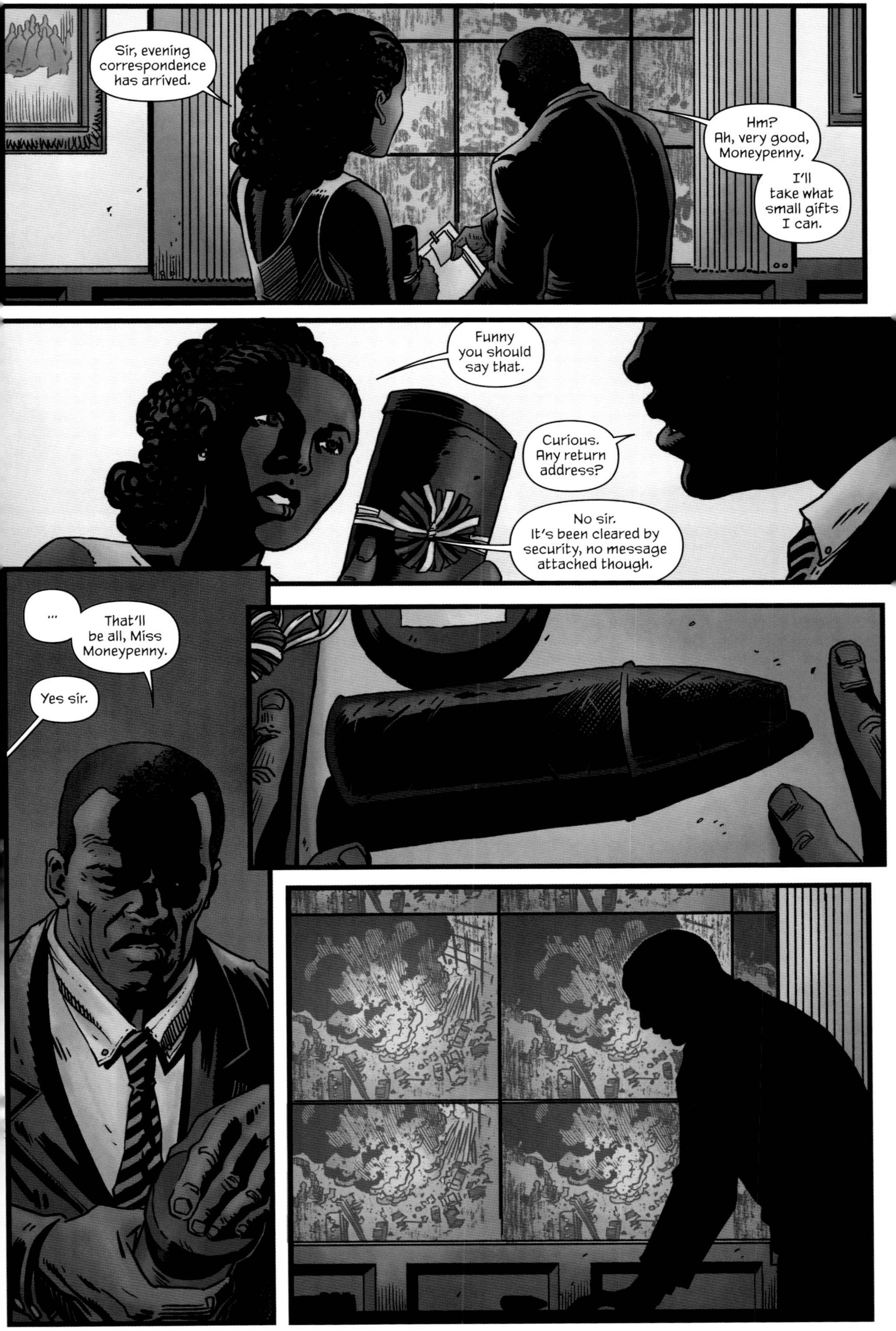
Sir, evening correspondence has arrived.
Hm? Ah, very good, Moneypenny.
I'll take what small gifts I can.
Funny you should say that.
Curious. Any return address?
No sir. It's been cleared by security, no message attached though.
...
That'll be all, Miss Moneypenny.
Yes sir.

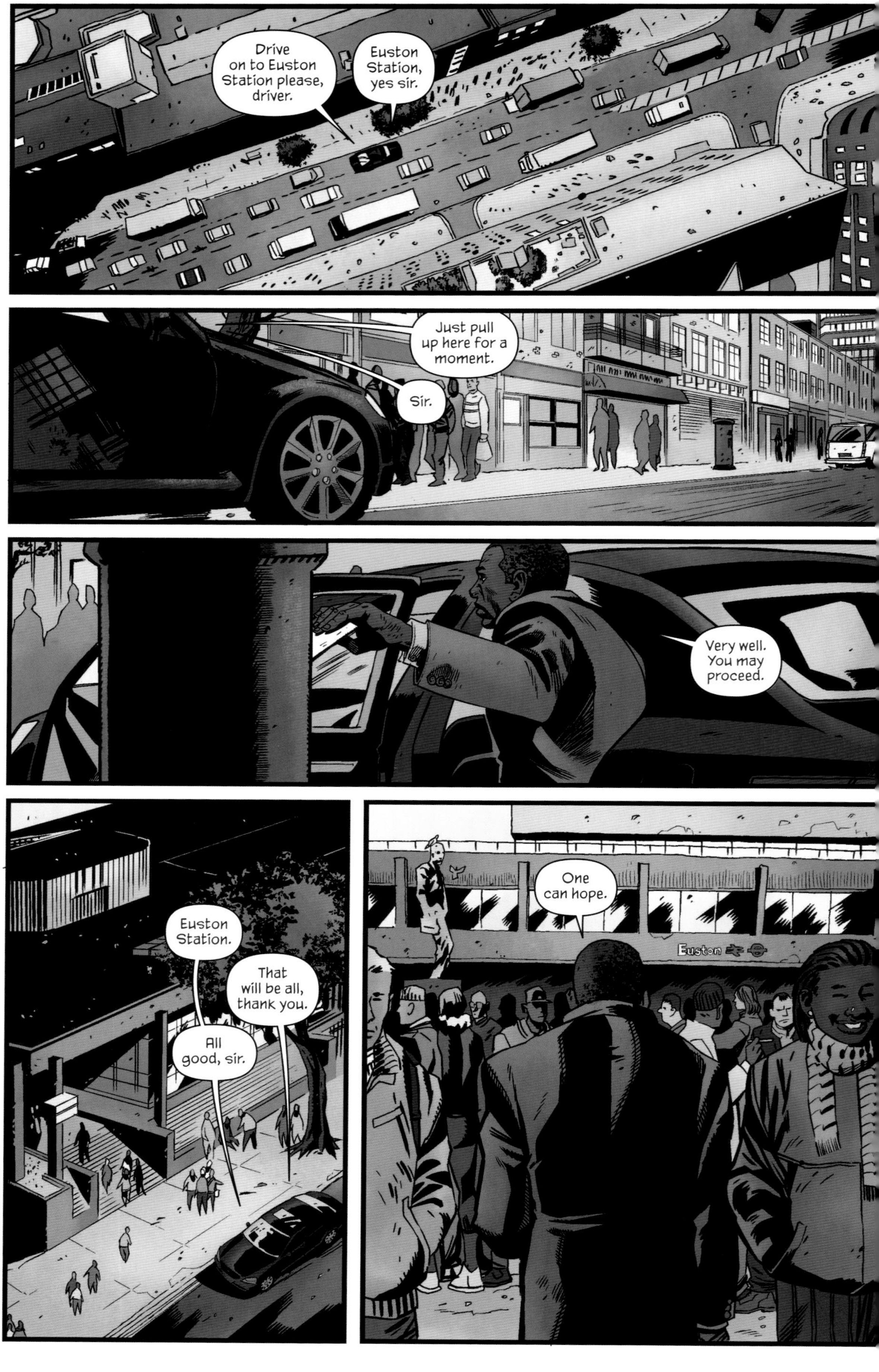
Drive on to Euston Station please, driver.
Euston Station, yes sir.
Just pull up here for a moment.
Sir.
Very well. You may proceed.
Euston Station.
That will be all, thank you.
All good, sir.
One can hope.
Euston

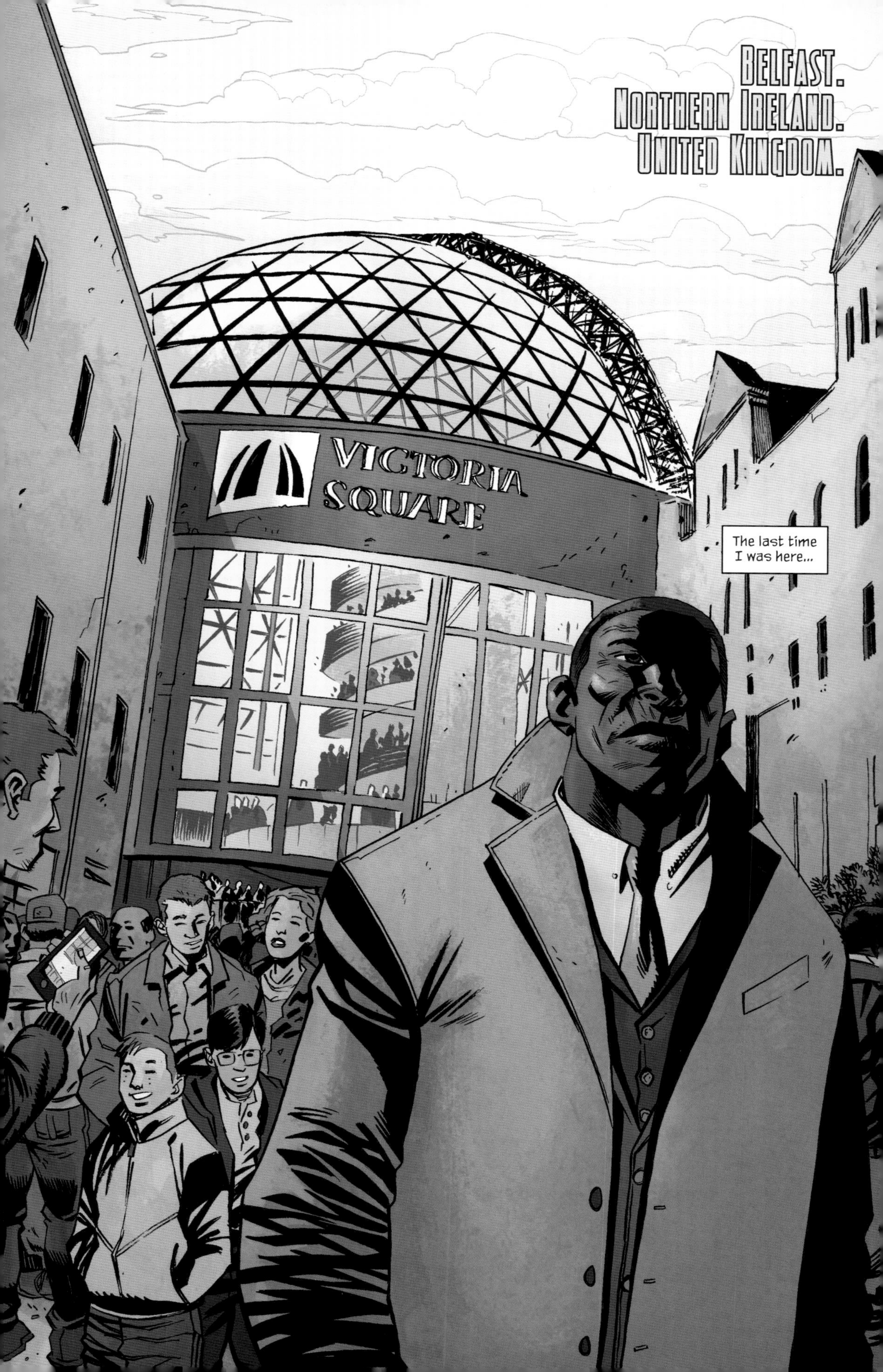
BELFAST.
NORTHERN IRELAND.
UNITED KINGDOM.
VICTORIA SQUARE
The last time I was here...

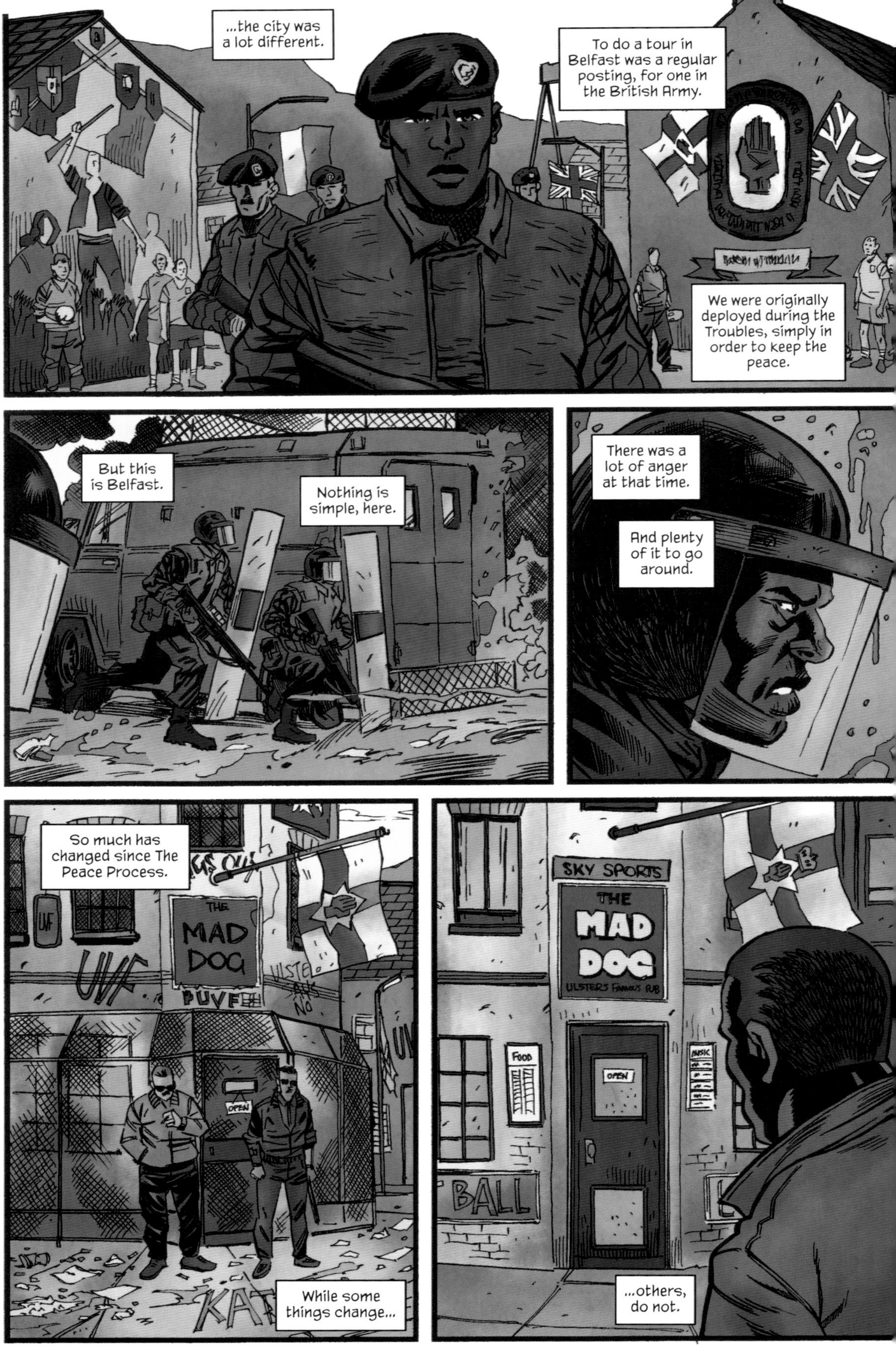

...the city was a lot different.
To do a tour in Belfast was a regular posting, for one in the British Army.
We were originally deployed during the Troubles, simply in order to keep the peace.
But this is Belfast.
Nothing is simple, here.
There was a lot of anger at that time.
And plenty of it to go around.
So much has changed since The Peace Process.
THE MAD DOG
UVF
OPEN
While some things change...
SKY SPORTS
THE MAD DOG
ULSTERS Famous PUB
FOOD
OPEN
BALL
...others, do not.

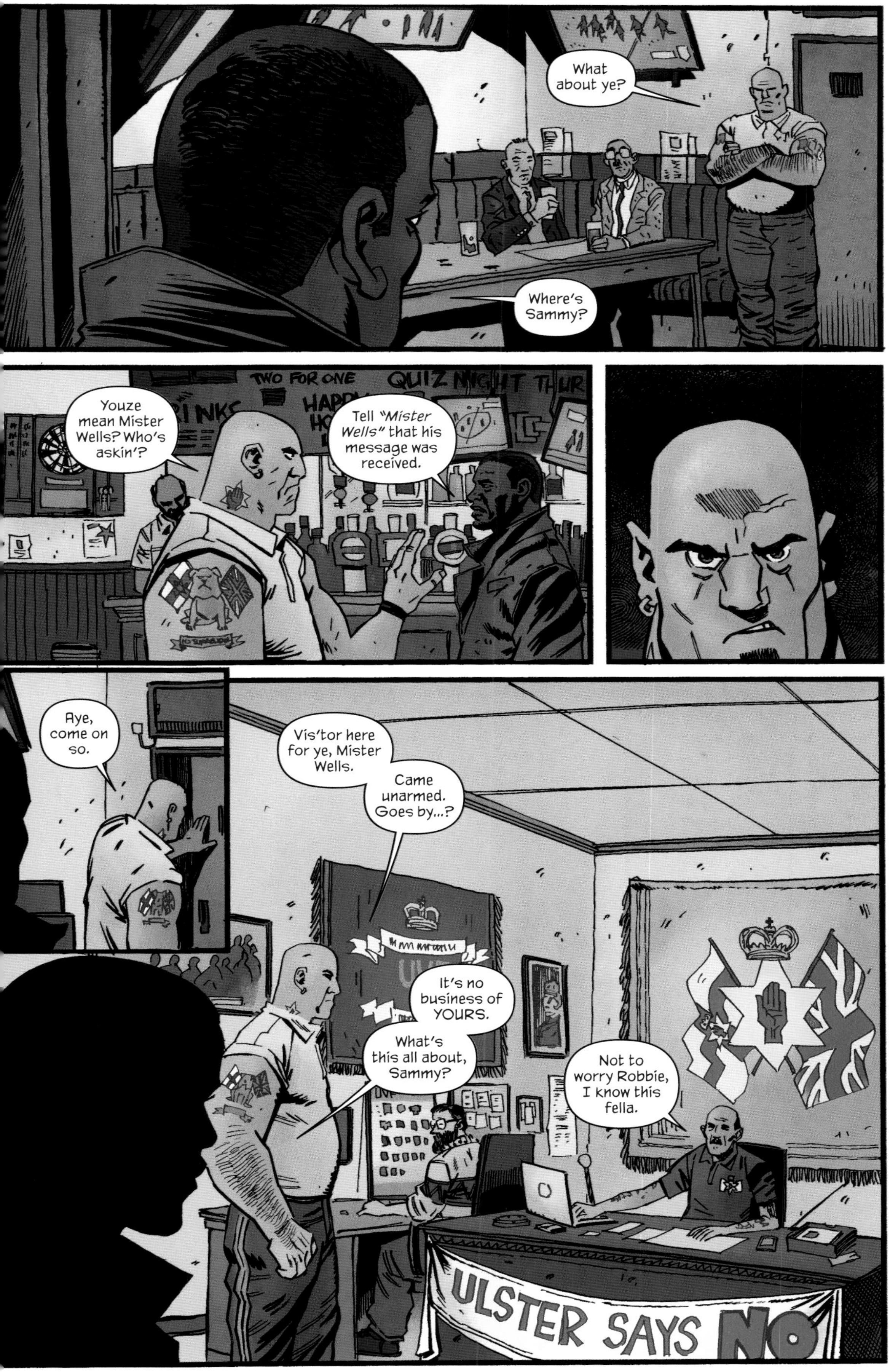
What about ye?
Where's Sammy?
TWO FOR ONE
QUIZ NIGHT THUR
Youze mean Mister Wells? Who's askin'?
Tell "*Mister Wells*" that his message was received.
Aye, come on so.
Vis'tor here for ye, Mister Wells.
Came unarmed. Goes by...?
It's no business of YOURS.
What's this all about, Sammy?
Not to worry Robbie, I know this fella.
ULSTER SAYS NO

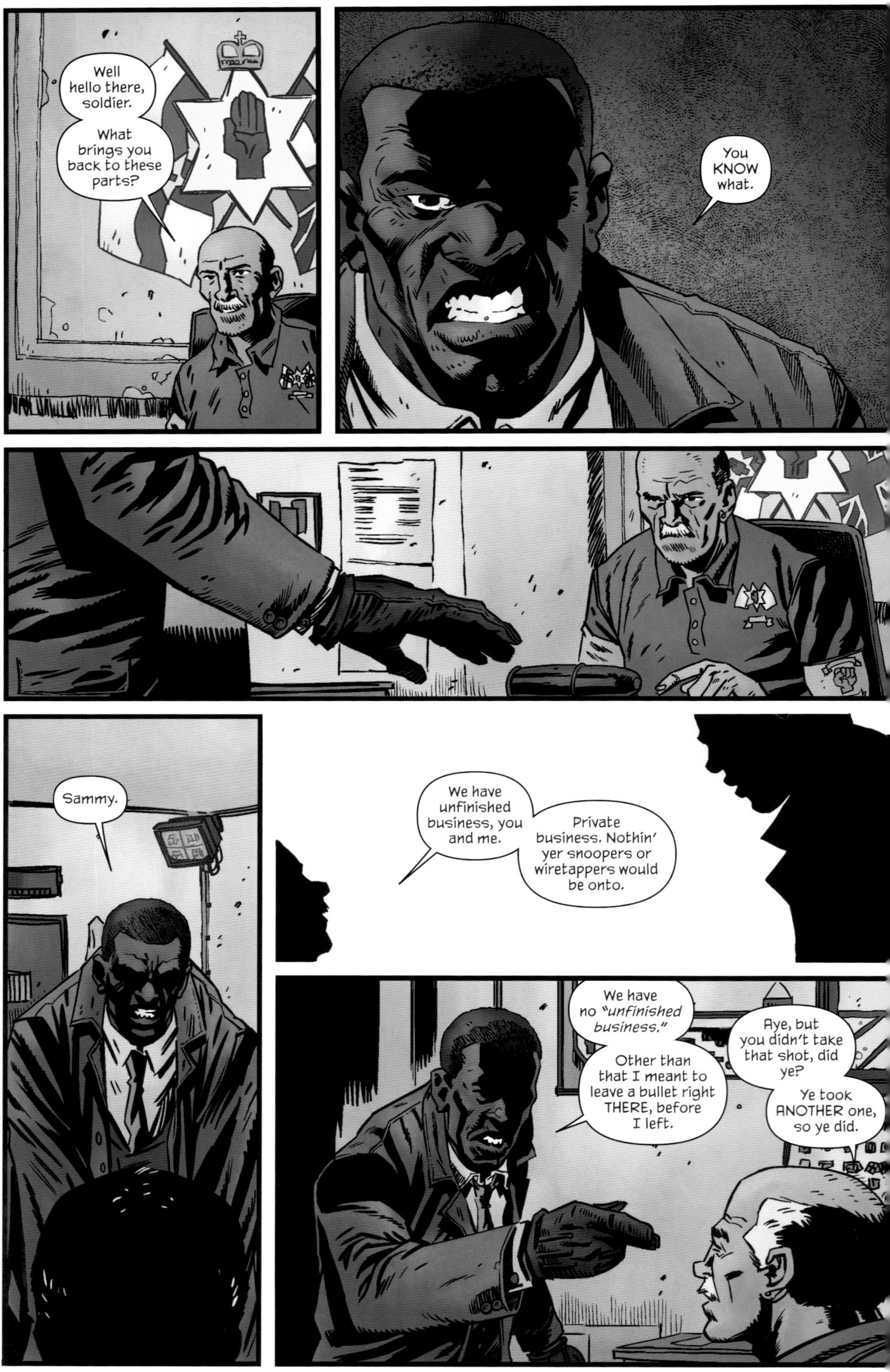
Well hello there, soldier.
What brings you back to these parts?
You KNOW what.
Sammy.
We have unfinished business, you and me.
Private business. Nothin' yer snoopers or wiretappers would be onto.
We have no "unfinished business."
Other than that I meant to leave a bullet right THERE, before I left.
Aye, but you didn't take that shot, did ye?
Ye took ANOTHER one, so ye did.

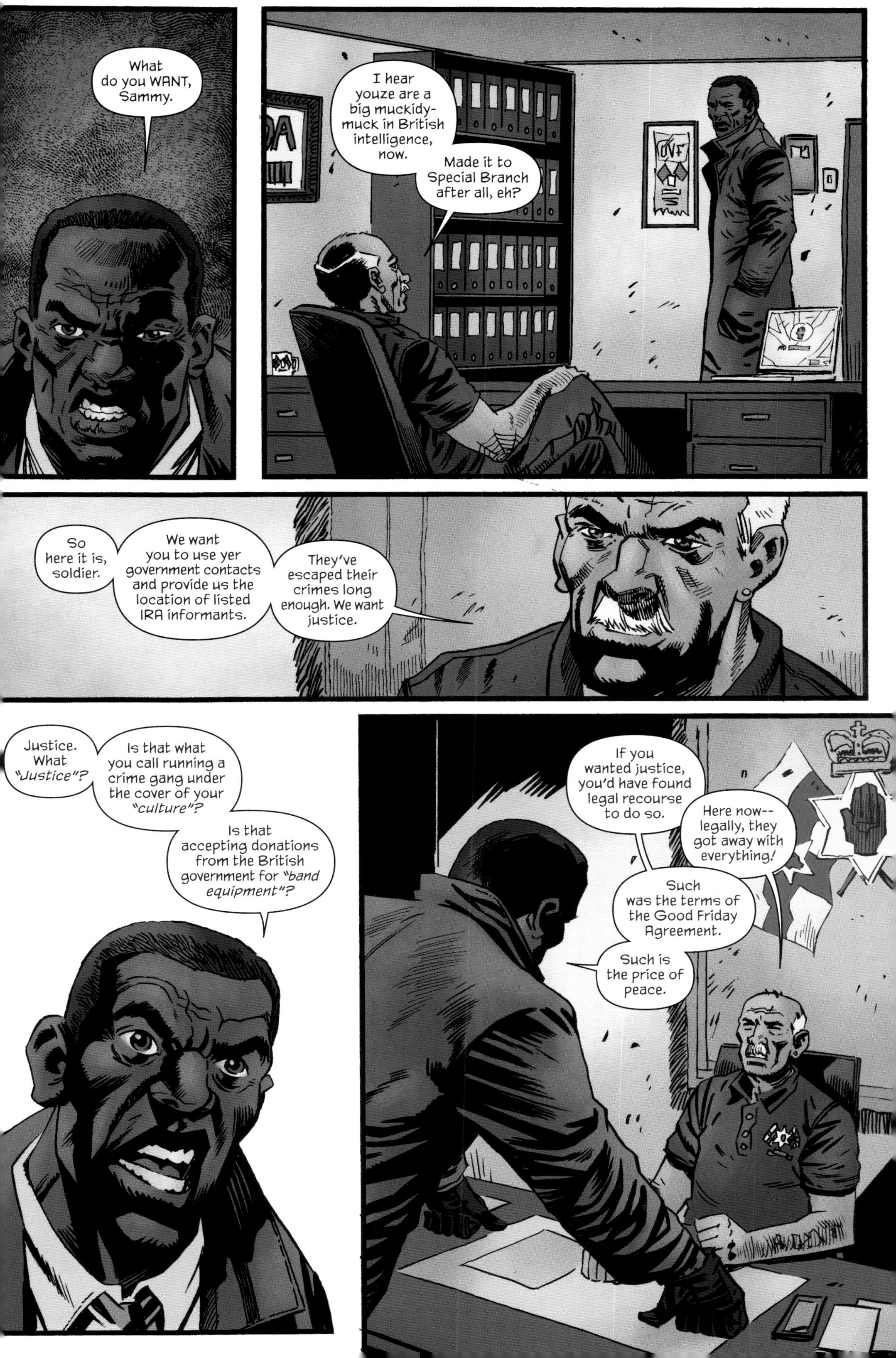

What do you WANT, Sammy.
I hear youze are a big muckidy-muck in British intelligence, now.
Made it to Special Branch after all, eh?
UVF
So here it is, soldier.
We want you to use yer government contacts and provide us the location of listed IRA informants.
They've escaped their crimes long enough. We want justice.
Justice. What "Justice"?
Is that what you call running a crime gang under the cover of your "culture"?
Is that accepting donations from the British government for "band equipment"?
If you wanted justice, you'd have found legal recourse to do so.
Here now-- legally, they got away with everything!
Such was the terms of the Good Friday Agreement.
Such is the price of peace.

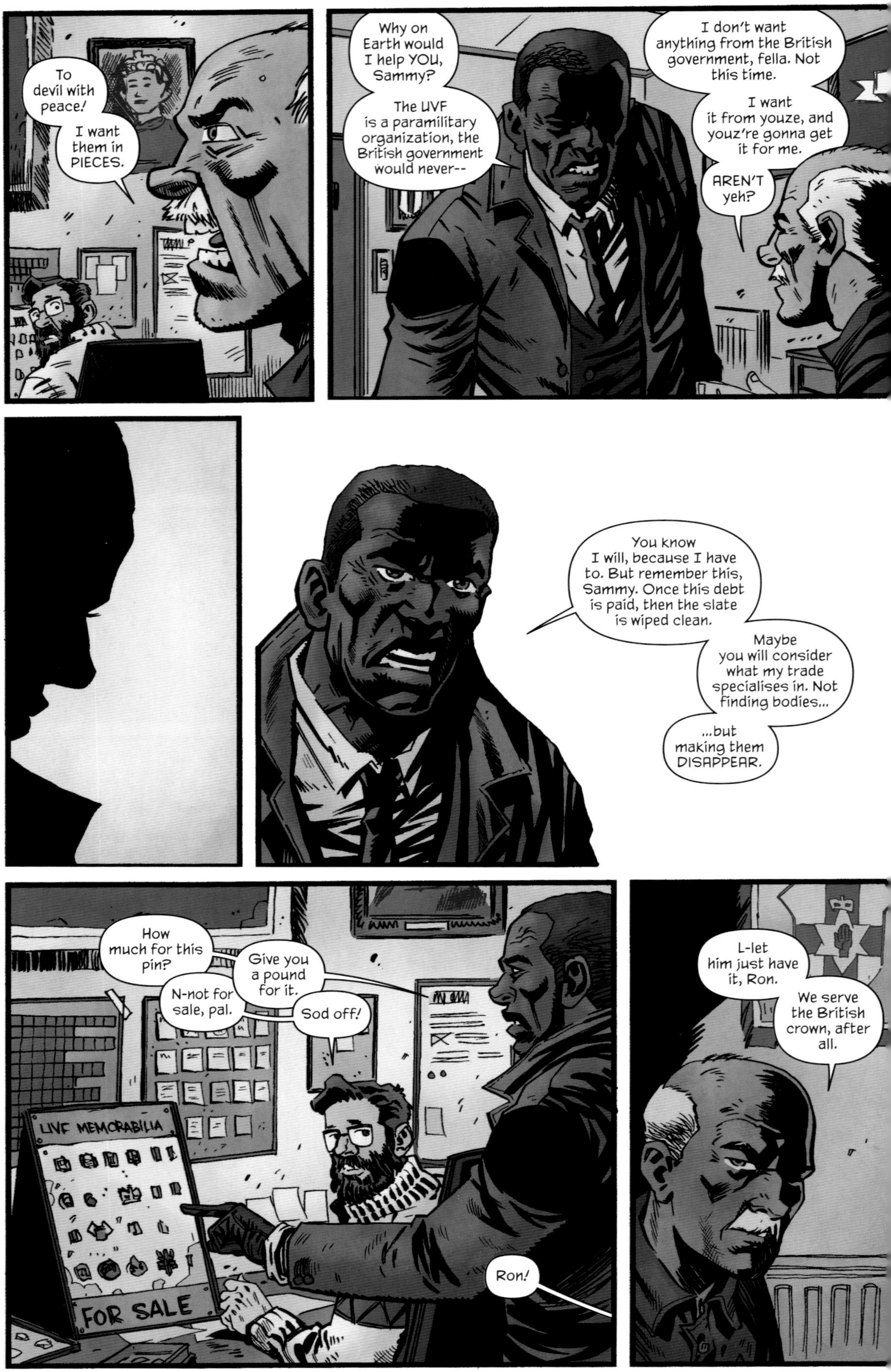
To devil with peace!
I want them in PIECES.
Why on Earth would I help YOU, Sammy?
The UVF is a paramilitary organization, the British government would never--
I don't want anything from the British government, fella. Not this time.
I want it from youze, and youz're gonna get it for me.
AREN'T yeh?
You know I will, because I have to. But remember this, Sammy. Once this debt is paid, then the slate is wiped clean.
Maybe you will consider what my trade specialises in. Not finding bodies...
...but making them DISAPPEAR.
How much for this pin?
N-not for sale, pal.
Give you a pound for it.
Sod off!
UVF MEMORABILIA
FOR SALE
Ron!
L-let him just have it, Ron.
We serve the British crown, after all.

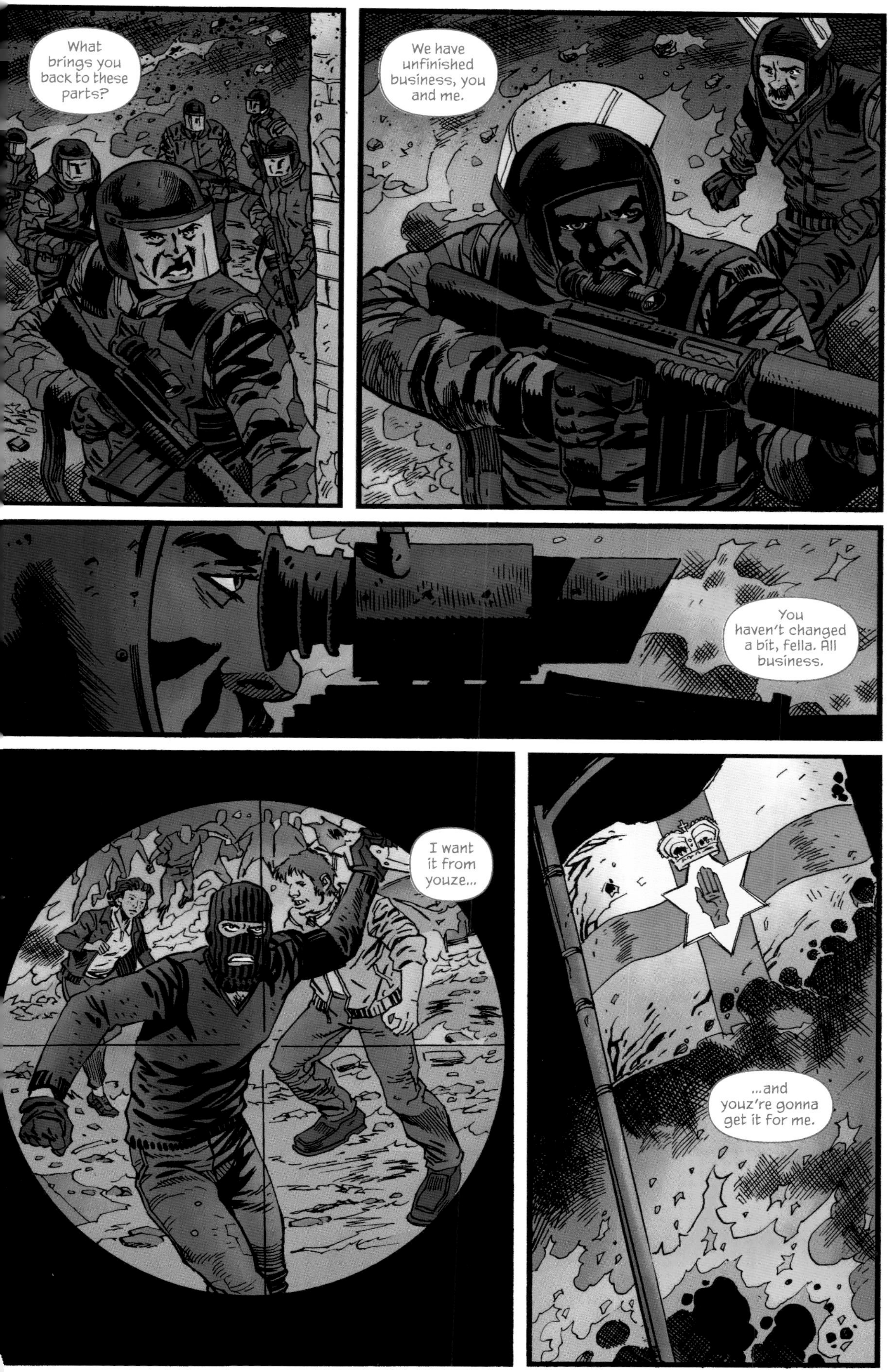
What brings you back to these parts?
We have unfinished business, you and me.
You haven't changed a bit, fella. All business.
I want it from youze...
...and youz're gonna get it for me.

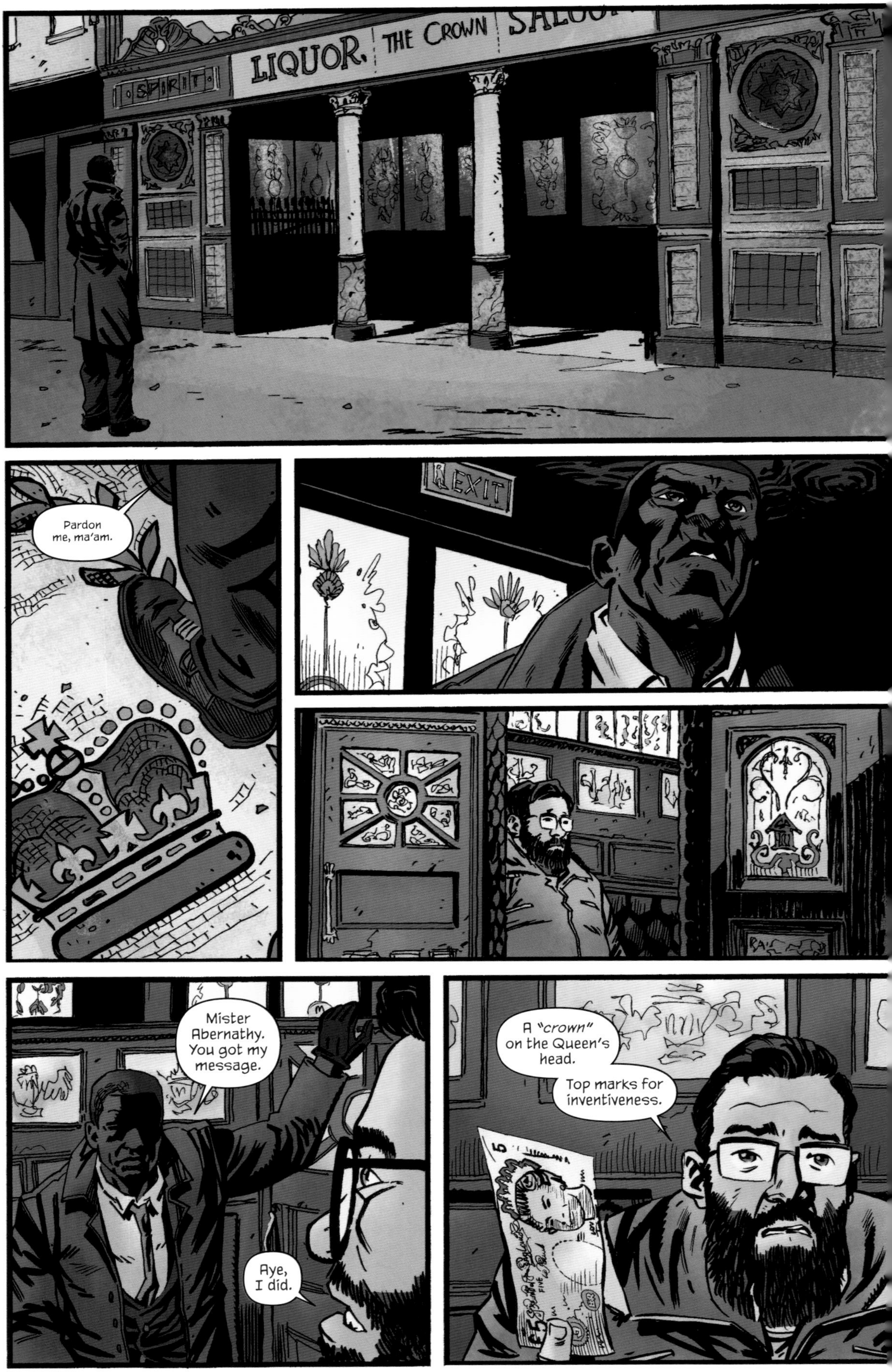
LIQUOR.
THE CROWN
SPIRIT
Pardon me, ma'am.
EXIT
Mister Abernathy. You got my message.
Aye, I did.
A "crown" on the Queen's head.
Top marks for inventiveness.

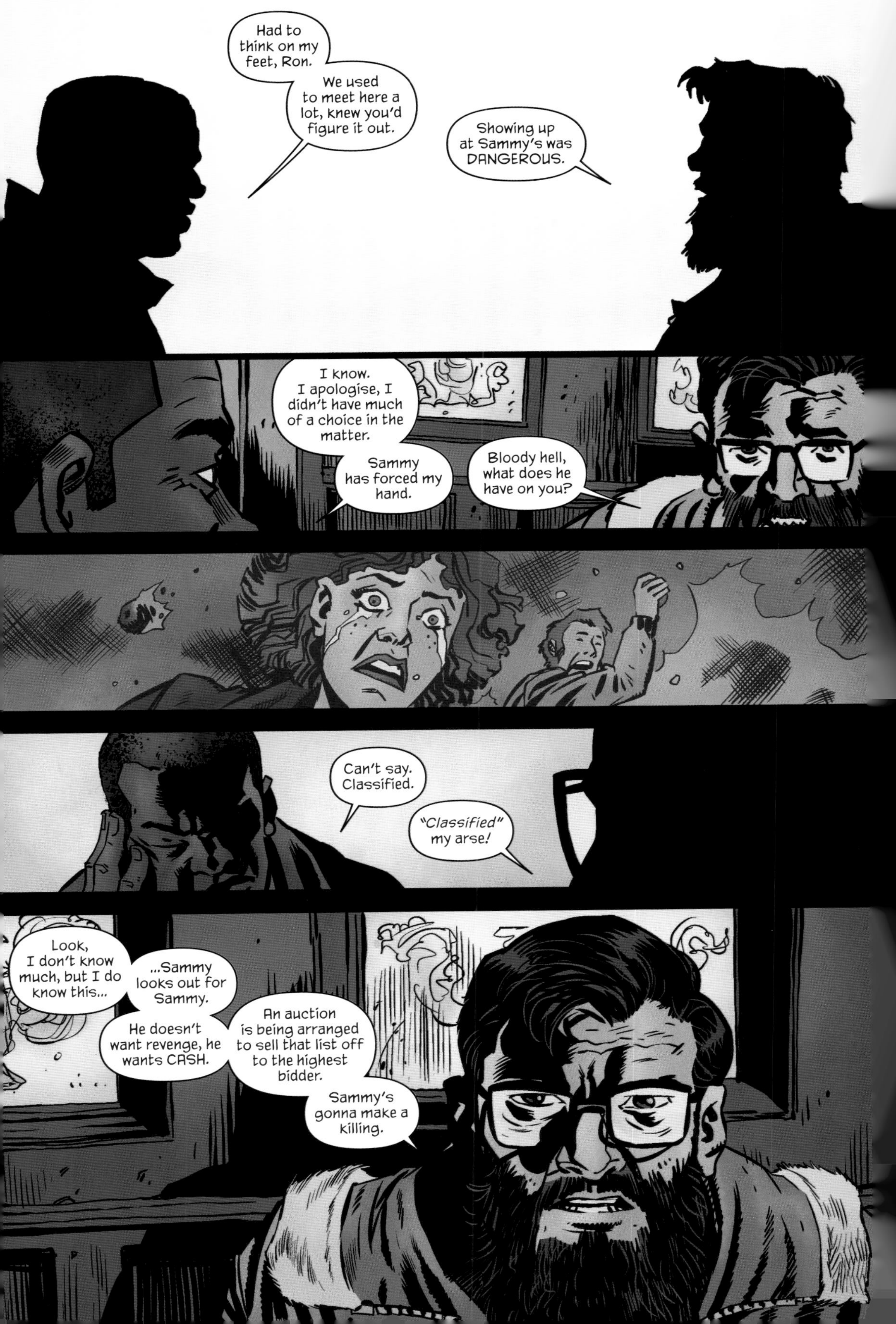
Had to think on my feet, Ron.
We used to meet here a lot, knew you'd figure it out.
Showing up at Sammy's was DANGEROUS.
I know. I apologise, I didn't have much of a choice in the matter.
Sammy has forced my hand.
Bloody hell, what does he have on you?
Can't say. Classified.
"Classified" my arse!
Look, I don't know much, but I do know this...
...Sammy looks out for Sammy.
He doesn't want revenge, he wants CASH.
An auction is being arranged to sell that list off to the highest bidder.
Sammy's gonna make a killing.

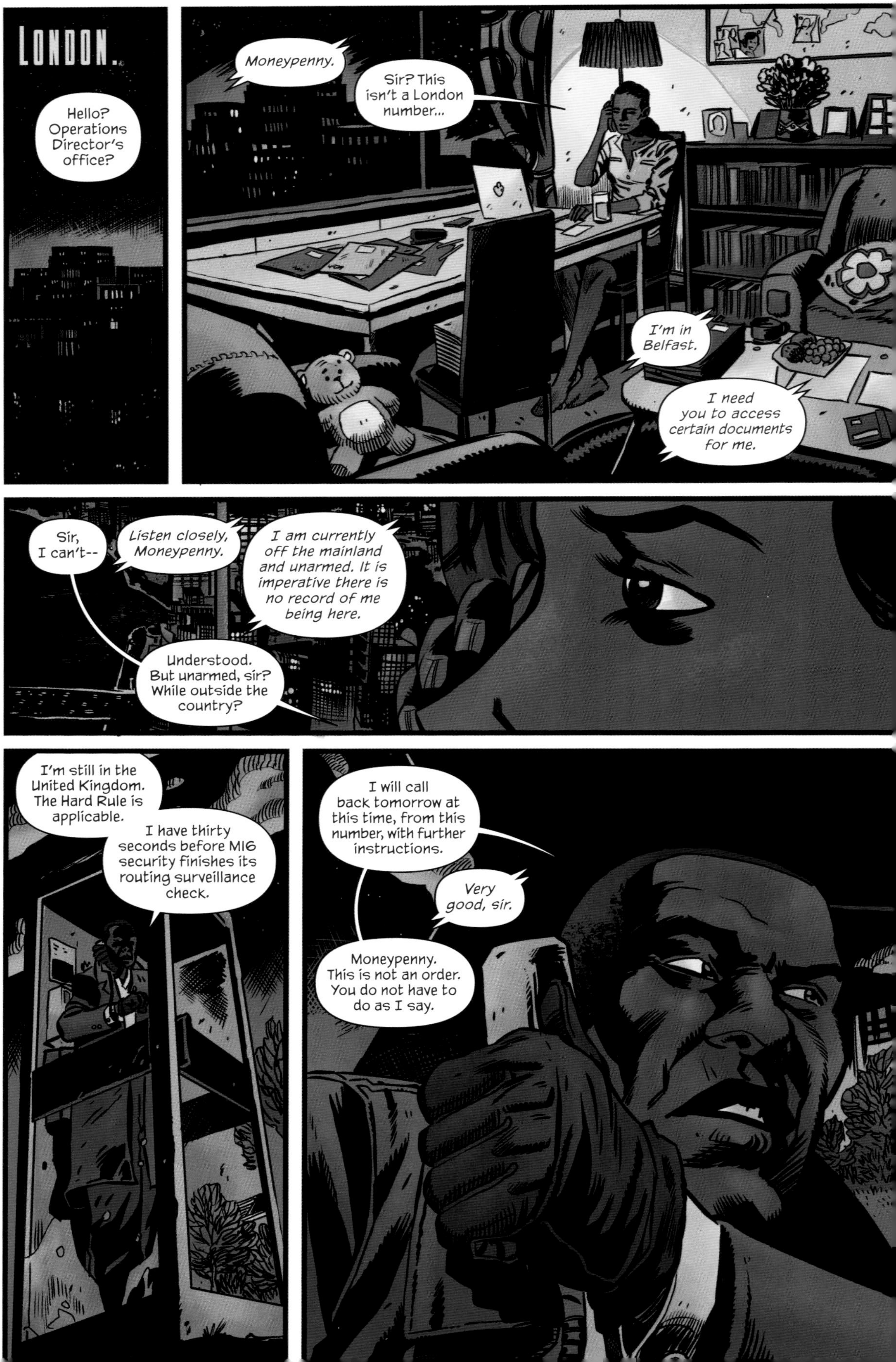
LONDON.
Hello? Operations Director's office?
Moneypenny.
Sir? This isn't a London number...
I'm in Belfast.
I need you to access certain documents for me.
Sir, I can't--
Listen closely, Moneypenny.
I am currently off the mainland and unarmed. It is imperative there is no record of me being here.
Understood. But unarmed, sir? While outside the country?
I'm still in the United Kingdom. The Hard Rule is applicable.
I have thirty seconds before MI6 security finishes its routing surveillance check.
I will call back tomorrow at this time, from this number, with further instructions.
Very good, sir.
Moneypenny. This is not an order. You do not have to do as I say.

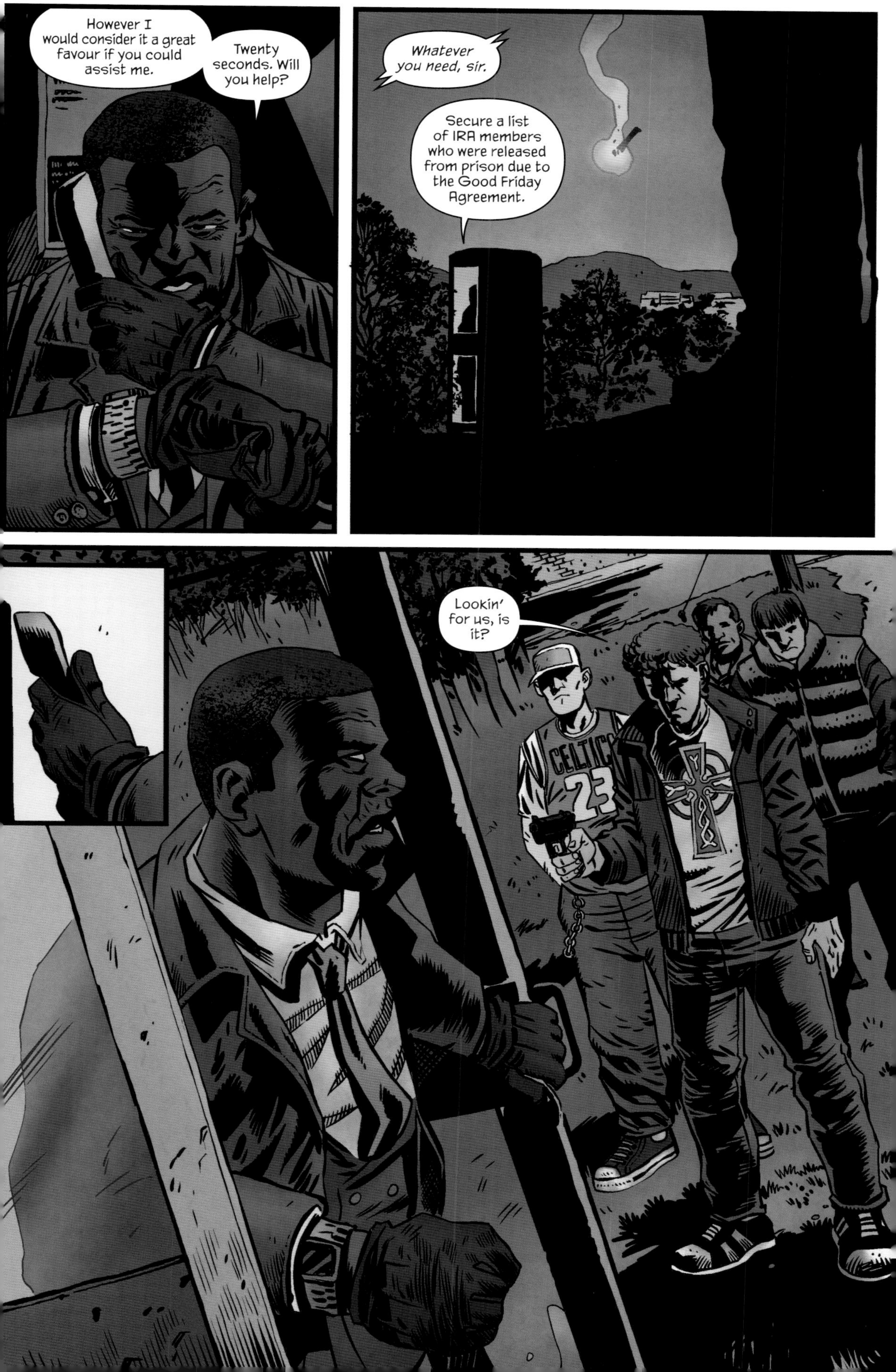
However I would consider it a great favour if you could assist me.
Twenty seconds. Will you help?
Whatever you need, sir.
Secure a list of IRA members who were released from prison due to the Good Friday Agreement.
Lookin' for us, is it?
CELTICS
23

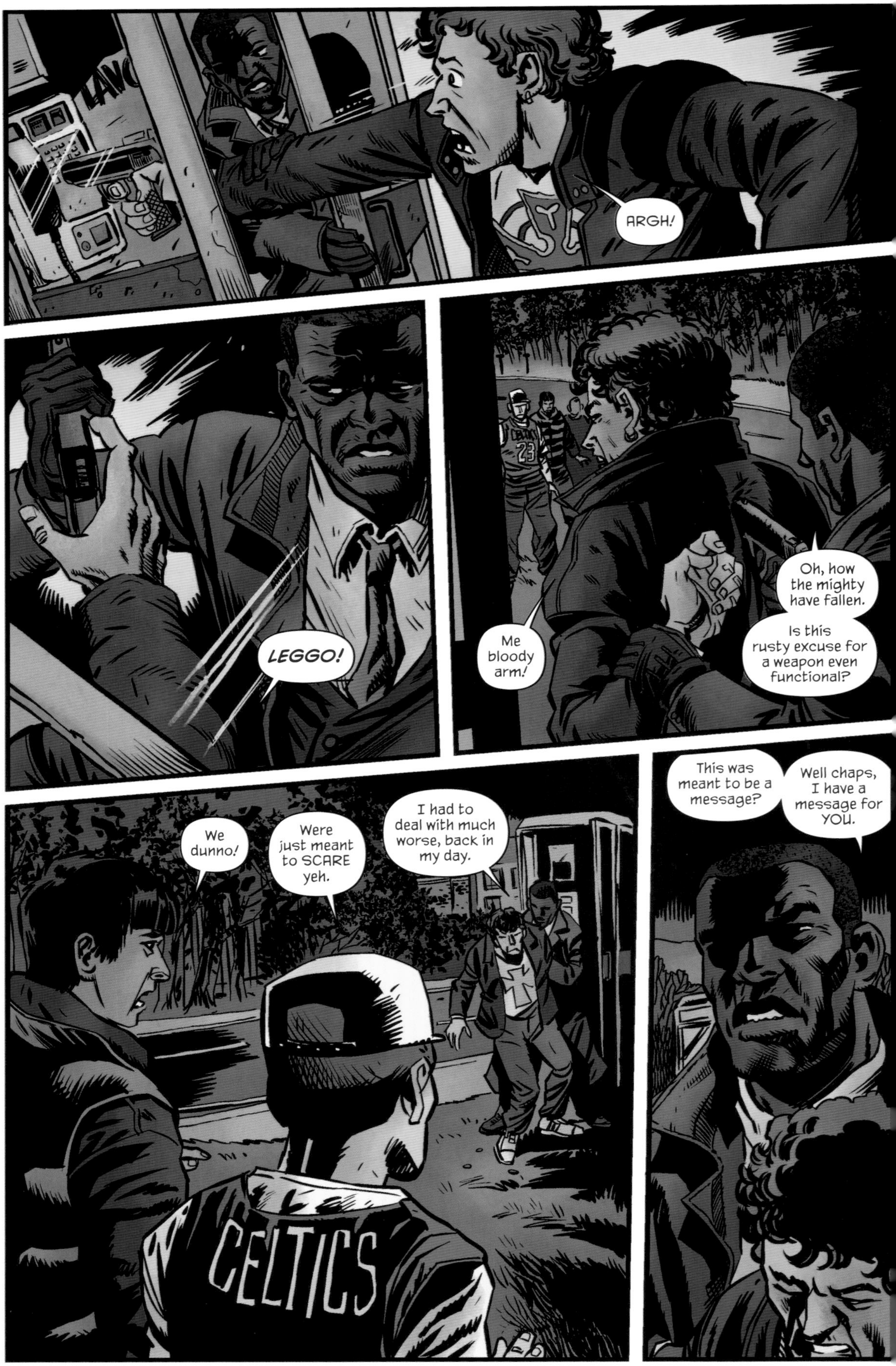
ARGH!
LEGGO!
Me bloody arm!
Oh, how the mighty have fallen.
Is this rusty excuse for a weapon even functional?
We dunno!
Were just meant to SCARE yeh.
I had to deal with much worse, back in my day.
This was meant to be a message?
Well chaps, I have a message for YOU.

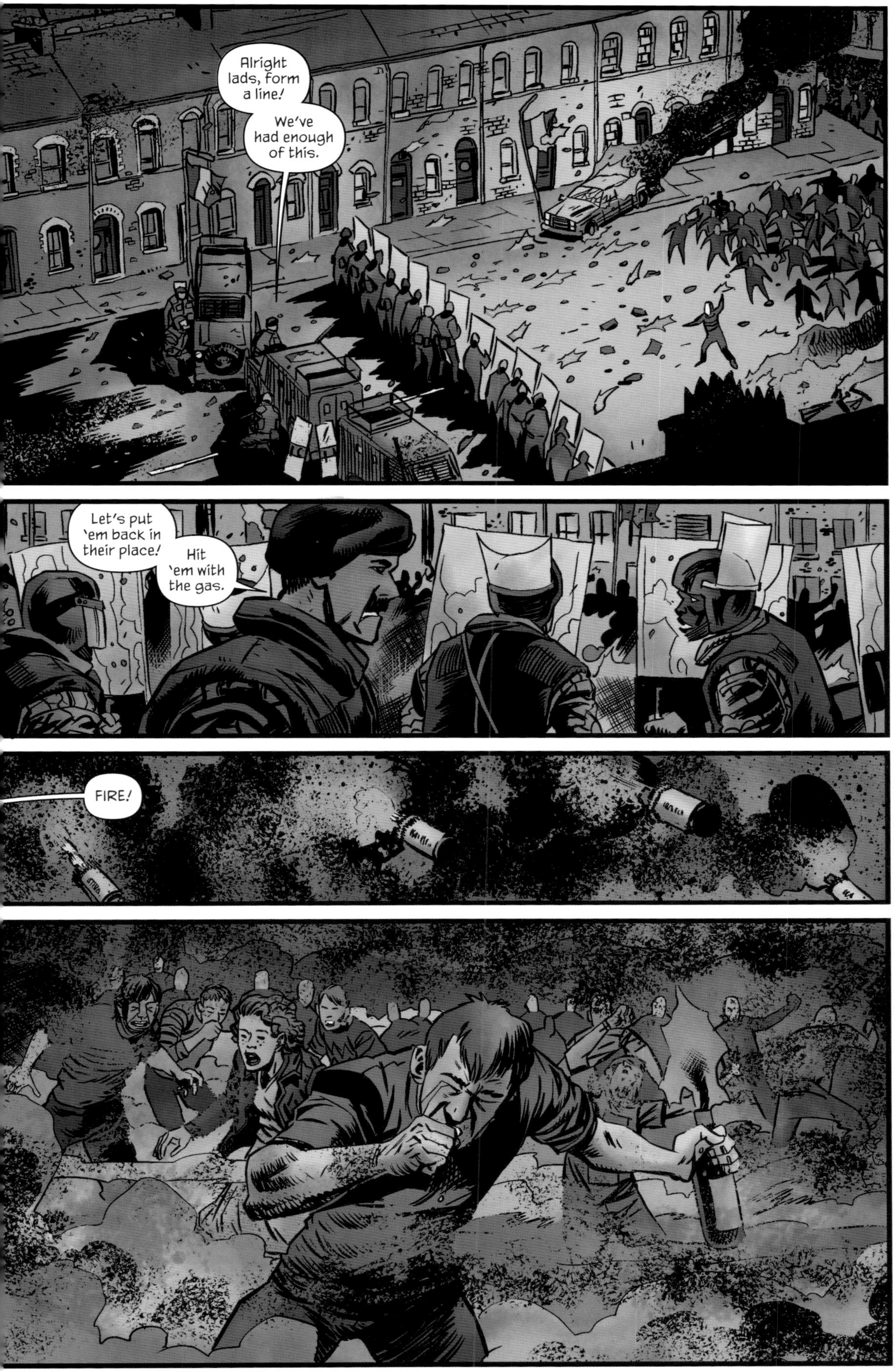
Alright lads, form a line!
We've had enough of this.
Let's put 'em back in their place!
Hit 'em with the gas.
FIRE!

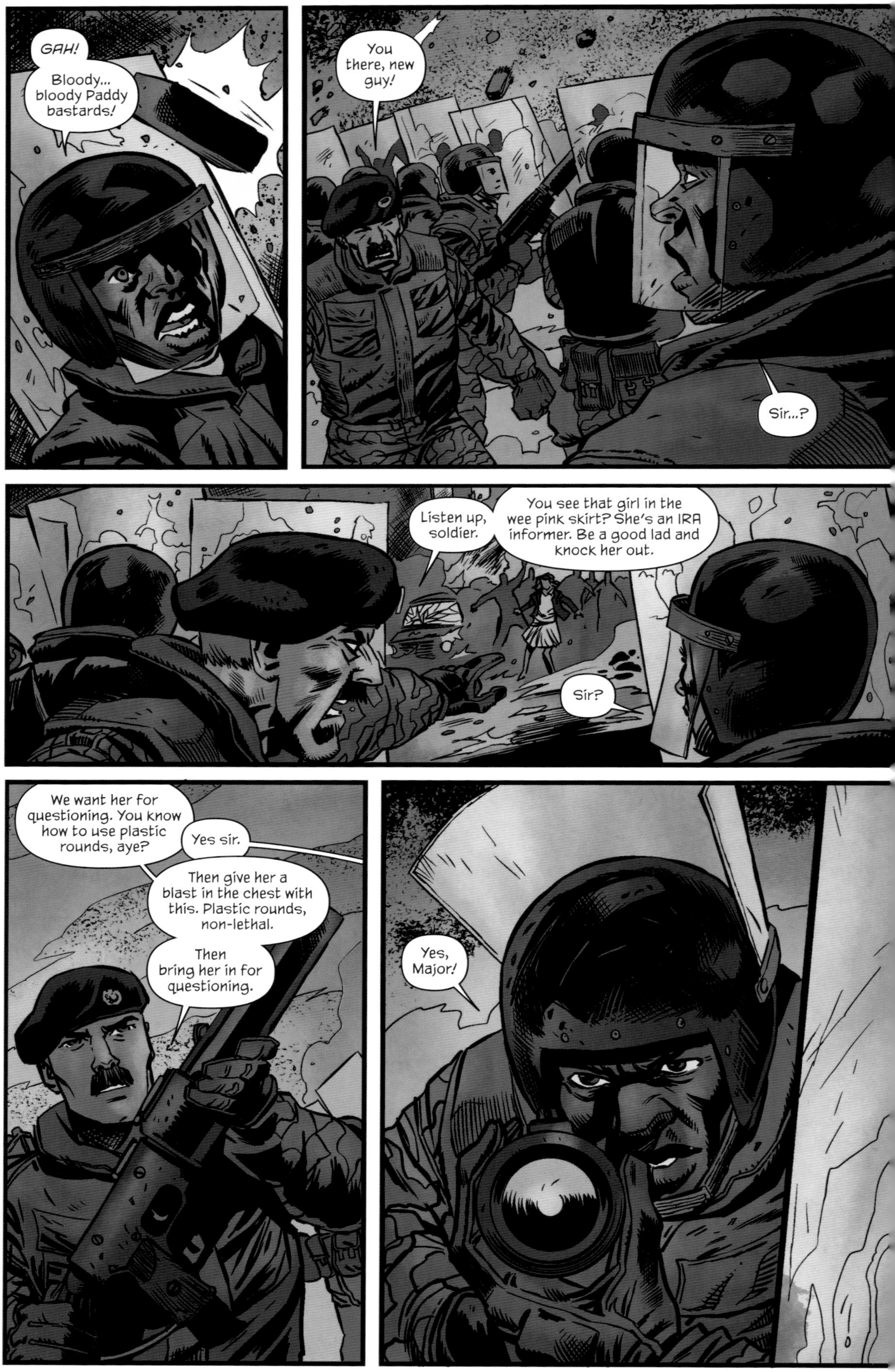
GAH!
Bloody... bloody Paddy bastards!
You there, new guy!
Sir...?
Listen up, soldier.
You see that girl in the wee pink skirt? She's an IRA informer. Be a good lad and knock her out.
Sir?
We want her for questioning. You know how to use plastic rounds, aye?
Yes sir.
Then give her a blast in the chest with this. Plastic rounds, non-lethal.
Then bring her in for questioning.
Yes, Major!

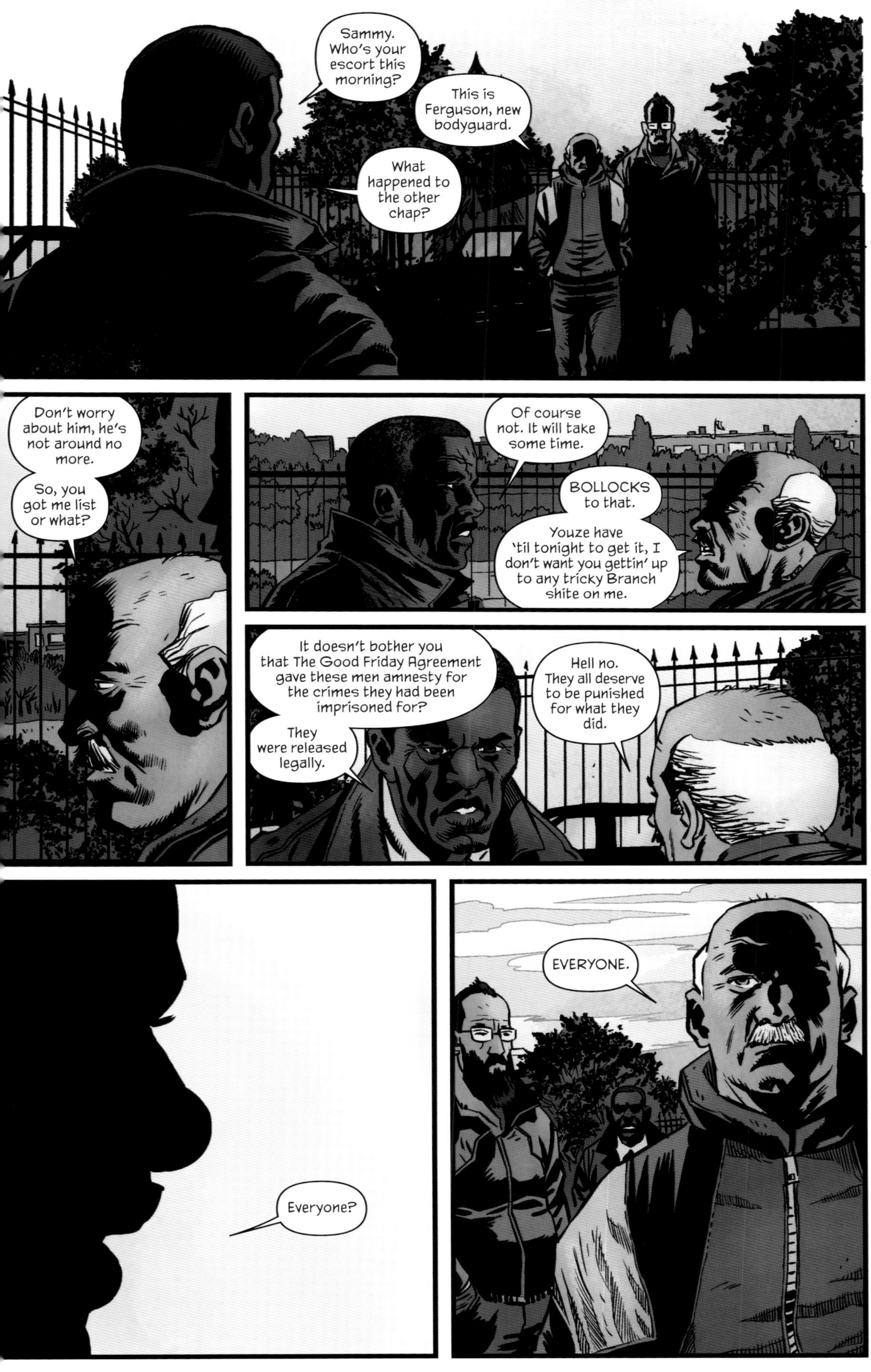
Sammy. Who's your escort this morning?
This is Ferguson, new bodyguard.
What happened to the other chap?
Don't worry about him, he's not around no more.
So, you got me list or what?
Of course not. It will take some time.
BOLLOCKS to that.
Youze have 'til tonight to get it, I don't want you gettin' up to any tricky Branch shite on me.
It doesn't bother you that The Good Friday Agreement gave these men amnesty for the crimes they had been imprisoned for?
They were released legally.
Hell no. They all deserve to be punished for what they did.
Everyone?
EVERYONE.

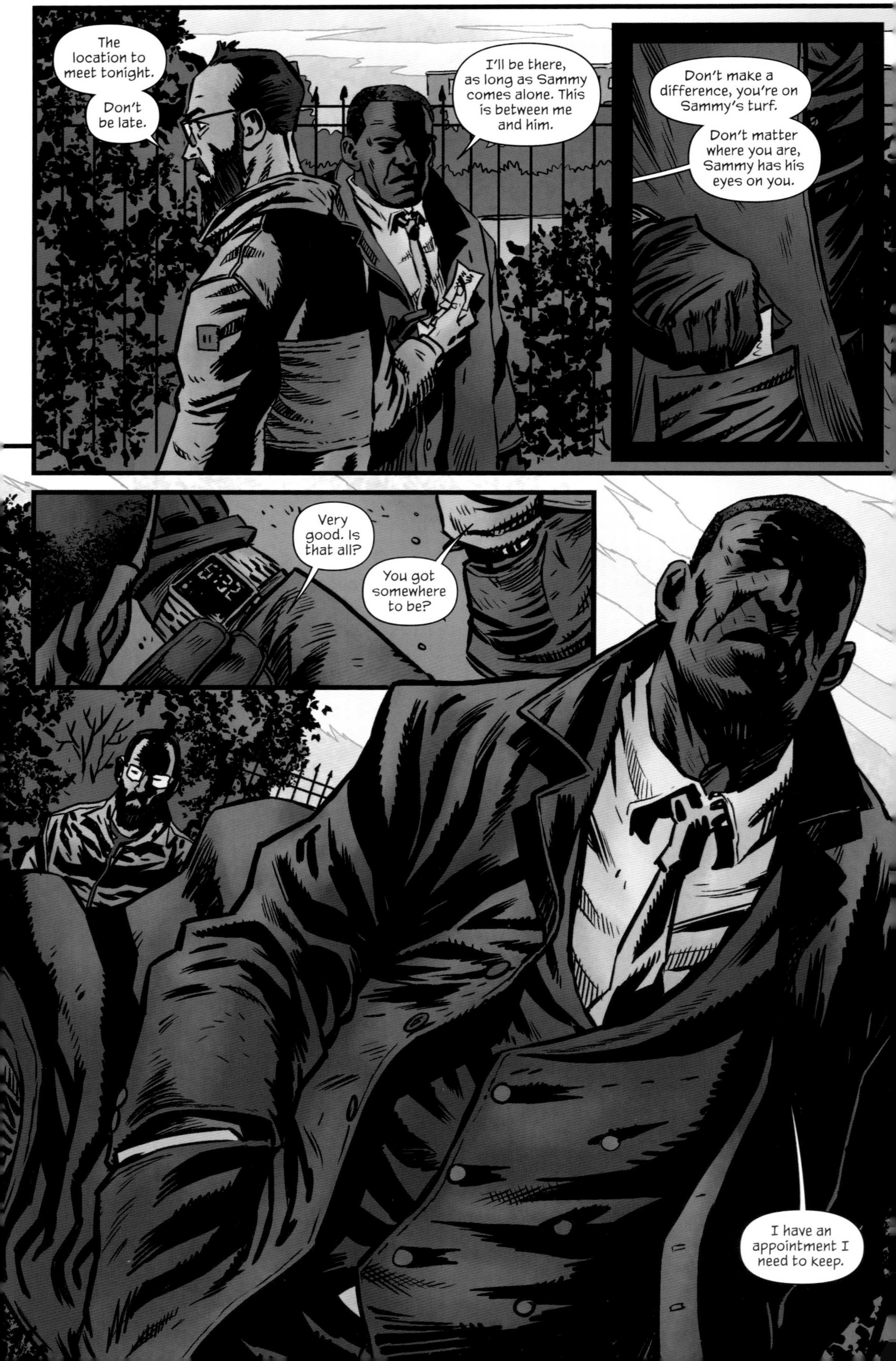
The location to meet tonight.
Don't be late.
I'll be there, as long as Sammy comes alone. This is between me and him.
Don't make a difference, you're on Sammy's turf.
Don't matter where you are, Sammy has his eyes on you.
Very good. Is that all?
You got somewhere to be?
I have an appointment I need to keep.

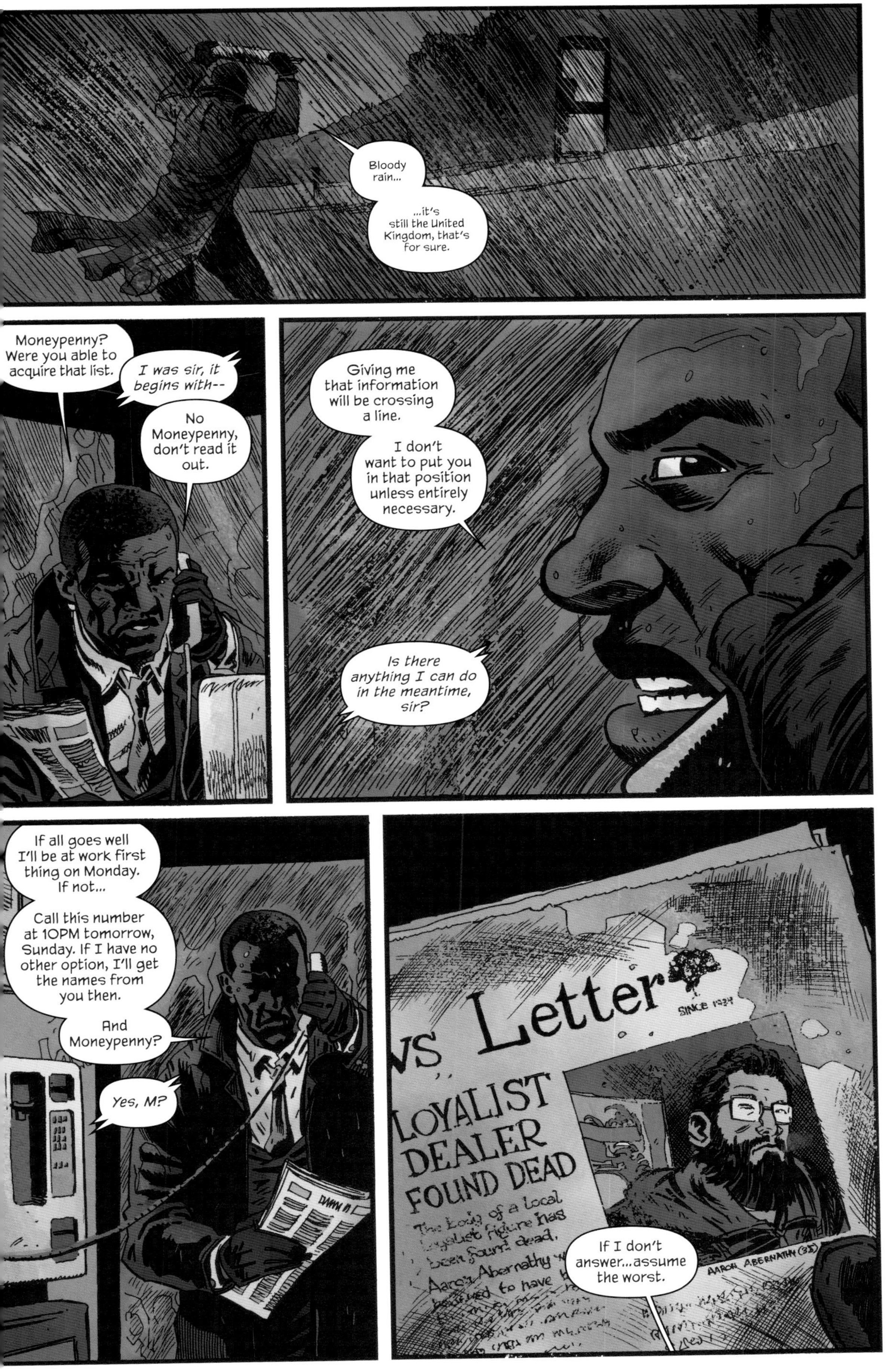
Bloody rain...
...it's still the United Kingdom, that's for sure.
Moneypenny? Were you able to acquire that list.
I was sir, it begins with--
No Moneypenny, don't read it out.
Giving me that information will be crossing a line.
I don't want to put you in that position unless entirely necessary.
Is there anything I can do in the meantime, sir?
If all goes well I'll be at work first thing on Monday. If not...
Call this number at 10PM tomorrow, Sunday. If I have no other option, I'll get the names from you then.
And Moneypenny?
Yes, M?
VS Letter
SINCE 1737
LOYALIST DEALER FOUND DEAD
The body of a local loyalist figure has been found dead.
AARON ABERNATHY (35)
If I don't answer...assume the worst.

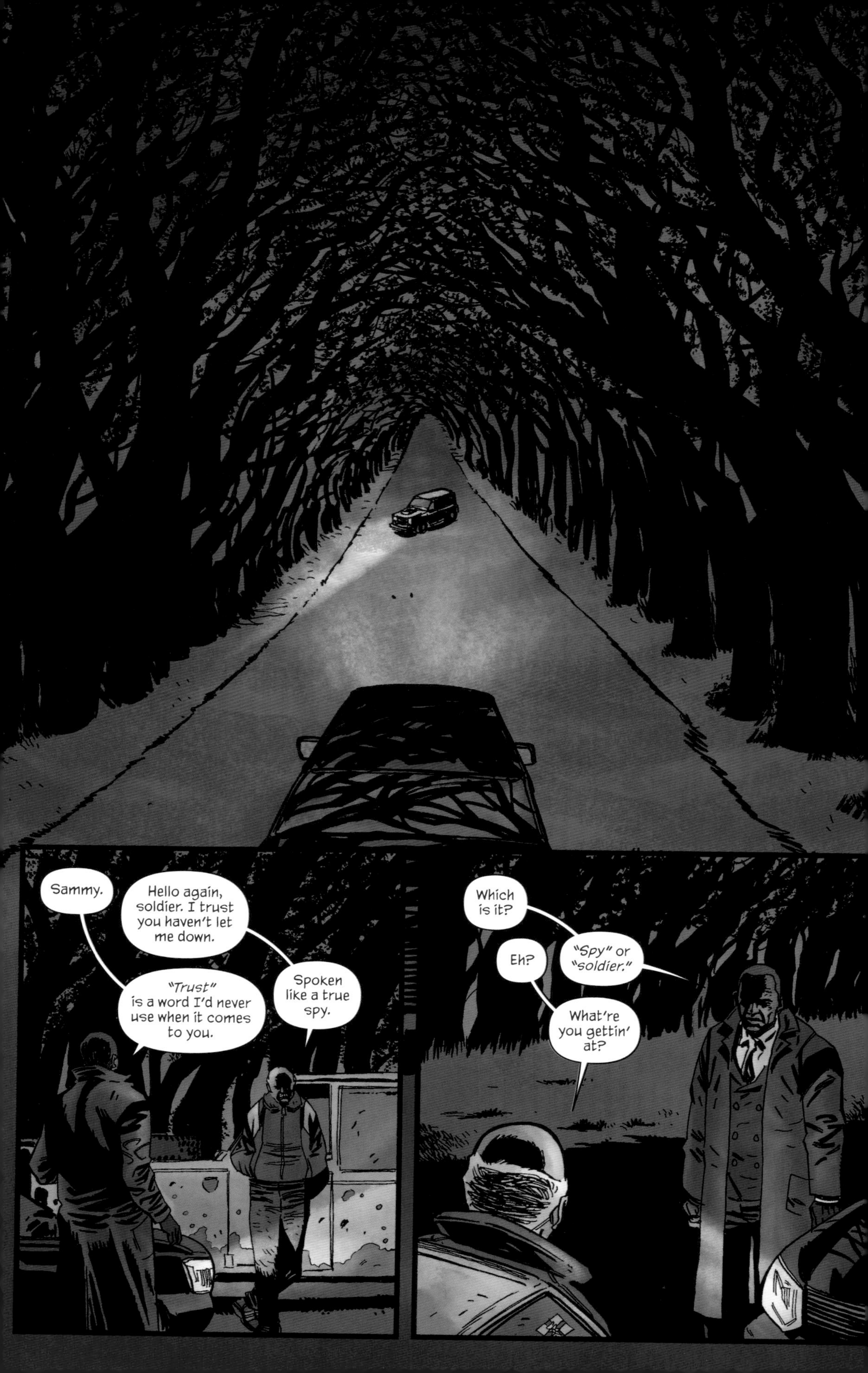
Sammy.
Hello again, soldier. I trust you haven't let me down.
"Trust" is a word I'd never use when it comes to you.
Spoken like a true spy.
Which is it?
"Spy" or "soldier."
Eh?
What're you gettin' at?

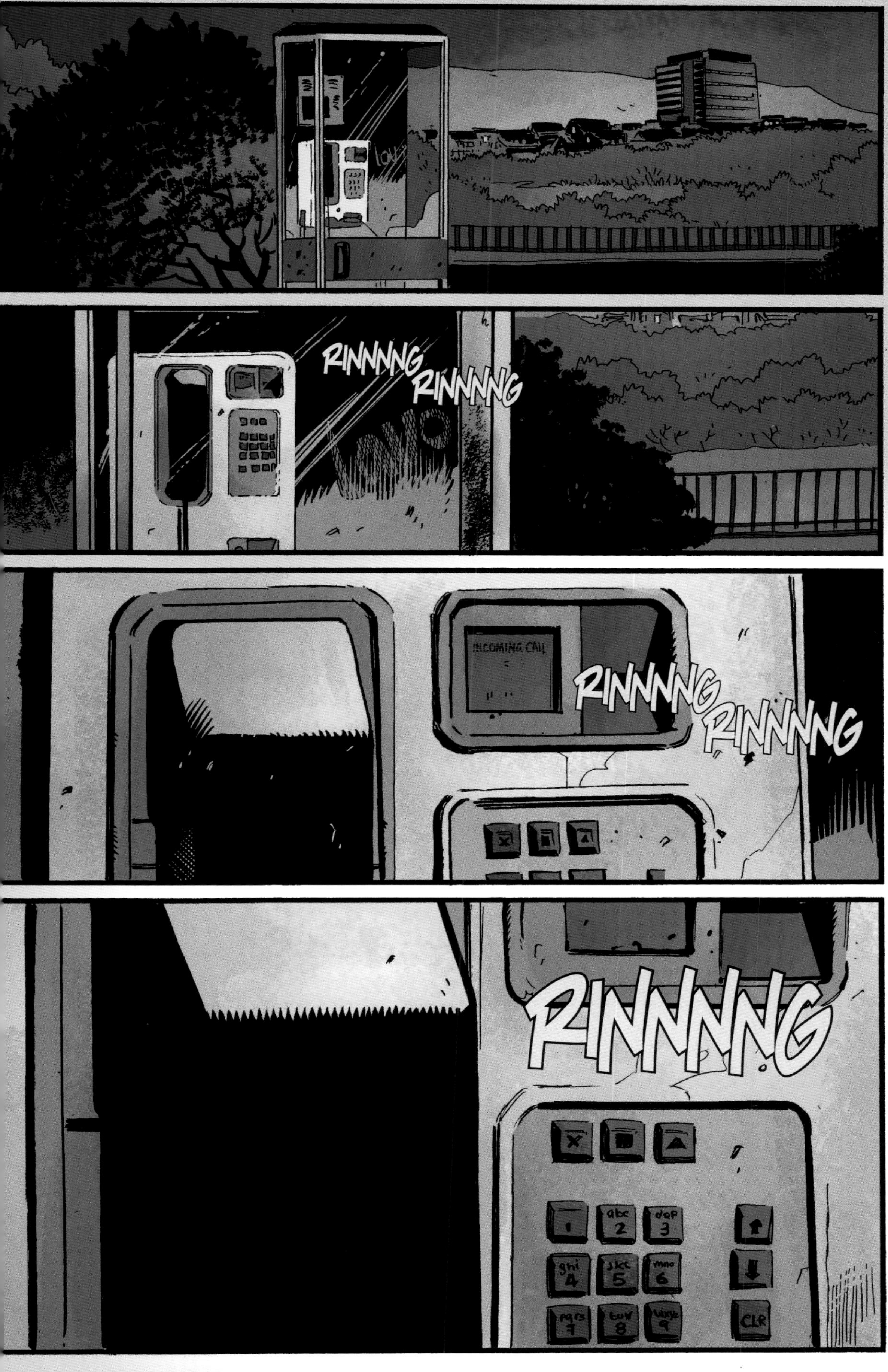
RINNNNG
RINNNNG
INCOMING CALL
RINNNNG
RINNNNG
RINNNNG

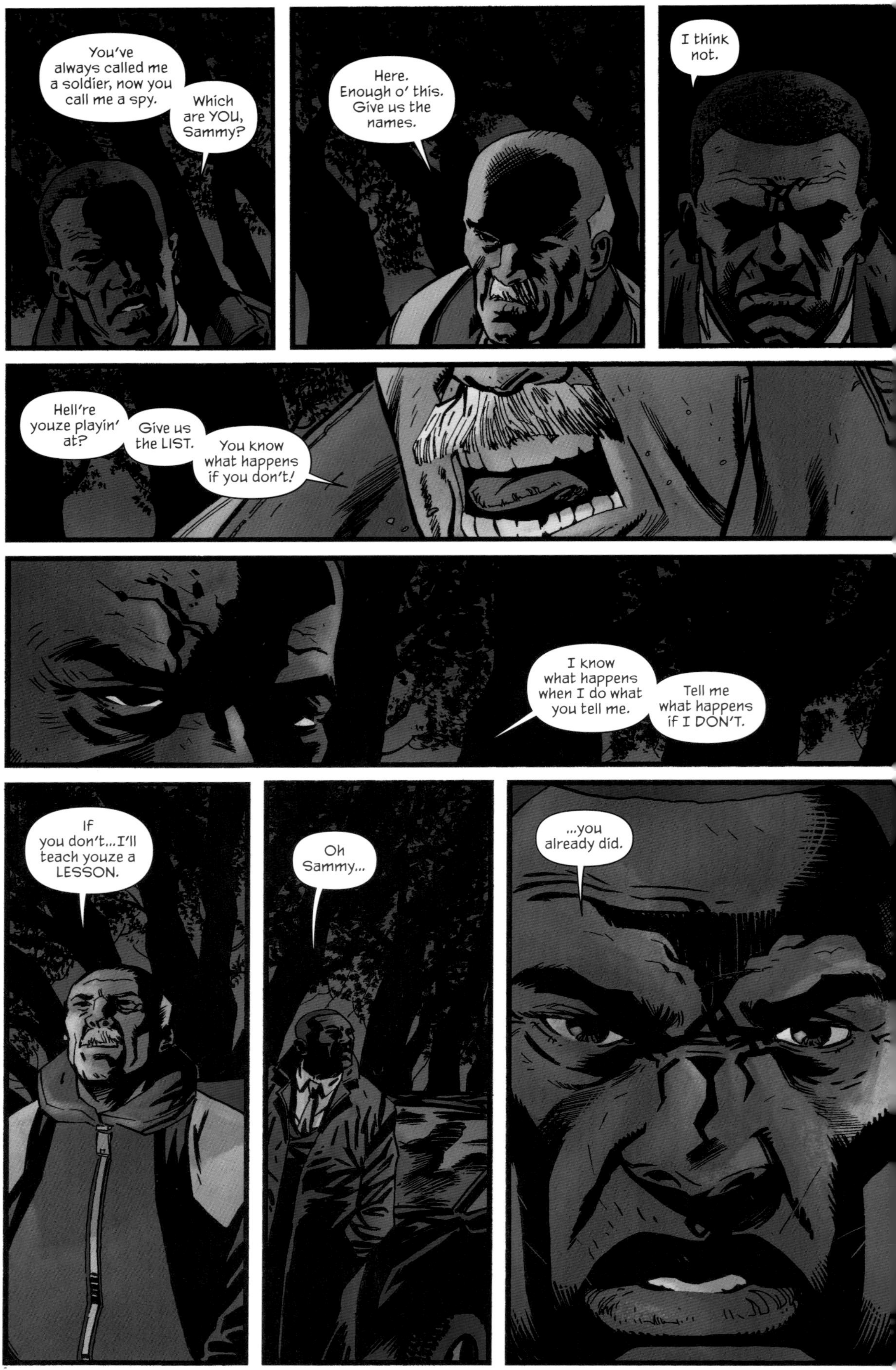
You've always called me a soldier, now you call me a spy.
Which are YOU, Sammy?
Here. Enough o' this. Give us the names.
I think not.
Hell're youze playin' at?
Give us the LIST.
You know what happens if you don't!
I know what happens when I do what you tell me.
Tell me what happens if I DON'T.
If you don't...I'll teach youze a LESSON.
Oh Sammy...
...you already did.

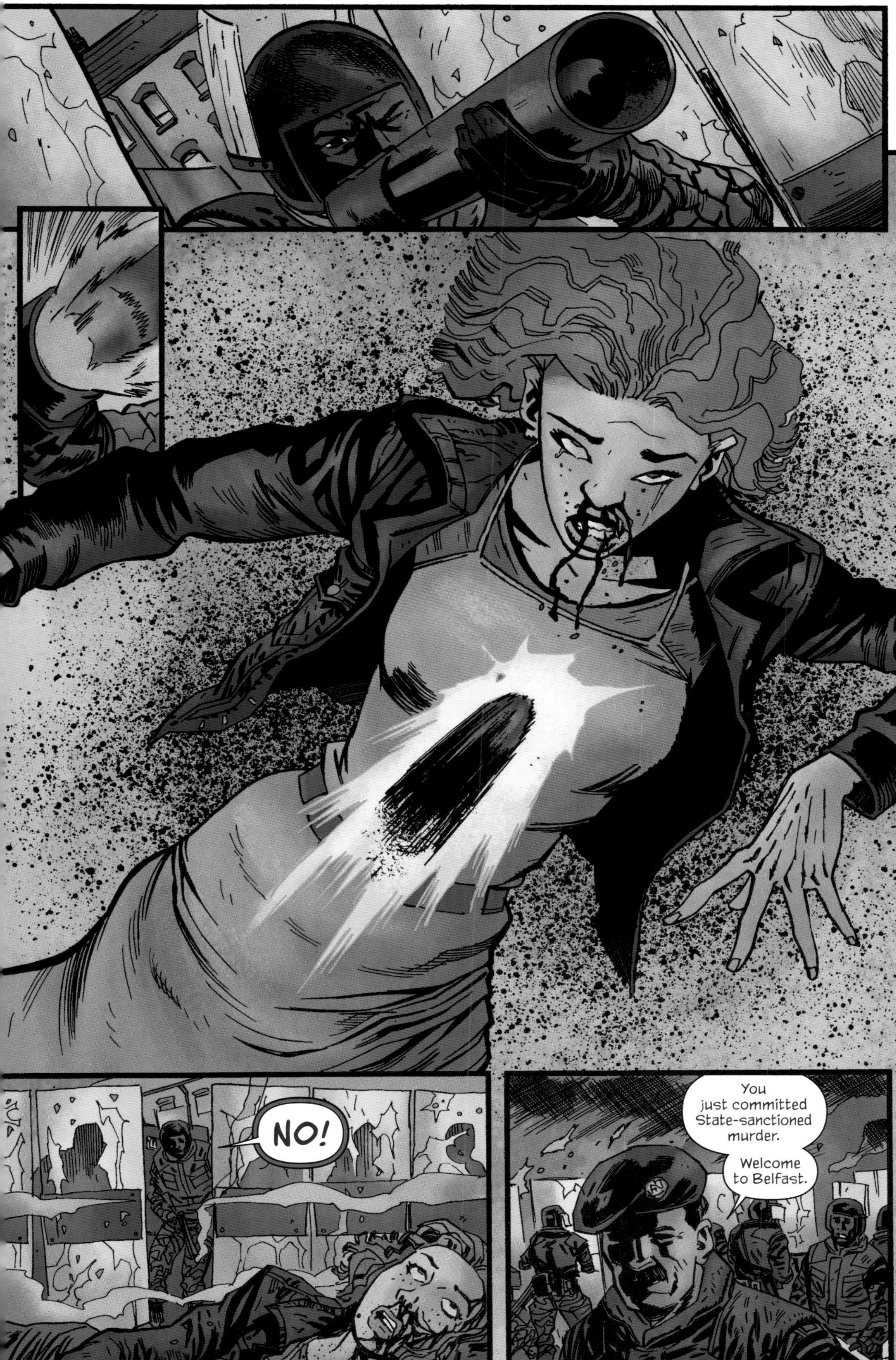
NO!
You just committed State-sanctioned murder.
Welcome to Belfast.

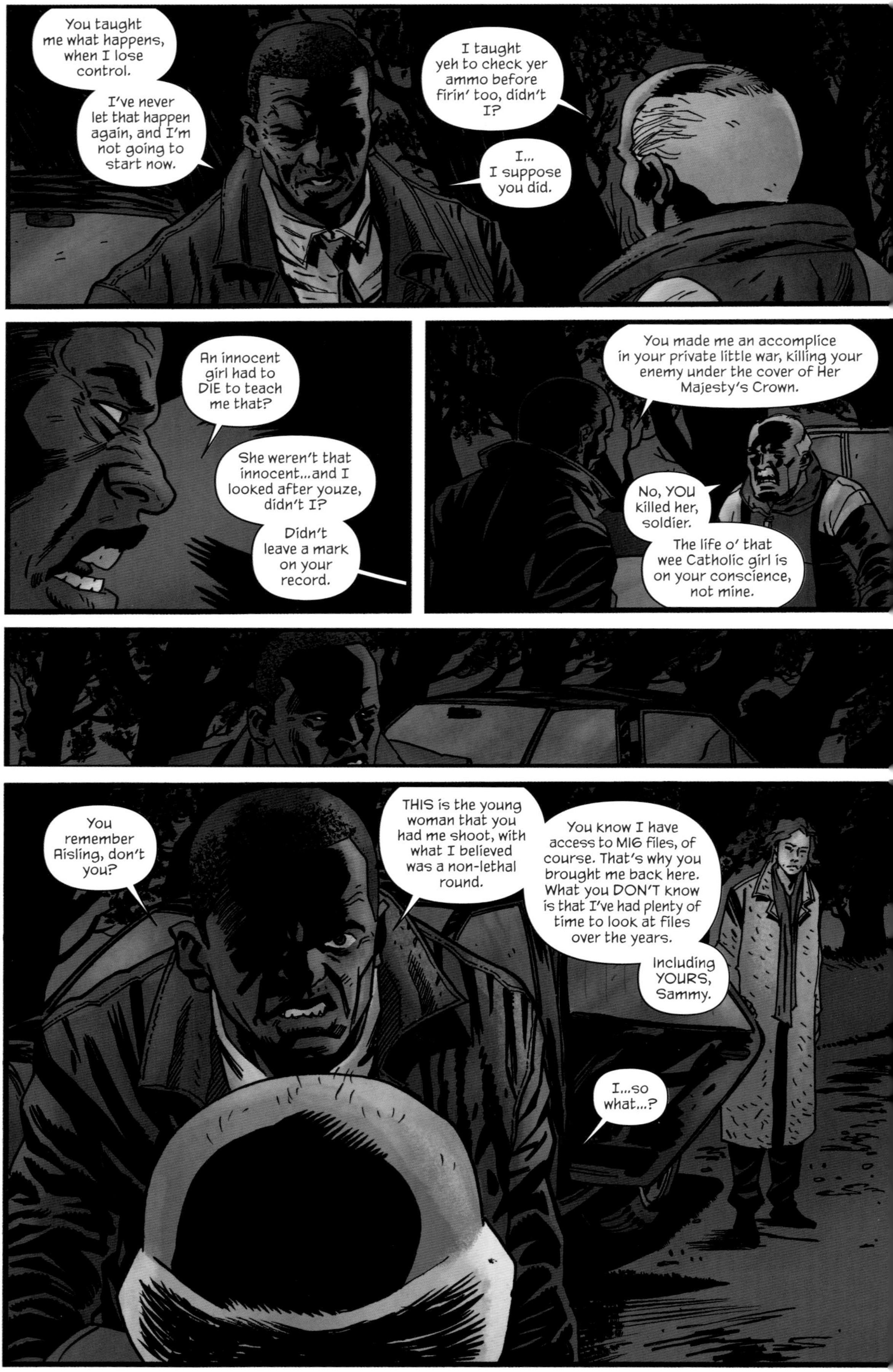
You taught me what happens, when I lose control.
I've never let that happen again, and I'm not going to start now.
I taught yeh to check yer ammo before firin' too, didn't I?
I... I suppose you did.
An innocent girl had to DIE to teach me that?
She weren't that innocent...and I looked after youze, didn't I?
Didn't leave a mark on your record.
You made me an accomplice in your private little war, killing your enemy under the cover of Her Majesty's Crown.
No, YOU killed her, soldier.
The life o' that wee Catholic girl is on your conscience, not mine.
You remember Aisling, don't you?
THIS is the young woman that you had me shoot, with what I believed was a non-lethal round.
You know I have access to MI6 files, of course. That's why you brought me back here. What you DON'T know is that I've had plenty of time to look at files over the years.
Including YOURS, Sammy.
I...so what...?

I found out she had been your INFORMANT. You promised to look after her brother if she fed you intel.

Until you were FINISHED with her. You USED me to clean up your dirty work.

Undercover MI6 agents pulled her out in time to save her life, issued a false Certificate of Death. She'd earned a new life, even if you were willing to let her bleed out on the street.

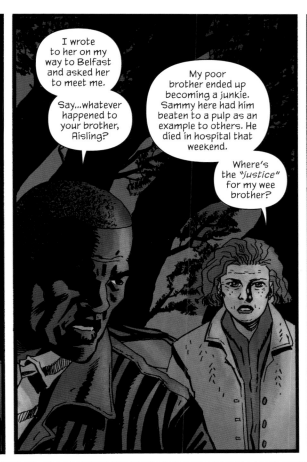

I wrote to her on my way to Belfast and asked her to meet me.

Say...whatever happened to your brother, Aisling?

My poor brother ended up becoming a junkie. Sammy here had him beaten to a pulp as an example to others. He died in hospital that weekend.

Where's the "justice" for my wee brother?

Listen, I don't know what your game is here, just gimme those 'RA names before I lose the head wi' yeh.

You want justice... for past crimes?

Aye.

Fine. Let's have some. Please get back in the car, Aisling.

I FOUND your IRA names.

What? Where are they?

We're here.

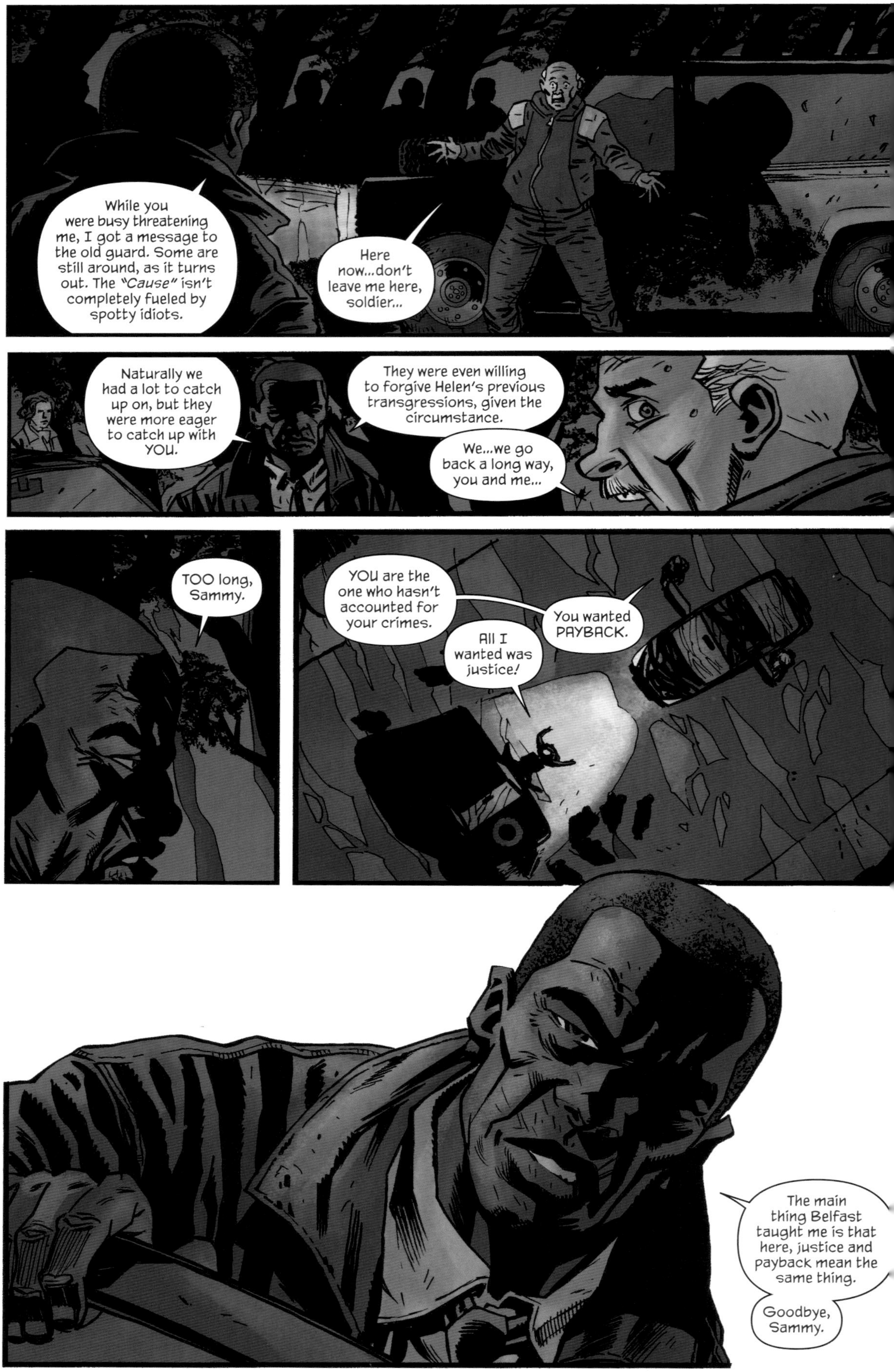
While you were busy threatening me, I got a message to the old guard. Some are still around, as it turns out. The "Cause" isn't completely fueled by spotty idiots.
Here now...don't leave me here, soldier...
Naturally we had a lot to catch up on, but they were more eager to catch up with YOU.
They were even willing to forgive Helen's previous transgressions, given the circumstance.
We...we go back a long way, you and me...
TOO long, Sammy.
YOU are the one who hasn't accounted for your crimes.
You wanted PAYBACK.
All I wanted was justice!
The main thing Belfast taught me is that here, justice and payback mean the same thing.
Goodbye, Sammy.

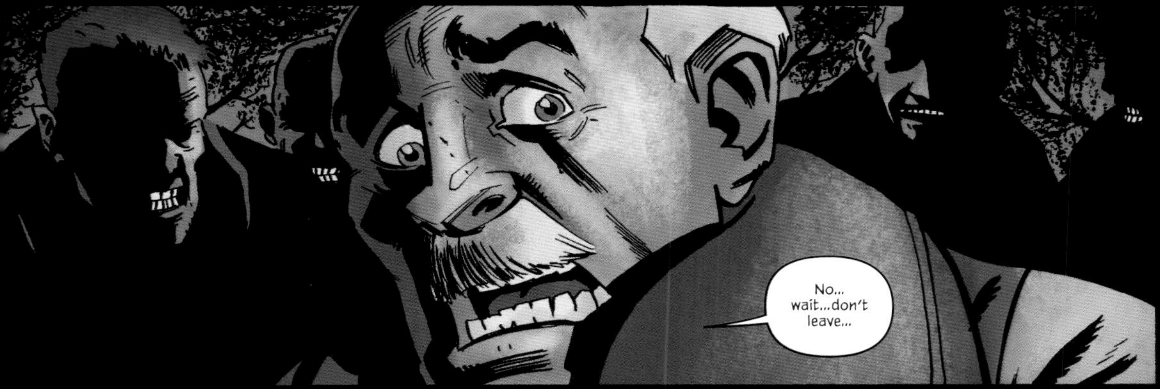
No... wait...don't leave...

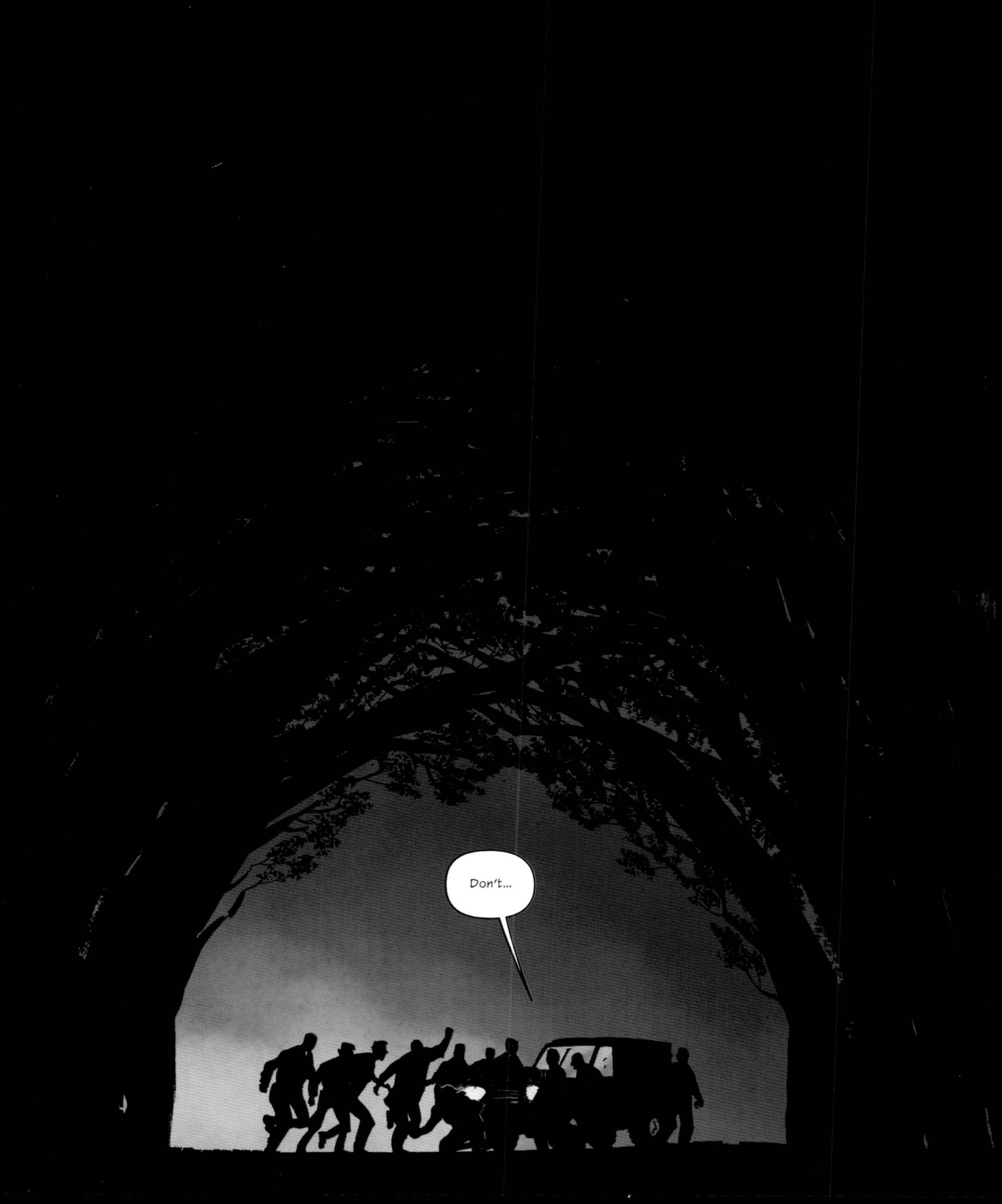
Don't...

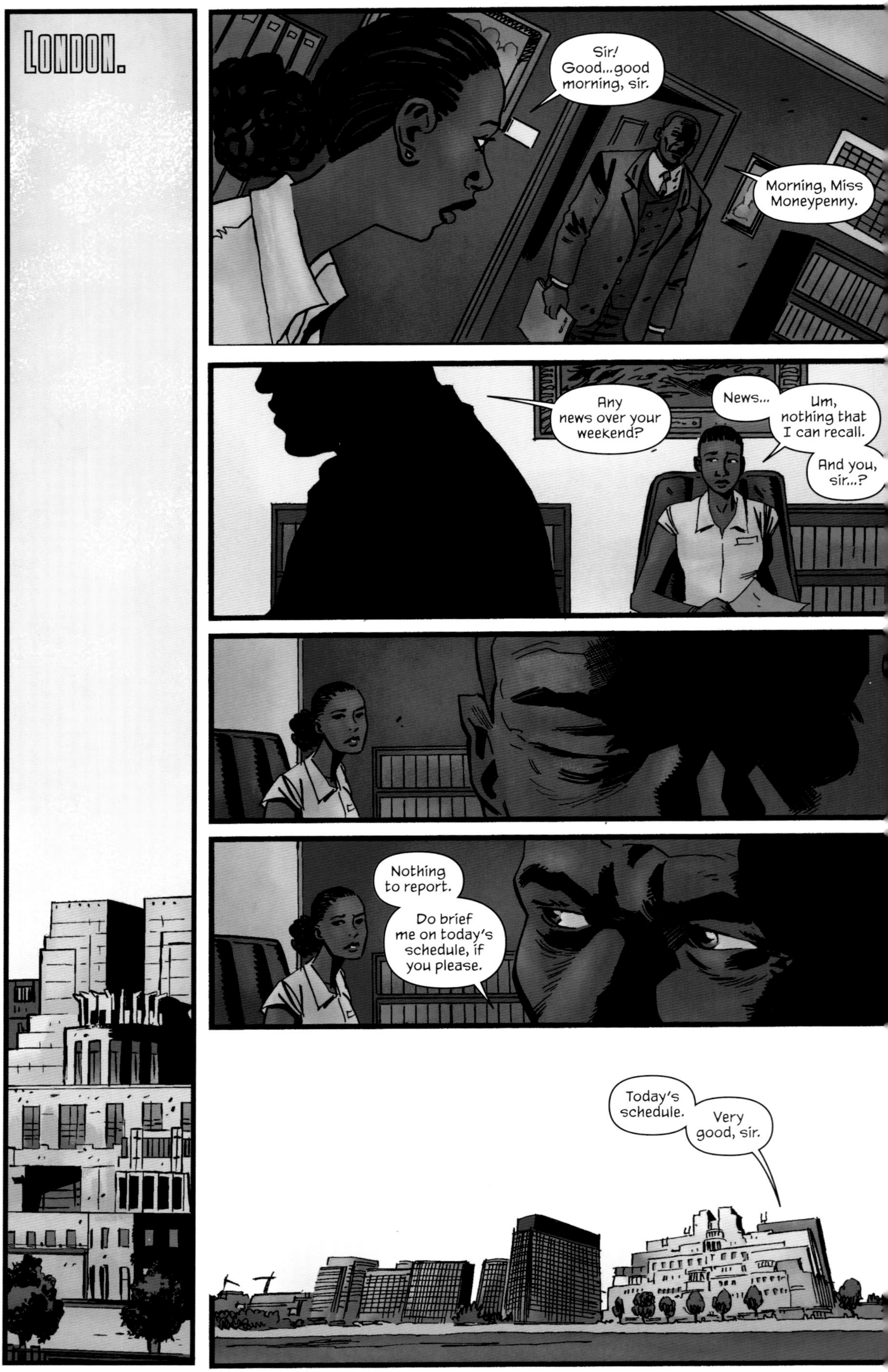
LONDON.
Sir! Good...good morning, sir.
Morning, Miss Moneypenny.
Any news over your weekend?
News...
Um, nothing that I can recall.
And you, sir...?
Nothing to report.
Do brief me on today's schedule, if you please.
Today's schedule.
Very good, sir.

BONUS
MATERIAL

IAN FLEMING'S

JAMES BOND: SERVICE

INKS AND CHARACTER SKETCHES BY IMBRAHIM MOUSTAFA

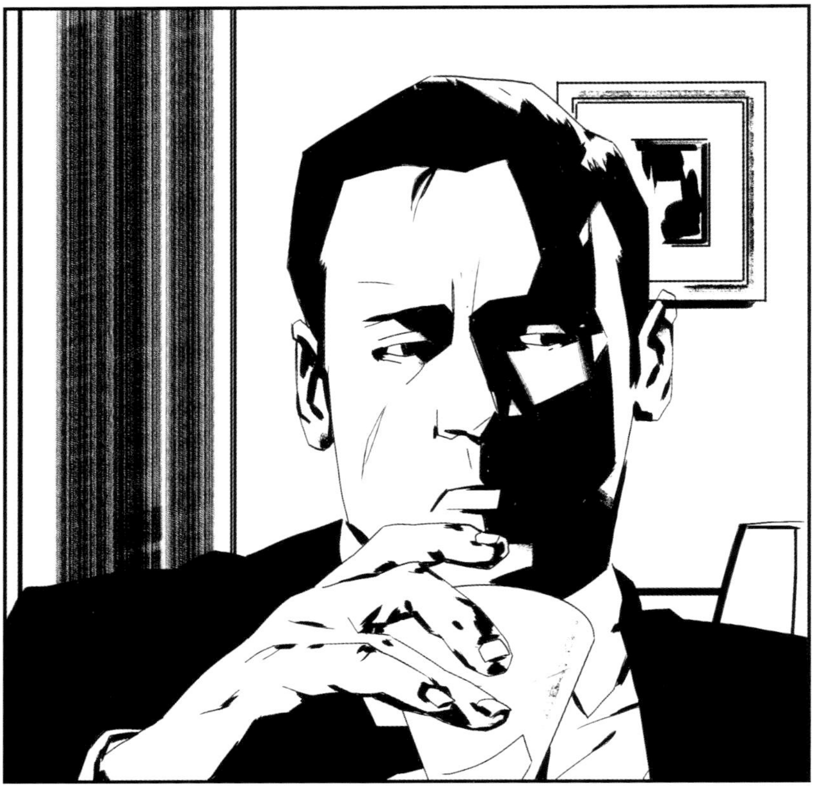

LEFT:

UNUSED PANEL FOR PAGE 1

BOTTOM:

JAMES BOND CHARACTER DESIGN BY ANTONIO FUSO

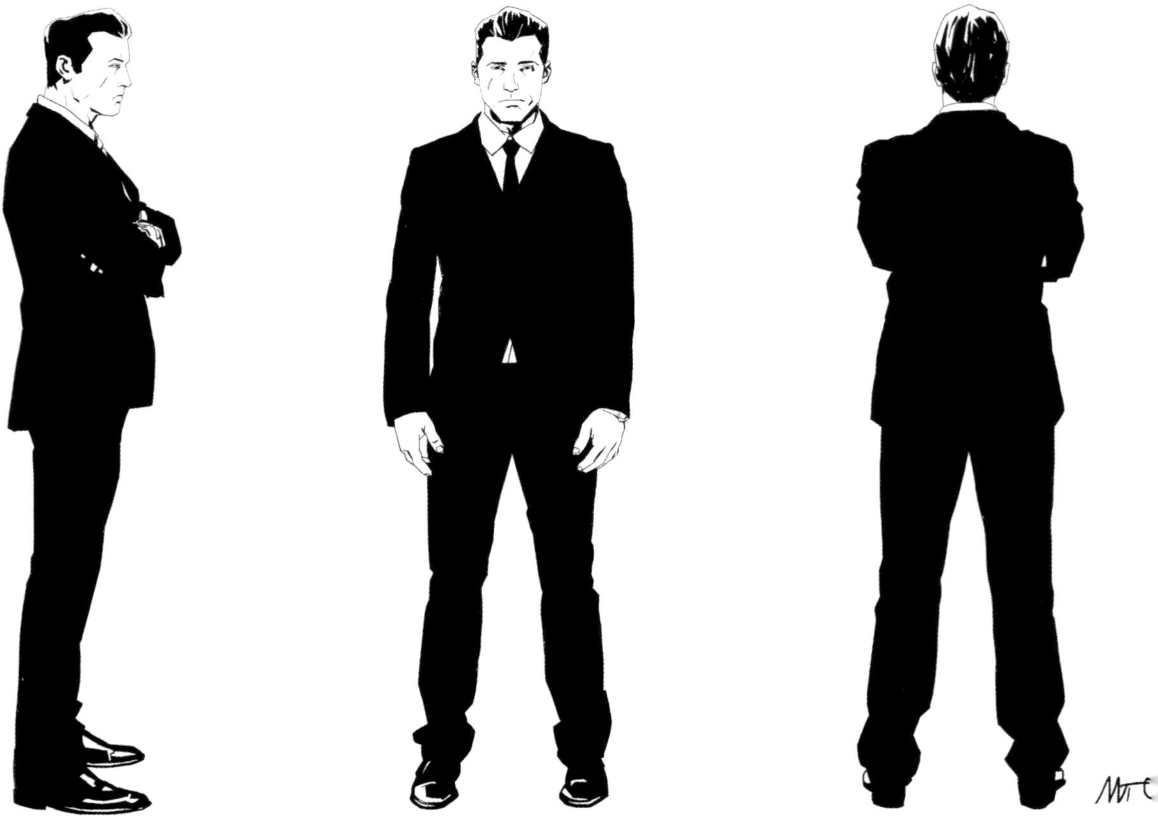

JAMES BOND PIN-UP
BY ANTONIO FUSO

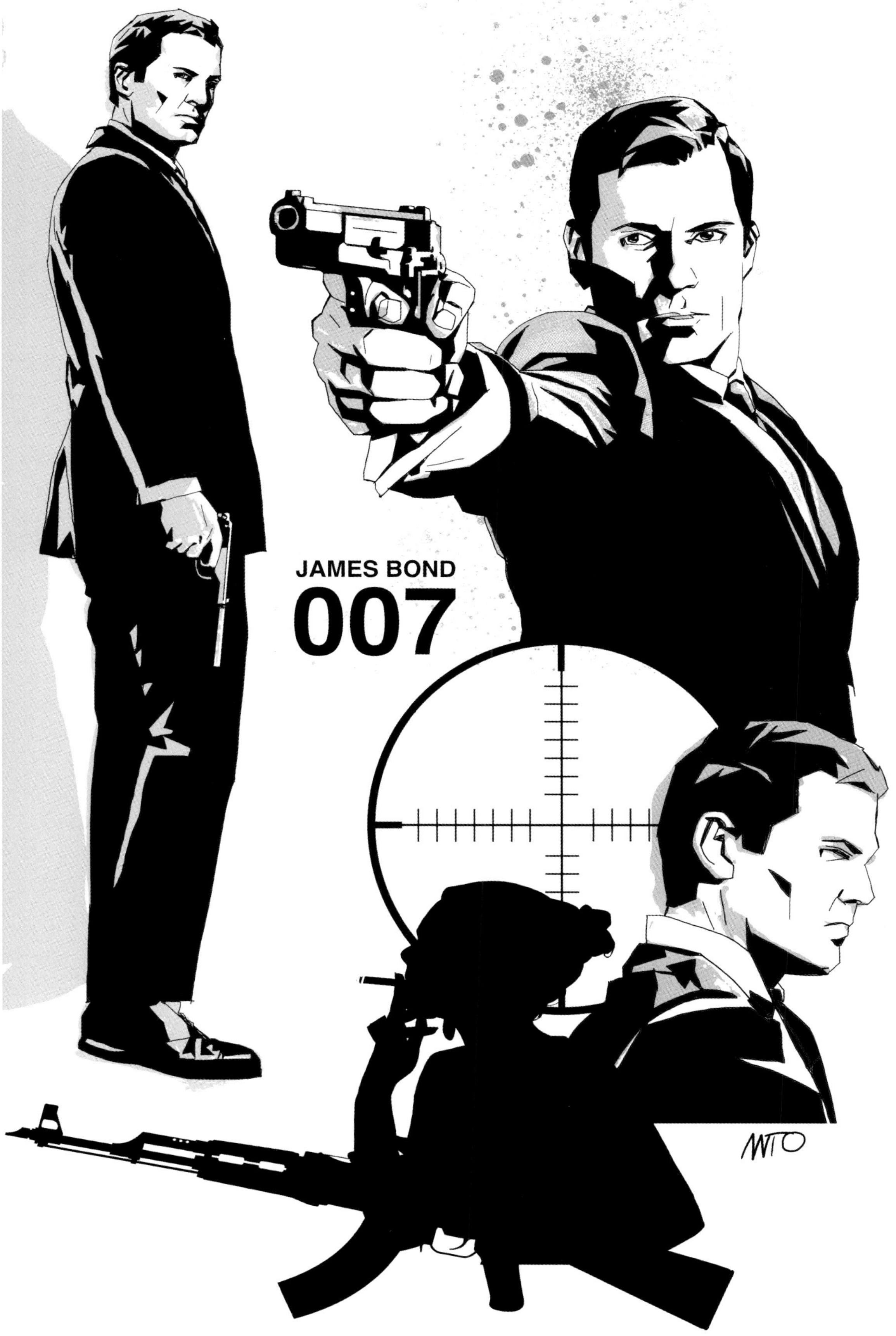
JAMES BOND
007

IAN FLEMING'S

JAMES BOND: SOLSTICE

ROUGH INKS; PAGES 1–12 BY IMBRAHIM MOUSTAFA

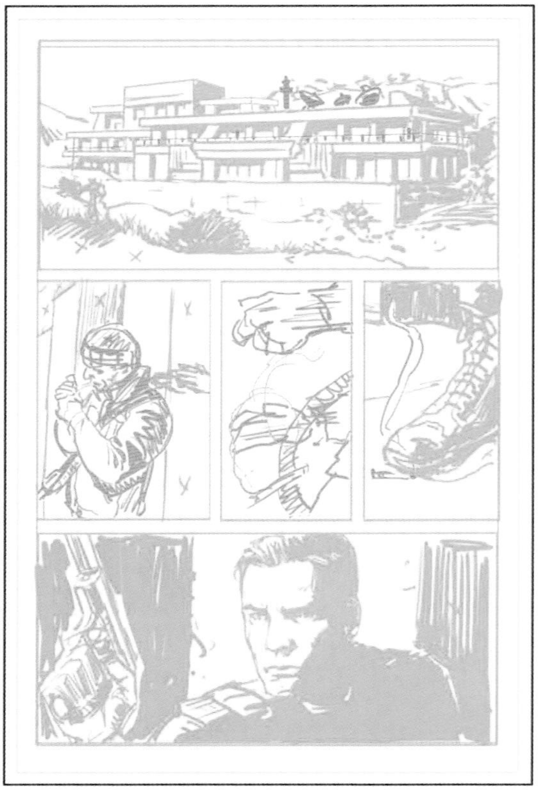

1

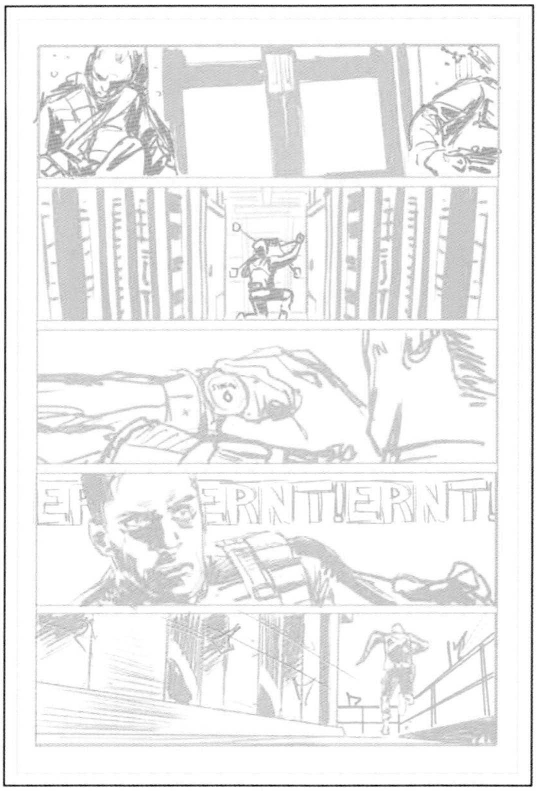

ERNT!ERNT!

2

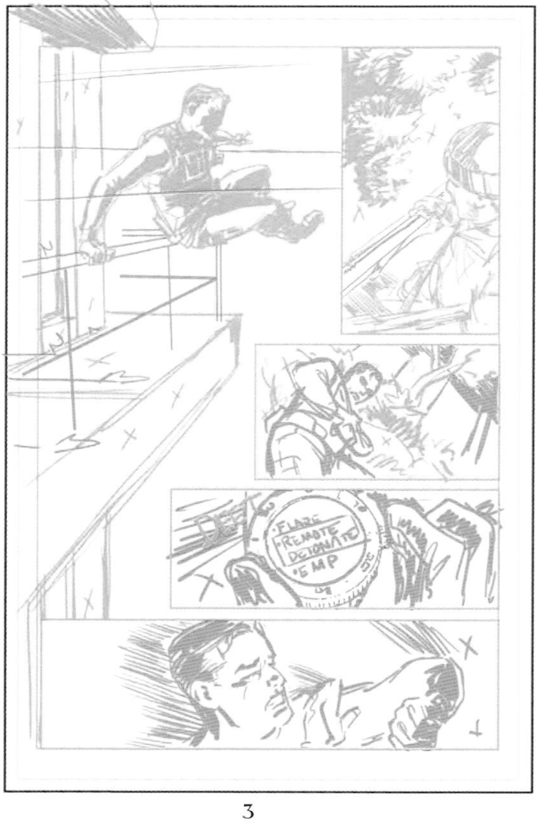

FLARE
REMOTE
DETONATE
EMP

3

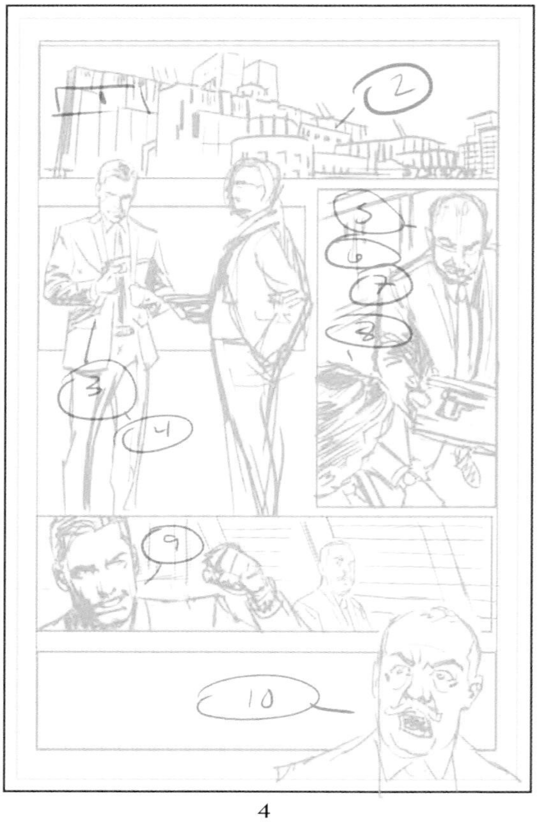

4

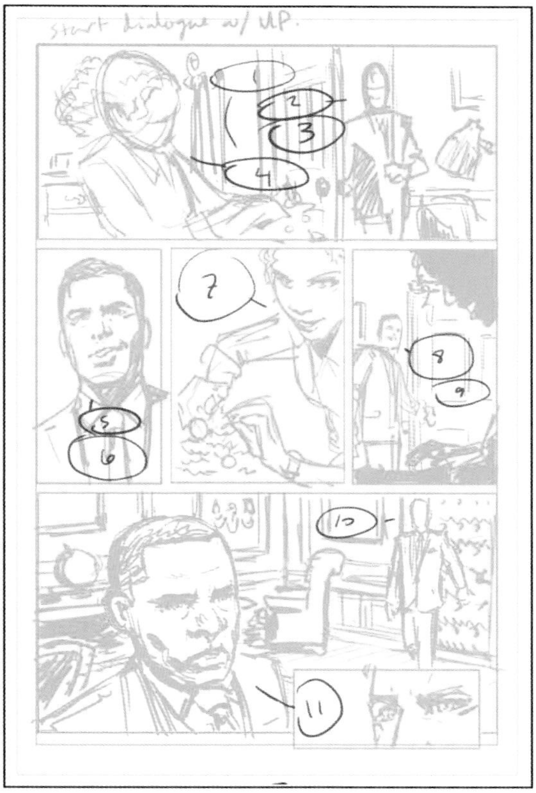
start dialogue w/ MP.

5

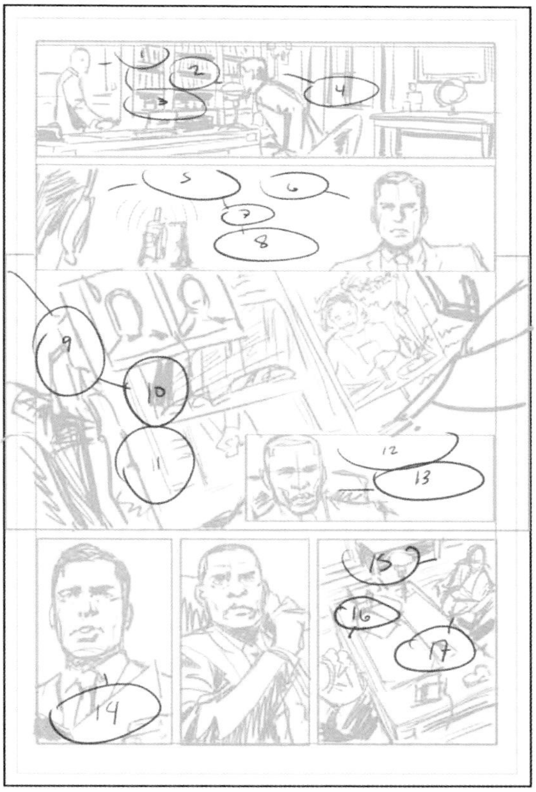

6

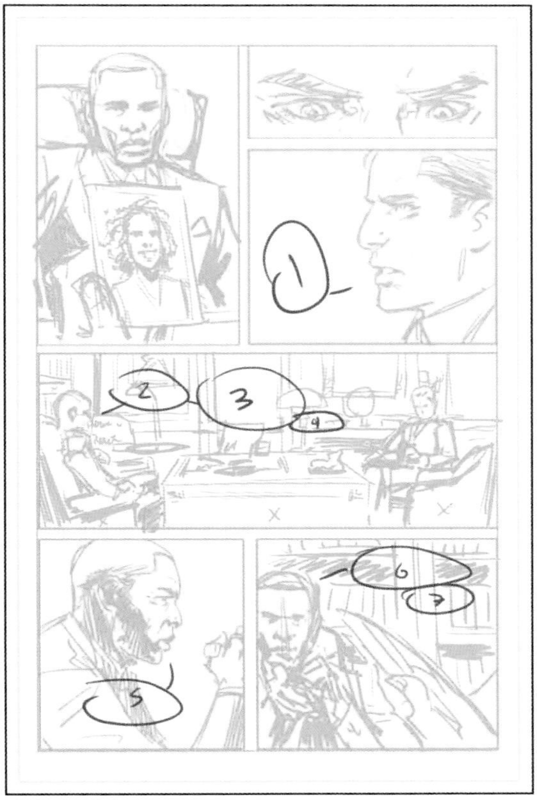

7

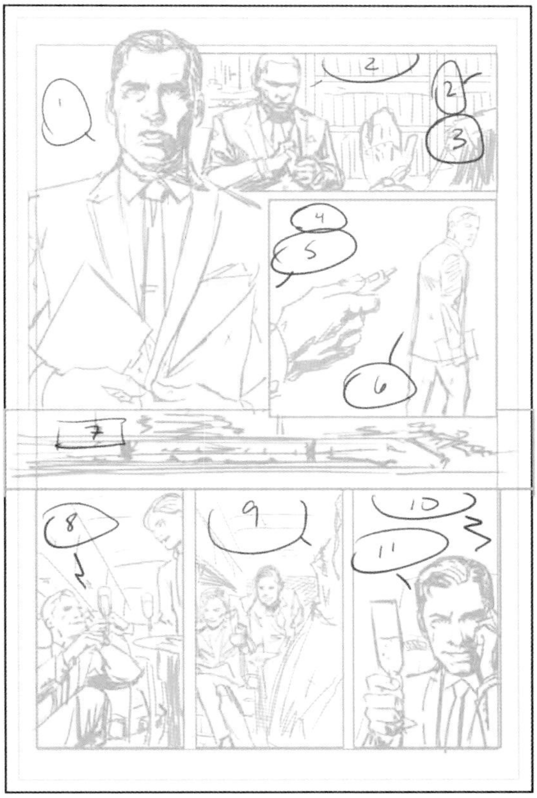

8

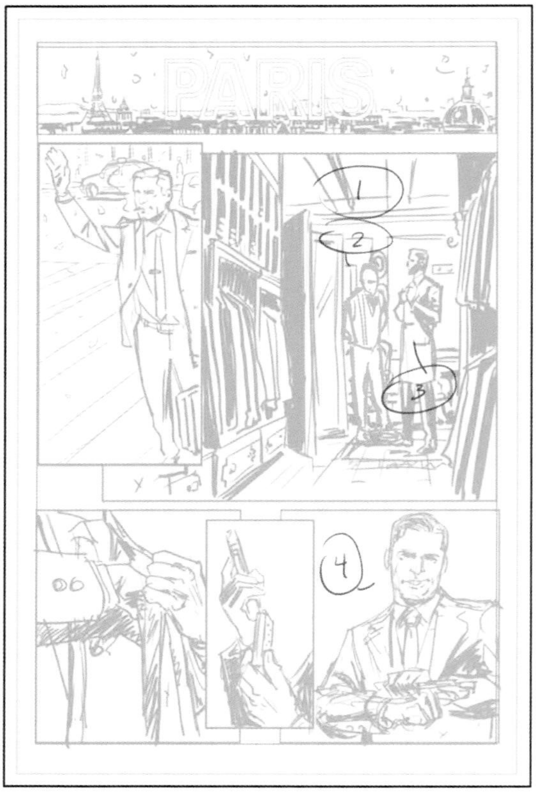
PARIS

9

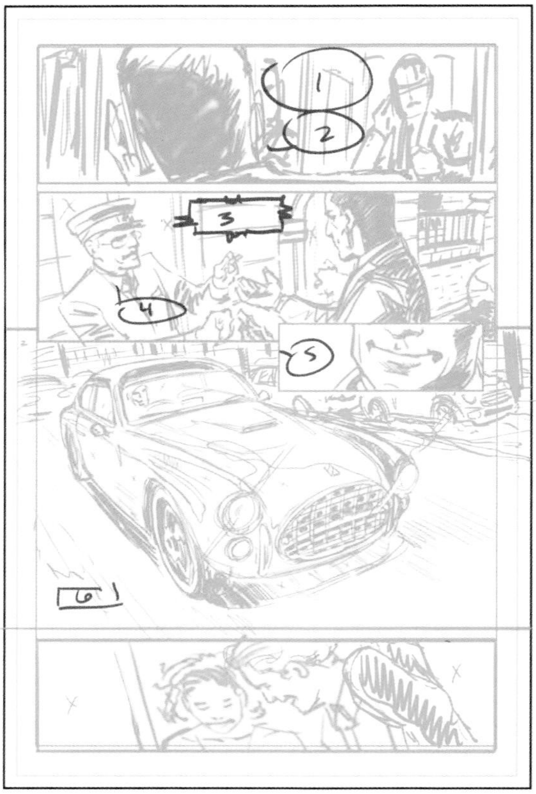

10

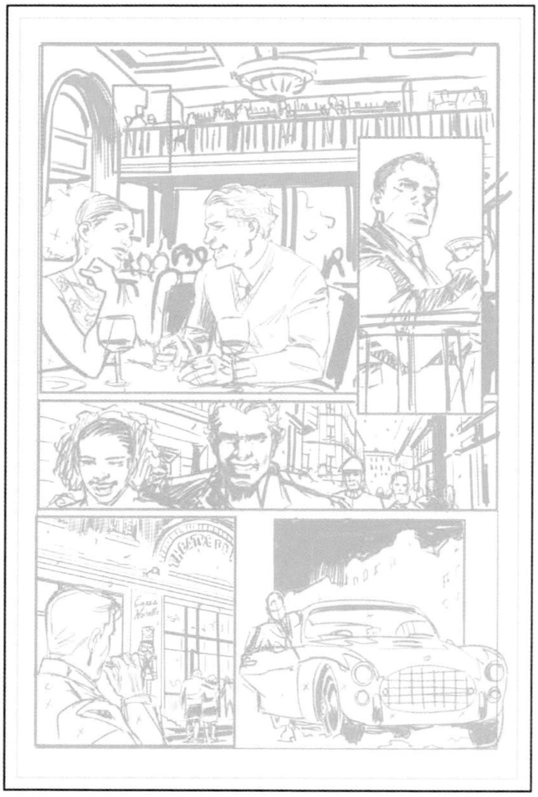

11

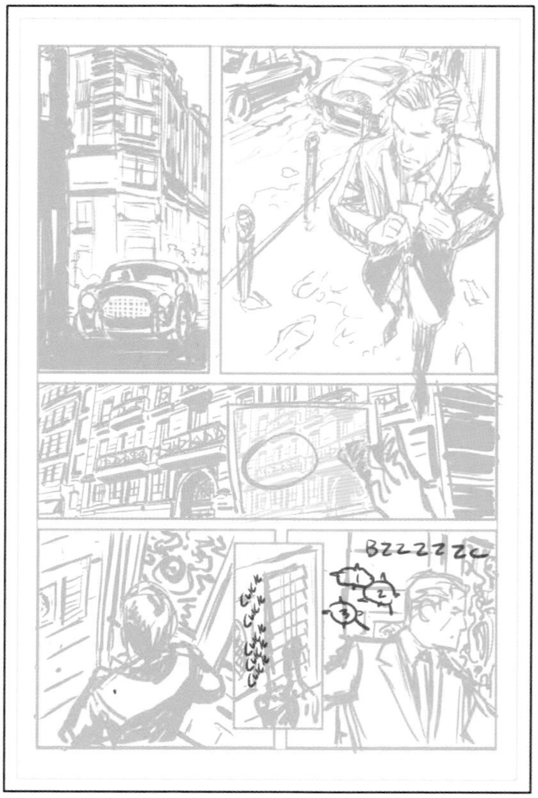
BZZZZZC

12

ORIGINAL COVER PITCHES
BY IBRAHIM MOUSTAFA

IAN FLEMING'S
JAMES BOND 007
SOLSTICE

IAN FLEMING'S
JAMES BOND 007
SOLSTICE

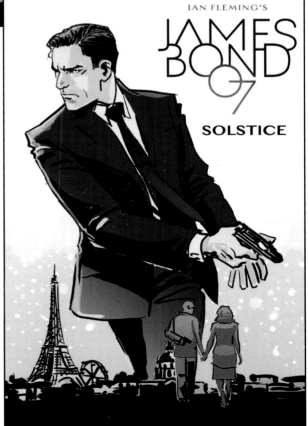

JAMES BOND: MONEYPENNY

ORIGINAL SCRIPT BY JODY HOUSER
PLUS: ROUGH INKS, FINAL INKS, AND FINAL COLORS
BY JACOB EDGAR AND DERBHLA KELLY

PAGE 33

Panel 1 – Carr moves over towards the
still-living people in the group. She keeps her eyes trained on the
professor.

CARR
They did know exactly where we were heading...

Panel 2 – Lane flanks M, whose expression
reveals nothing.

LANE
He is the reason you're here, sir.

Panel 3 – Moneypenny however doesn't look at the professor. She
meets eyes with M.

MONEYPENNY
I ran the background. He's clean.

Panel 4 – Collins, still looking rather freaked out, almost trips over
the words.

COLLINS
But, but you could have missed something, right?

Panel 5 – Moneypenny immediately fixes her gaze on Collins.

MONEYPENNY
You should have stuck with killing the last
witness.

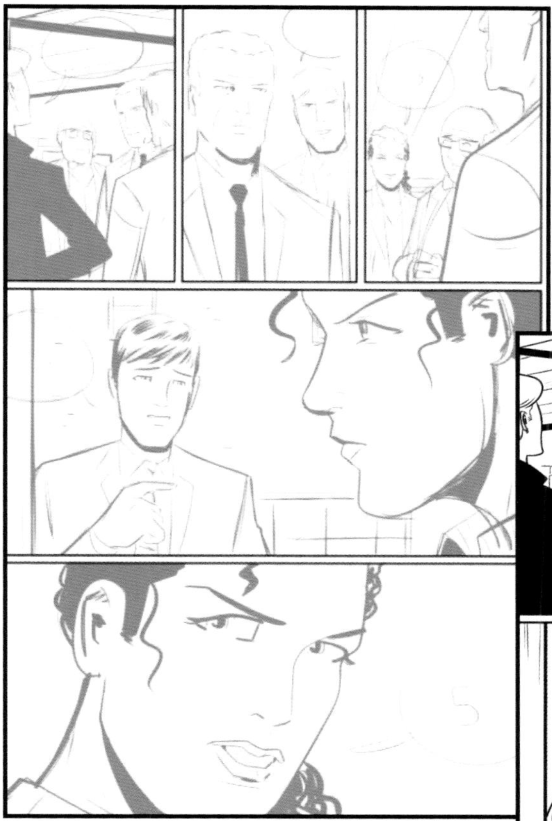

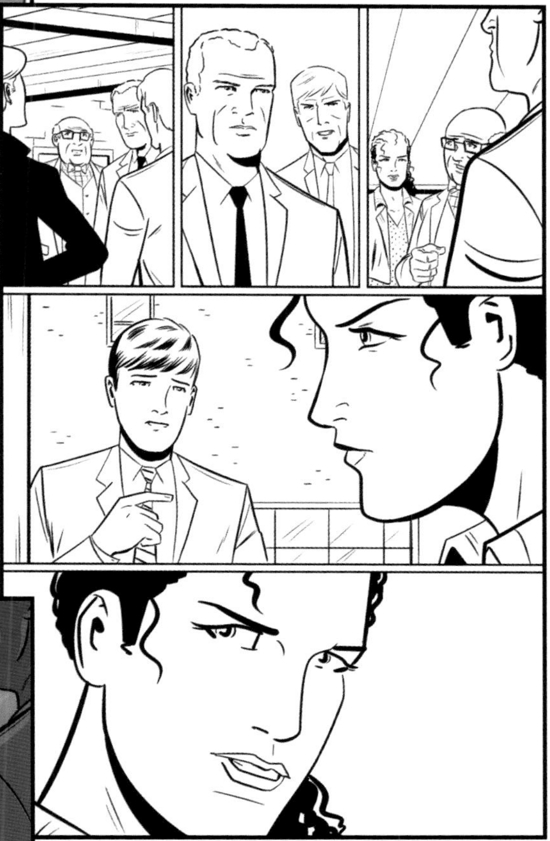

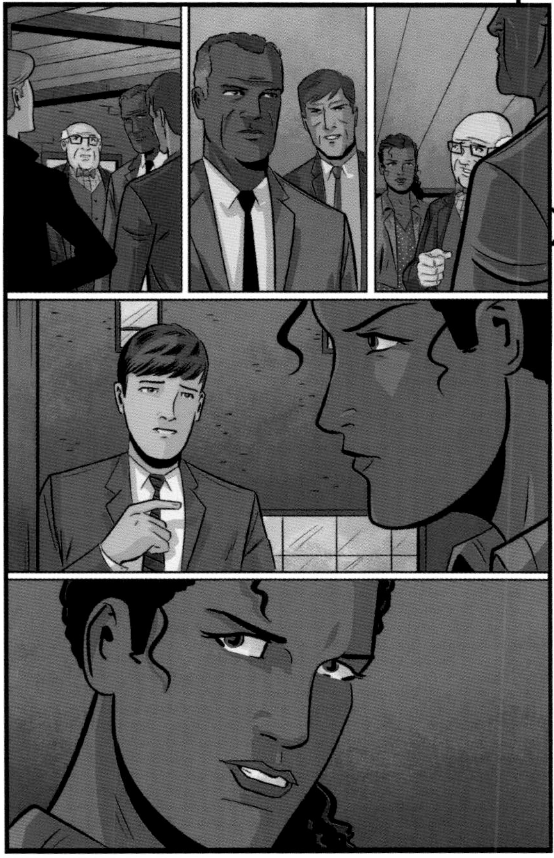

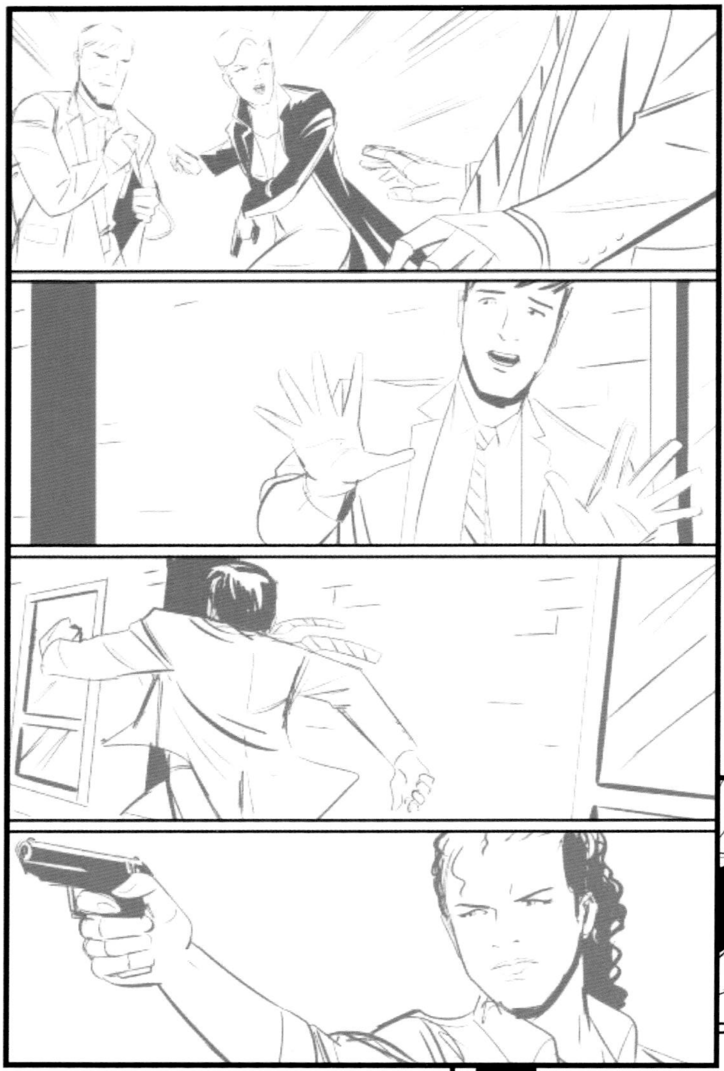
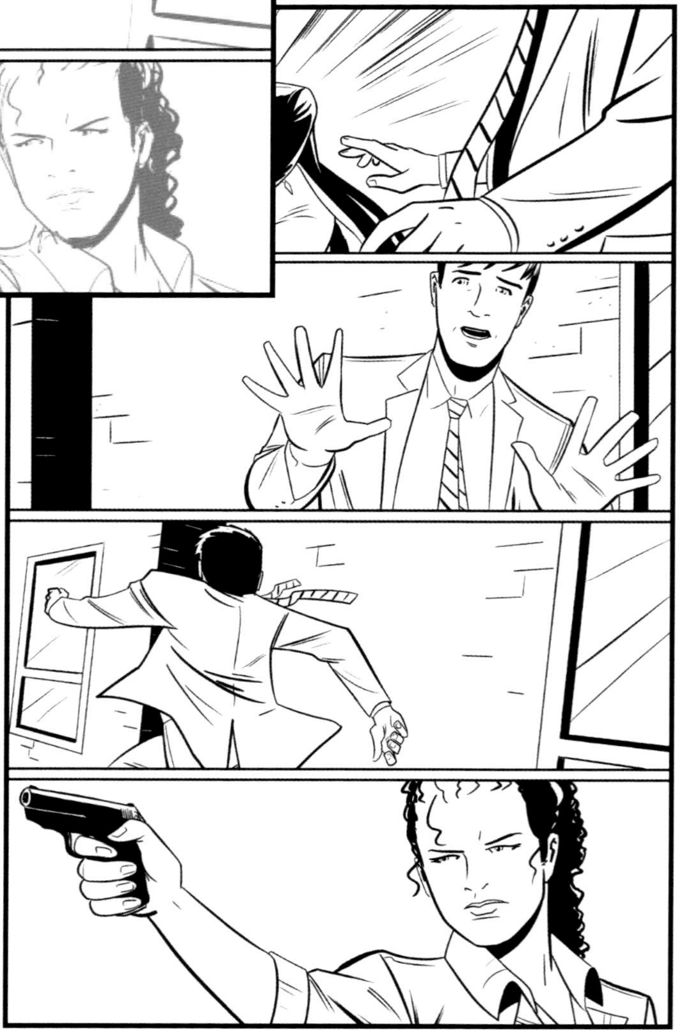

Panel I – Carr and Lane have the realization at the same time. Reaching for their weapons.

Panel 2 – Collins takes a step backwards, still looking terrified.

COLLINS
I... I didn't...

Panel 3 – And then he turns, running.

Panel 4 – Moneypenny aims her gun...

JAMES BOND: M

COMMENTARY BY DECLAN SHALVEY (FEATURED ON BLEEDINGCOOL.COM)
INKS BY PJ HOLDEN

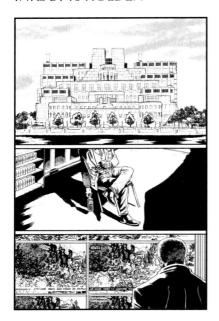

PAGE 1

Hey, this is a James Bond comic, I should open this up with a bombastic action sequence, right? Wrong. This story concentrates on M, and M is a very different character than James Bond, which is a very important part of this story. So, we open our story with M looking at a botched mission. The repercussions of the work they do. He's chewing out a 00 agent who is...

PAGE 2

...NOT James Bond. PJ did a great job of misleading us in the first page, so that we think this is a much more arrogant Bond. James Bond has been described as a blunt instrument, but he gets the job done. This agent M is dealing with is someone who is reckless to the point of disaster. We know M and Bond clash, but it was important we understand why M is the way he is... he demands control. Over the course of this story, we will find out why that is so.

PAGE 3

This is where we call back to Belfast. The Unionist/ Union Jack color of the package reminds M of Ulster, and the botched mission footage suddenly are in a different context, and are reminiscent of the footage we remember from Troubles-era Belfast.

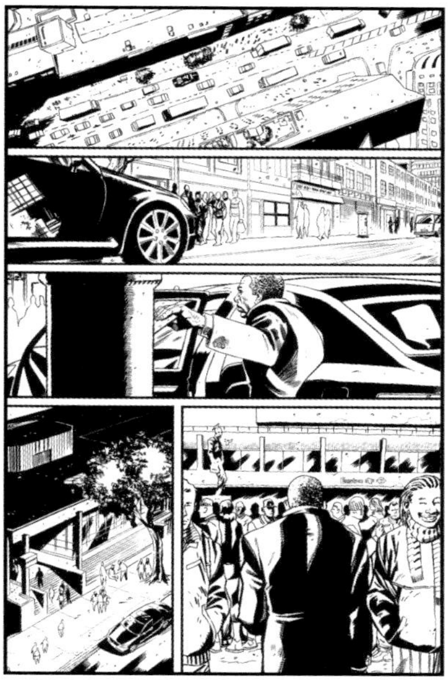

PAGE 4

Arguably, this is a very basic page that doesn't show us much (though it will ultimately set up a plot point for later), but I wanted to show the simplicity it would take to get to Belfast. No fancy private planes or yachts. Just a train and a ferry. Belfast is right under London's nose, I wanted to show that this IS still part of the United Kingdom, even though it is another land entirely.

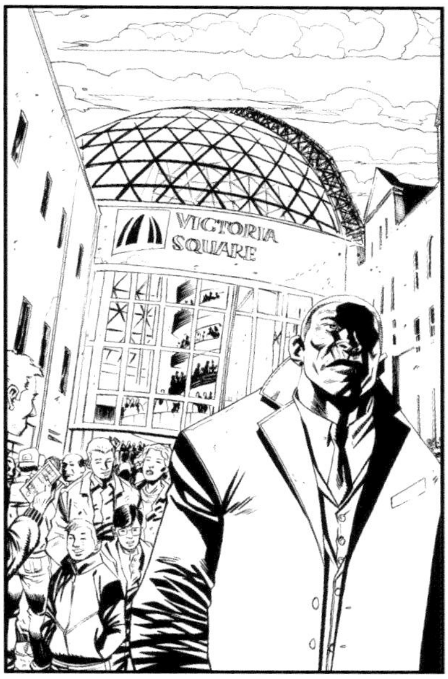
VICTORIA SQUARE

PAGE 5

BELFAST. I felt it was important for the reader to see contemporary Belfast here, to fly in the face of any preconceptions the they might have. It's not all soldiers on the streets any more, no army check-points, etc. From the conversation PJ and I had, he wanted to get Victoria Square in to the story – it's such a big impressive, futuristic looking building, the Dome is the tip of the iceberg. It shows there's a thriving cosmopolitan element to the city now that many are probably unaware of. We will be cutting back to the Troubles from time to time, but we're a couple of decades into the Peace Process now, thing have changed. As has M.

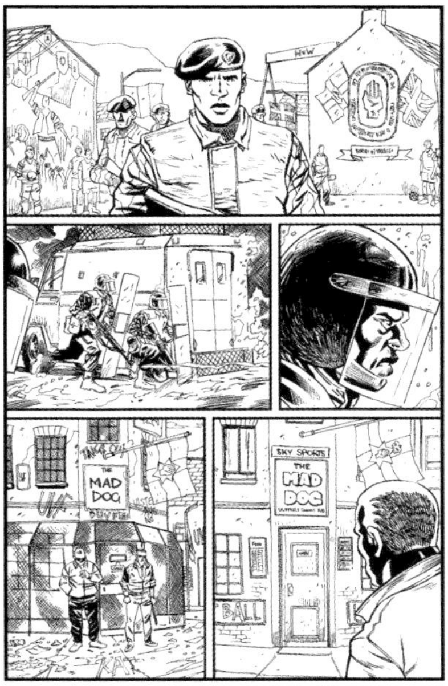
THE MAD DOG
SKY SPORTS
THE MAD DOG

PAGE 6

We flashback to the Troubles. I was really looking forward to seeing PJ draw all this stuff. PJ is from Belfast himself, so I knew he more than anyone else would be able to depict the old Belfast and the new. Though I've been to Belfast many times, I made the time to have a proper chat with PJ about how things have changed, and it informed a lot of the locations and content of the story. I love seeing PJ draw all the soldiers and army gear, he's so great at it. Also, these scenes nicely punctuate the visuals of the book overall, which is very much a restrained spy story. Dearbhla also did something really interesting with the colors here. There's a subtle color hold on the artwork, but it's all been graded in grey, with more important aspects like the young M, and the fire popping out.

The bar in the last two panels, The Mad Dog, is a name taken from an infamous UDA leader, is modelled on PJs memories of Belfast bars in the '80s.

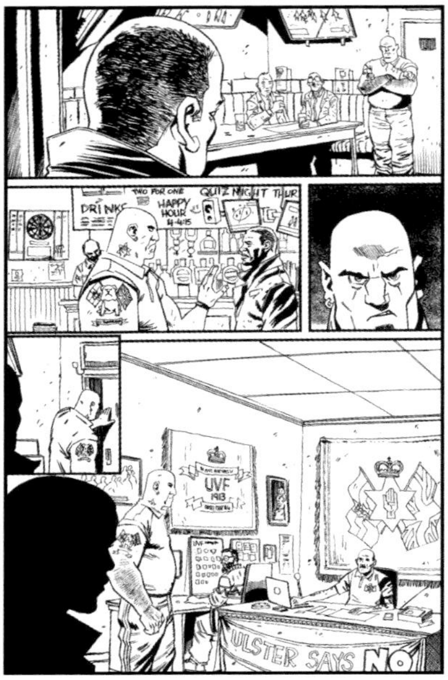
DRINKS
HAPPY HOUR
QUIZ NIGHT
UVF
ULSTER SAYS NO

PAGE 7

Whenever a story is set in Belfast, it generally revolves around the IRA. I wanted to subvert that a little... there was a line in Skyfall about M having been held captive by the IRA, so I kind of accepted that into M's past, but didn't make it the central part of this story. I wanted to show the UVF more, which is another paramilitary organization, just as corrupt and culpable as the IRA, but were fighting on the other side. For those who don't know, the UVF were made up of Loyalists; those who consider themselves loyal to the British crown. And were willing to kill to prove it...

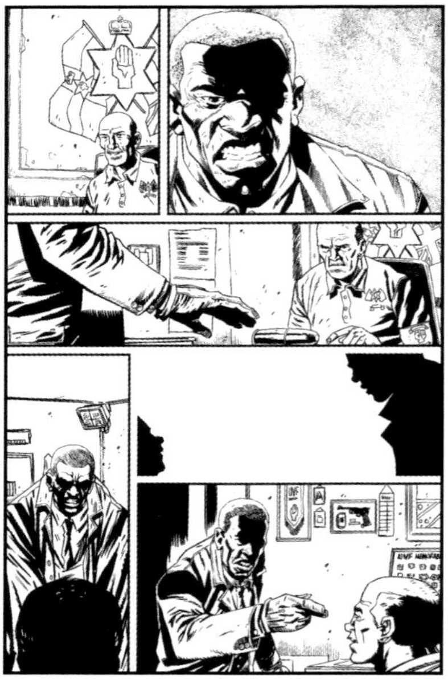

PAGE 8

...While it would be clear that as a soldier M would have run-ins with the IRA, I wanted to show how interlinked Loyalists were working within British institutions (the army, police force, etc.) and also paramilitary organizations. Nothing was simple back then...

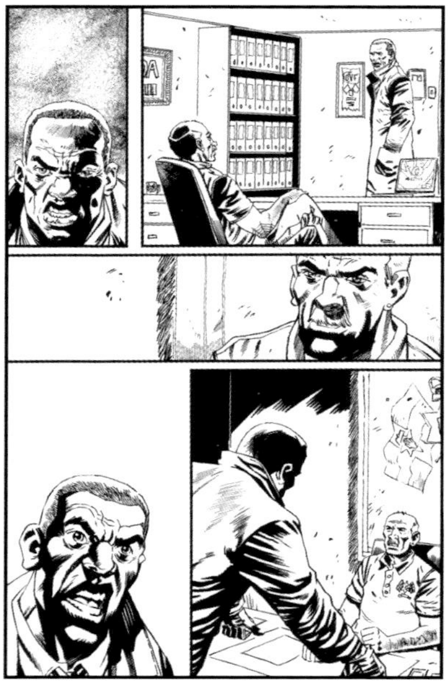

PAGE 9

...Here, we meet Sammy, the head of the Loyalist gang and clearly someone who has a history with M. He has something on M, something he wants to exploit in the name of "justice"....

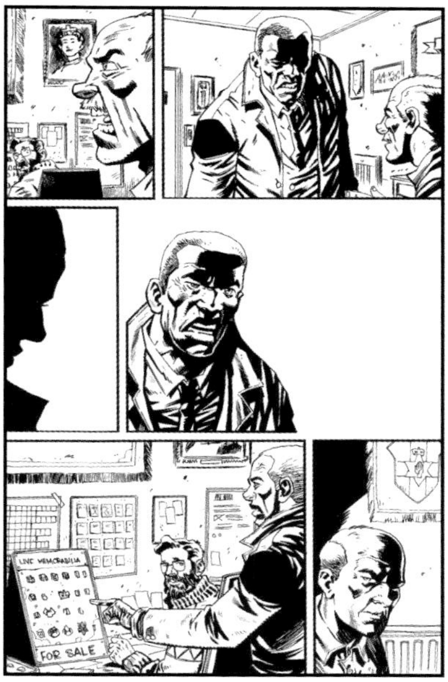
FOR SALE

PAGE 10

...I like how visually interesting this scene is composed by PJ. What could arguably be a boring talking heads scene moves around the page with a healthy flow. I also love how much Dearbhla worked in the colors of the Union Jack in this scene.
Lots of reds and whites and blues.

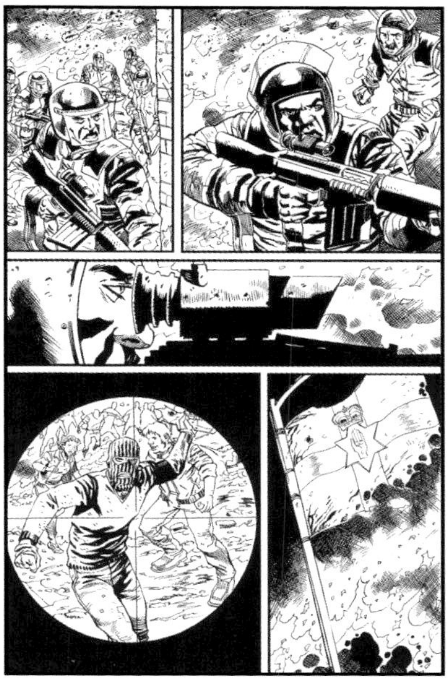

PAGE 11

Another flashback. Again, love the limited color palette here, and I just love how PJ draws the big chunky army gear. I think his background in drawing Judge Dredd really comes across here. While we're telling one story in the present, I tried to make sure we're slowly chipping through the backstory. Everyone else seems to know what happened other than the reader, and I wanted to create some tension and build up to it, while also breaking up the main story with some bolder visual scenes.

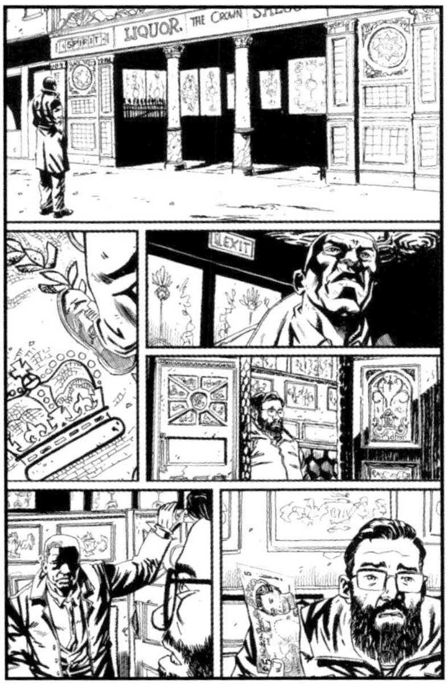
LIQUOR
THE CROWN
EXIT

PAGE 12

We cut from a shot of an Ulster flag with a crown on it, to The Crown Pub in the heart of Belfast.
This is a real pub, PJ told me a story where one of the old owners put a crown in the tiles of the floor as a subtle way of walking on it. Here, M respectfully avoids that. I understand The Crown is even more baroque and fancy looking that the art here would suggest. I'm told if you were in there at any time in the early '90s you'd have probably stumbled across Garth Ennis and Steve Dillon having a drink...

PAGE 13

...Again, Belfast is a place with a murky past. We see that Abernathy, the Loyalist in Sammy's office was an old informant of M's from back in the day. They arranged this meet right under Sammy's nose. Abernathy confirms M's suspicions, Sammy is only working in self-interest. It was something I wanted to get across to readers who wouldn't know much about The North or the Troubles, in all the politics and extremism at the end of the day, both terrorist organizations were more interested in lining their pockets.

PAGE 14

While M is the focus of this story, he wouldn't be able to get anything done without Moneypenny. While not the type to dole out praise, he clearly trusts her and it is really only her who can help him operate incognito on this personal mission. Moneypenny's living room is based on PJ's living room. He denies the teddy is his, but I don't believe him.

Also, I really miss phone booths! They're fast disappearing, I couldn't resist writing a scene in a phone booth, especially considering how they've been often used in the spy genre. This phone booth is referenced from the phone booth down the street from PJs house. PJ was entertained that the locations both these characters are in are really only about a hundred yards away from each other.

PAGE 15

Everyone's scared of the big bad IRA, but I wanted to show how the younger generation who find themselves attracted to republicanism, are just a bunch of fools. As I said before, this isn't an action story in any way but I wanted to show M could clearly handle himself if need be. He could bust some heads and get some answers if he had to... but he chooses not to...

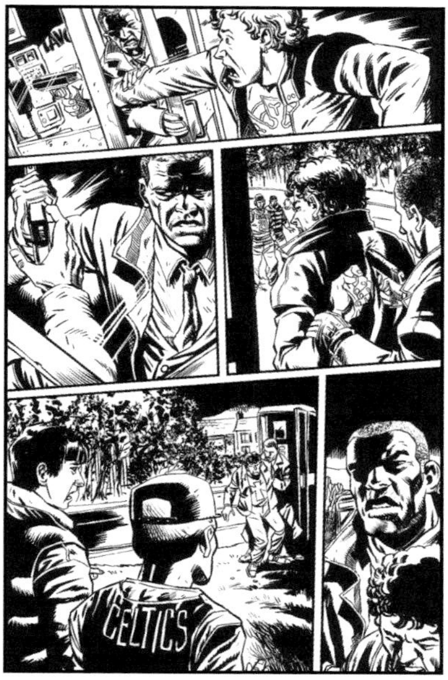
CELTICS

PAGE 16

...I love how dopey PJ drew these lads too.

PAGE 17

Again, using the flashbacks to add more context to M's current motivations. We know it's not going to end well, but we're not exactly sure what's going to happen...

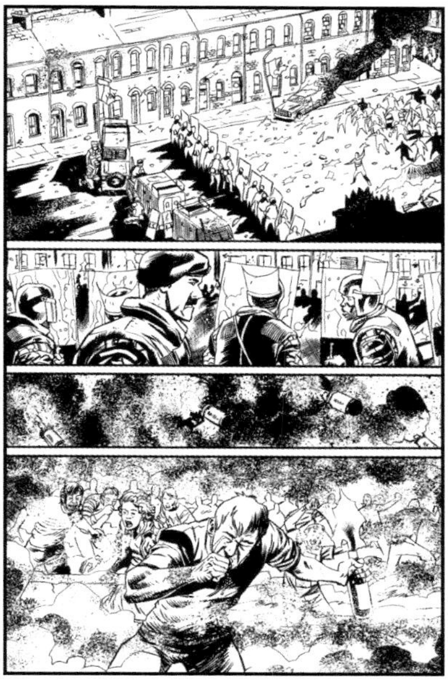

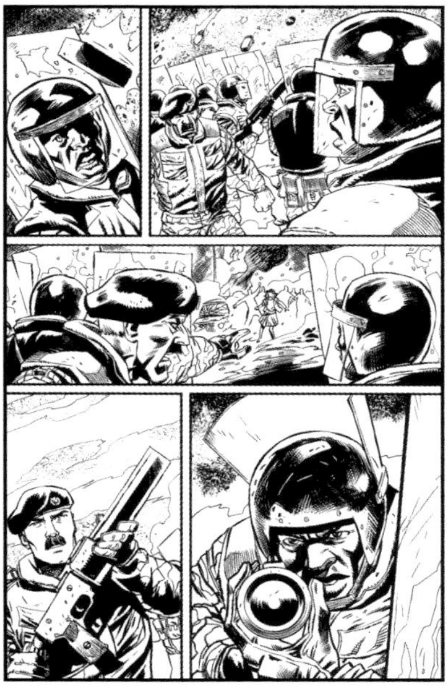

PAGE 18

...That backstory is slowly being revealed bit by bit. I think these also worked so that every time the current plot develops, we're given more "time" between scenes.

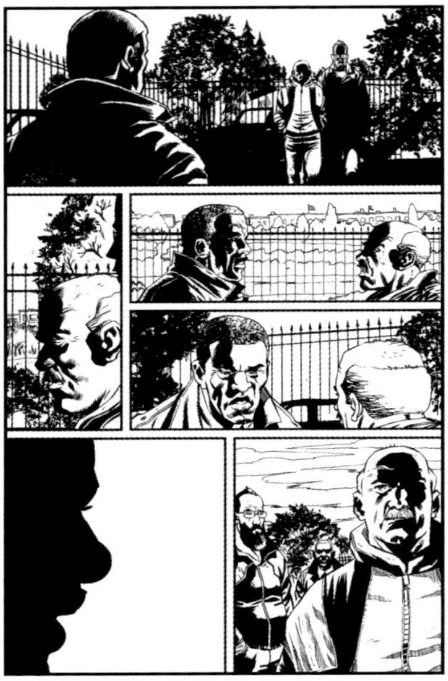

PAGE 19

Writing a spy story, how could I resist writing a “two spies in the park” scene? PJ based this park on the Botanic Gardens in Belfast...

PAGE 20

...I was trying to raise the stakes a little more at the end, and increase the intrigue with more questions, like making us ask what happened to Abernathy.

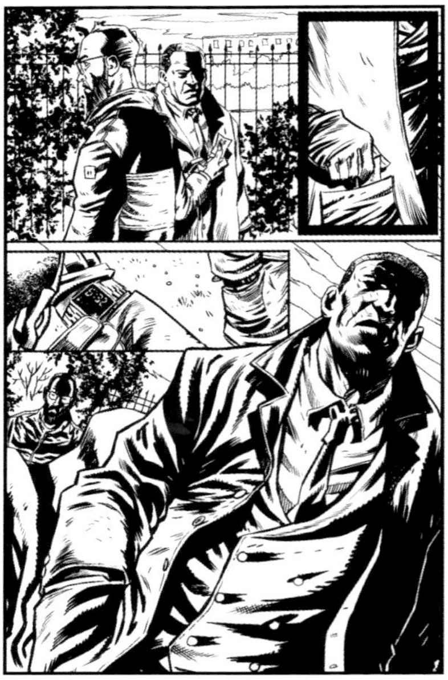

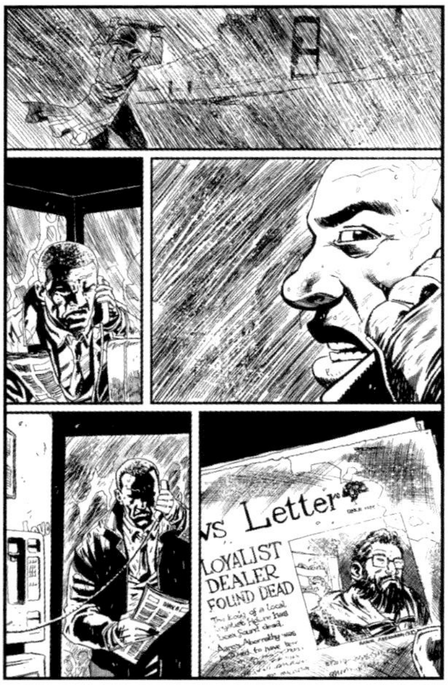
Letter
LOYALIST DEALER FOUND DEAD

PAGE 21

More danger, walls closing in. Abernathy’s fate revealed; we’re reminded of the repercussions in this line of work. Also, I felt that we need a change in weather, to break up the scenes a little, add a bit more miserableness and also, reflect our irritable climate patterns.

PAGE 22

For the main end scene, I wanted a location that was different from all the city stuff we had before, something a lot more imposing and moody. I think it was PJ who suggested the Dark Hedges to me... they're more famous for being a location in Game Of Thrones, but just on their own, they're so visually appealing and make a great background location.

PAGE 23

We cut to the phone booth as Moneypenny tries to reach M. Nothing like a ringing phone to raise tensions. The building in the background is Belfast City Hospital...

PAGE 24

...I love that PJ did such a great job of setting this story in so many real locations. With a story like this that is rooted in serious real life politics, that sense of authenticity is very important.

PAGE 25

We lead up to and reveal the moment that changed everything for M. He followed orders, but had he not lost control in the first place, he wouldn't have been in that position.

M shot the young woman with a Plastic Bullet, like the gift we saw in the opening scene. Designed to be "non-lethal", it was found, not long after their introduction, that improper use at close range could lead to fatalities. There were 17 people killed by plastic bullet rounds during the Troubles. Eight of them were children.

This is where M became trapped in Sammy's web. Why M has returned to Belfast today, to be free of this secret.

PAGE 26

Or is it? The young woman is alive, having been sent a notice earlier (told you there was a reason for that scene in the car earlier). She, like many informants during the Troubles, was put into GHJGHJ. M would of course have access to that classified information and would have had the time and resources to track her down. So why has M returned? For justice, possibly revenge. He's cleaning up past messes for sure, and using the IRA to do so, keeping his hands clean...

PAGE 27

I liked the idea of using the IRA sparingly, showing the new generation to be a shower of idiots, but still respecting the threat the old guard, letting them be the boogeymen of this story...

PAGE 28

...I really like how Dearbhla is still getting in reds and blues even in this scene. It's more subtle, but a wonderful storytelling device.

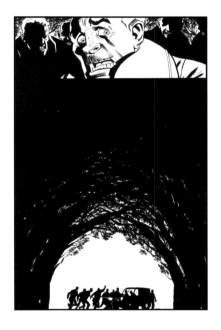

PAGE 29

A gloriously terrifying page. ALL THE BLACK. Love it.

PAGE 30

Back to work for both M and Moneypenny. It was important to retain that classic British stiff-upper-lip in the dialogue, but I think PJ did a fantastic job on showing the character's emotions... they're saying one thing, but they're communicating another. We get to end on a note of formality, but also hopefully a more tender moment between the two also.

THESE GREAT JAMES BOND COLLECTIONS ALSO AVAILABLE

ELLIS · MASTERS
IAN FLEMING'S
JAMES BOND 007
VARGR
DYNAMITE

JAMES BOND: VARGR
HARDCOVER: 978-1-60690-901-0
TRADE PAPERBACK: 978-1-5241-0480-1

ELLIS · MASTERS
IAN FLEMING'S
JAMES BOND 007
EIDOLON
DYNAMITE

JAMES BOND: EIDOLON
HARDCOVER: 978-1-5241-0272-2
TRADE PAPERBACK: 978-1-5241-0694-2

PERCY · LOBOSCO
IAN FLEMING'S
JAMES BOND 007
BLACK BOX
DYNAMITE

JAMES BOND: BLACK BOX
HARDCOVER: 978-1-5241-0409-2

DIGGLE · CASALANGUIDA
IAN FLEMING'S
JAMES BOND 007
HAMMERHEAD
DYNAMITE

JAMES BOND: HAMMERHEAD
HARDCOVER: 978-1-5241-0322-4

DIGGLE · CASALANGUIDA
IAN FLEMING'S
JAMES BOND 007
KILL CHAIN
DYNAMITE
AVAILABLE SIGNED BY ANDY DIGGLE!

JAMES BOND: KILL CHAIN
HARDCOVER: 978-1-5241-0595-2

JAMES BOND 007
FELIX LEITER
ROBINSON | CAMPBELL
DYNAMITE

JAMES BOND: FELIX LEITER
HARDCOVER: 978-1-5241-0470-2

Ian Fleming's
JAMES BOND
Agent 007
CASINO ROYALE
adapted by Van Jensen and Dennis Calero
AVAILABLE SIGNED BY VAN JENSEN! ALSO AVAILABLE SIGNED & REMARKED BY DENNIS CALERO!

JAMES BOND: CASINO ROYALE
HARDCOVER: 978-1-5241-0068-1

VARGR:

"This is classic Bond here."

– Bleeding Cool

EIDOLON:

"Not only are the characters great, the story itself is engaging as hell."

– Newsarama

BLACK BOX:

"Percy's got the voice right for Bond and Lobosco definitely has some really strong design work here with characters and locations."

– The Fandom Post

HAMMERHEAD:

"This comic is all the best parts of a Fleming book accompanied with visuals that only a comic can provide."

– Weird Science

KILL CHAIN:

"Dynamite Entertainment continues to show that when it comes to James Bond, nobody does it better."

- Comic Crusaders

FELIX LEITER:

"James Bond: Felix Leiter...still stands as a neatly compact solo outing for the fan-favorite co-star."

– Newsarama

CASINO ROYALE:

"The bourbon is gone. The triumph of "Casino Royale" remains."

– The Oregonian

Ian Fleming™

IAN FLEMING PUBLICATIONS LIMITED

DYNAMITE®

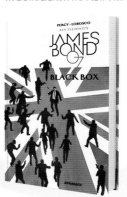

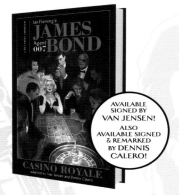